LEARN, TEACH...

SUCCEED...

CHECK FOR
DISC IN POCKET

With **REA's NYSTCE Multi-Subject CST (002)**
test prep, you'll be in a class all your own.

WE'D LIKE TO HEAR FROM YOU!

Visit **www.rea.com** to send us your comments
or email us at **info@rea.com**

NYSTCE® MULTI-SUBJECT CST (002)

NEW YORK STATE TEACHER CERTIFICATION EXAMINATIONS™

TestWare® Edition

Contributing Authors
Norman Levy and Joan Levy
Educational Consultants
Albertson, NY

The Editors of
Research & Education Association

Research & Education Association

Visit our Educator Support Center: www.rea.com/teacher

Updates to the test and this book: www.rea.com/NYSTCE/multi002.htm

Research & Education Association
61 Ethel Road West
Piscataway, New Jersey 08854
E-mail: info@rea.com

NYSTCE® Multi-Subject Content Specialty Test (002) with TestWare® on CD-ROM, 2nd Edition

Library of Congress Control Number 2011933137

ISBN-13: 978-0-7386-0996-6
ISBN-10: 0-7386-0996-X

The NYSTCE Multi-Subject Content Specialty Test Objectives presented in this book were created and implemented by the New York State Education Department and Pearson Education, Inc. For further information visit the NYSTCE website at *www.nystce.nesinc.com*. NYSTCE and New York State Teacher Certification Examinations are trademarks of the New York State Education Department and and Pearson Education, Inc. or its affiliate(s). Windows® is a registered trademark of Microsoft Corporation. All other trademarks cited in this publication are the property of their respective owners.

REA® and TestWare® are registered trademarks of Research & Education Association, Inc.

H11-0101

CONTENTS

Contents

About Research & Education Association

Founded in 1959, Research & Education Association is dedicated to publishing the finest and most effective educational materials—including software, study guides, and test preps—for students in middle school, high school, college, graduate school, and beyond.

REA's Test Preparation series includes books and software for all academic levels in almost all disciplines. Research & Education Association publishes test preps for students who have not yet completed high school, as well as for high school students preparing to enter college. Students from countries around the world seeking to attend college in the United States will find the assistance they need in REA's publications. For college students seeking advanced degrees, REA publishes test preps for many major graduate school admission examinations in a wide variety of disciplines, including engineering, law, and medicine. Students at every level, in every field, with every ambition can find what they are looking for among REA's publications.

REA's practice tests are always based upon the most recently administered exams and include every type of question that you can expect on the actual exams.

REA's publications and educational materials are highly regarded and continually receive an unprecedented amount of praise from professionals, instructors, librarians, parents, and students. Our authors are as diverse as the fields represented in the books we publish. They are well-known in their respective disciplines and serve on the faculties of prestigious high schools, colleges, and universities throughout the United States and Canada.

Today, REA's wide-ranging catalog is a leading resource for teachers, students, and professionals.

We invite you to visit us at *www.rea.com* to find out how "REA is making the world smarter."

Acknowledgments

We would like to thank REA's Larry B. Kling, Vice President, Editorial, for supervising development; Pam Weston, Publisher, for setting the quality standards for production integrity and managing the publication to completion; John Paul Cording, Vice President, Technology, for coordinating the design, development, and testing of REA's TestWare®; Kathleen Casey, Senior Editor, for project management and editorial preflight review; Diane Goldschmidt, Senior Editor, for post-production quality assurance; Heena Patel, software project manager, for her software testing efforts; Christine Saul, Senior Graphic Artist, for cover design; and Maureen Mulligan, Production Graphic Artist, for typesetting revisions.

We gratefully acknowledge David M. Myton, Ph.D., Renay M. Scott, Ph.D., Karen Bondarchuck, M.F.A., John A. Lychner, Ph.D., Janet E. Rubin, Ph.D., Ellen R. Van't Hof, M.A., Nelson Maylone, Ph.D., and Ginny Muller, Ph.D., for providing foundational material for this book. We also thank Al Davis, M.A., M.S., for editing this book in accordance with New York's NYSTCE standards, Anita Price Davis, Ed.D., for editorial contributions, and Joan and Norman Levy for creating Practice Test 2.

We also gratefully acknowledge Caragraphics for page composition.

Teach...
Lead...
Inspire...

Introduction

With this book in hand, you've taken an important step toward becoming a certified teacher in the State of New York. REA's NYSTCE (New York State Teacher Certification Examinations) Multi-Subject Content Specialty Test (CST) preparation book is designed to help candidates master the multi-subject CST subject matter for a PreK–9 license. The CST Multi-Subject test is composed of the following subareas: English Language Arts; Mathematics; Science and Technology; Social Sciences; The Fine Arts; Health and Fitness; Family and Consumer Science and Career Development; and Foundations of Reading: Constructed-Response Assignment.

Each subtest area that appears on the official test is comprehensively reviewed, and two full-length practice tests are provided to hone your knowledge. Following the tests, you will find an answer key with detailed explanations designed to help you more completely understand the test material and its difficulty. When you successfully complete this book, you will be well equipped with the knowledge, practice, and strategies to pass this most important exam.

About the Test

What is the NYSTCE Multi-Subject Content Specialty Test and what is it used for?

The NYSTCE Multi-Subject CST (Field 002) must be taken by individuals seeking certification as a PreK–9 public school teacher in the State of New York. It is a criterion-referenced test, meaning that it is designed to measure a candidate's knowledge and skills in relation to an established standard, rather than in relation to the performance of other candidates. The explicit purpose of the test is to help identify for certification those candidates who have demonstrated the appropriate level of knowledge and skills that are important for performing the responsibilities of a teacher in the New York State public schools.

If I apply for licensure in New York after having prepared in another state, do I have to take the test?

Yes, you must hold a New York State certificate to teach in the state's public schools. Reciprocity under the Interstate Agreement of Qualification of Educational Personnel is limited to coursework requirements only. Also, it applies only to the first-level regular certificate a member state issues. You must complete any examination requirements a member state may have. The New York State testing requirements for specific teaching certificates are available from the Office of Teaching Initiatives. For more information, visit their Web site at *http://OHE32.nysed.gov* and click the link for Office of Teaching Initiatives.

How is the test content determined?

Each test in the NYSTCE program is designed to measure areas of knowledge called subareas. Within each subarea, statements of important knowledge and skills, called objectives, define the content of test. The test objectives were developed for the NYSTCE in conjunction with committees of New York State educators. Test questions matched to the objectives were developed using, in part, textbooks; New York State learning standards and curriculum guides; teacher education curricula; and certification standards. The test questions were developed in consultation with committees of New York State teachers, teacher educators, and other content and assessment specialists.

Who administers the test?

All the NYSTCE tests are administered by the New York State Education Department.

When and where is the test given?

The New York teacher certification exams are given throughout the year. A current schedule of dates can be found on the Web at *www.nystce.nesinc.com.* Click on "Before You Register" for information about dates, test sites, and all the information you need. There are currently 19 test sites across New York State, one in New Jersey, one in Canada, and one in Puerto Rico, with other test sites in cities across the U.S.

Candidates may register by Internet, by mail, or by telephone for most tests:

NYSTCE
Evaluation Systems
Pearson
P. O. Box 660
Amherst, MA 01004-9008
Telephone: (413) 256-2882
www.nystce.nesinc.com

SSD Accommodations for Students with Disabilities

Alternative testing arrangements may be provided for examinees. Requirements can be found on the web at *www.nystce.nesinc.com.*

Is there a registration fee?

To take the NYSTCE Multi-Subject CST there is a fee. A complete summary of the registration fees can be found at the Web site above, or by calling the number above.

How to Use This Book and TestWare®

What do I study first?

Read over our review material, and then take the first practice test on the included CD-ROM. This will help you pinpoint your areas of weakness. Study those sections in which you had the most difficulty first, and then move on to those areas that presented less of a challenge to you. Our CD-ROM features two full-length practice tests that correlate with book tests 1 and 2. **We strongly recommend that you begin your preparation with the TestWare® tests.** The software provides the added benefit of instantaneous, accurate scoring and enforced time conditions.

Wisely scheduling your study time is also a key component to your success on the test. To best utilize your study time, follow our flexible study schedule at the end of this section. The schedule is based ideally on a seven-week program, but can be condensed if needed.

Format of the Multi-Subject CST

What is the basic format of the NYSTCE Multi-Subject CST?

The Multi-Subject CST contains approximately 90 multiple-choice questions and one constructed-response (written) assignment. The content of the test is organized into **subareas**. These subareas define the major content domains of the test. Subareas typically consist of several **objectives**. Objectives provide specific information about the knowledge and skills that are assessed by the test. Each objective is elaborated in **focus statements**. The focus statements provide examples of the range, type, and level of content that may appear on the test. **Test questions** are designed to measure specific test objectives. The number of objectives within a given subarea generally determines the number of questions that will address the content of that subarea on the test. In other words, the subareas that consist of more objectives will receive more emphasis on the test and contribute more to a candidate's test score than the subareas that consist of few objectives.

Scoring the Multi-Subject CST

The approximate percentages of the test corresponding to each subarea are as follows: Subarea I is 21%; II is 18%; III is 13%; IV is 15%; V is 8%; VI is 8%; VII is 7%; VIII—which includes the constructed-response assignment—is 10%.

An examinee's performance on a test is evaluated against an established standard. The passing requirement for each test is established by the New York State Commissioner of Education based on the professional judgments and recommendations of New York State educators.

The following characteristics guide the scoring of responses to the written assignment: (1) Purpose—fulfill the charge of the assignment, (2) Application of Content—accurately and effectively apply the relevant knowledge and skills, (3) Support—support the response with appropriate examples and/or reasoning reflecting an understanding of the relevant knowledge and skills.

The Multi-Subject CST scores are reported using a 1-through-4 scale, 4 being the best score. The total test score is reported in a range from 100 to 300 and is based on performance on all sections of the test. An examinee's multiple-choice score and scores on any constructed-response assignments are combined to obtain the total test score. A score of 220 represents the minimum passing score. An examinee with a total test score of 220 or above passes the test. An examinee with a total test score below 220 does not pass the test. Candidates who do not pass a test may retake it as often as necessary until a passing score is achieved. Candidates must reregister each time they retake a test. For more information about score reporting, visit the NYSTCE Web site at *www.nystce.nesinc.com*.

To gauge how well you score on REA's practice tests, if you score 75% correct or above you have passed the test.

Score Results

Your test scores will be reported to you, the NYSED (and are automatically added to your certification application file), and, if applicable, the institution that you indicated when you registered. Your score report will be mailed on the score report date published in the Test Dates section of the NYSTCE Web site at *www.nystce.nesinc.com*.

Test-Taking Strategies

Although you may not be familiar with tests like the Multi-Subject CST, this book will help acquaint you with this type of exam and help alleviate test-taking anxieties. Here are the key ways you can more easily get into the correct state of mind:

Become comfortable with the format of the Multi-Subject CST. Practice tests are the best way to learn the format. When you take a practice test, try to simulate the environmental conditions of the actual testing facility. Remember, you are in training for the Multi-Subject CST, and simulated testing conditions will only help you perform better. Stay calm and pace yourself. After simulating a test even once, you boost your chances of doing well, and you will be able to sit down for the actual test with much more confidence.

Read all the possible answers. Examine each answer choice to ensure that you are not making a mistake. Jumping to conclusions without considering all the answers is a common test-taking error.

Use the process of elimination. GUESS if you do not know. If you do not know the answer immediately after reading the answer choices, try to eliminate as many of the answers as possible. Eliminating just one or two answer choices gives you a far better chance of selecting the right answer.

Do not leave an answer blank. There is no penalty for wrong answers, and you might even get it right if you had to guess at the answer.

Familiarize yourself with the test's directions and content. Familiarizing yourself with the directions and content of the Multi-Subject CST not only saves you valuable time, but can also aid in reducing anxiety before the test. Many mistakes are caused by anxiety. It's simply better to go in knowing what you will face.

Mark it right! Be sure that the answer oval you mark corresponds to the appropriate number in the test booklet. The test is multiple-choice and is graded by machine. Marking just one answer in the wrong place can throw off the rest of the test. Correcting an error like this will deprive you of precious test time.

After the Test

When you finish your test, hand in your materials and you will be dismissed. Then, you are free. Go home and relax. Meet with friends. Go out to dinner. Or go shopping. Whatever you do, make it a great day! After all you have done to get this far, you deserve it!

NYSTCE Multi-Subject CST Study Schedule

The following study schedule allows for thorough preparation to pass the NYSTCE Multi-Subject CST. This is a suggested seven-week course of study. This schedule can, however, be condensed if you have less time available to study, or expanded if you have more time. Whatever the length of your available study time, be sure to keep a structured schedule by setting aside ample time each day to study. Depending on your schedule, you may find it easier to study throughout the weekend. No matter which schedule works best for you, the more time you devote to studying for the Multi-Subject CST, the more prepared and confident you will be on the day of the test.

Week	Activity
1	Take the first practice test on CD-ROM as a diagnostic exam. Your score will indicate where your strengths and weaknesses lie. Try to take the test under simulated exam conditions, and review the explanations for the questions you answered incorrectly.
2	Study the Multi-Subject test objectives to get a better idea of the content on which you will be tested. You should make a list of the objectives that you know you will have the most trouble mastering so that you can concentrate your study on those areas.
3	Study the review sections in this book. Take notes on the sections as you work through them, as writing will aid in your retention of information. Keep a list of the subject areas for which you may need additional aid.
4	Identify and review references and sources. Textbooks for college composition, science, social studies, arts, and mathematics courses will help in your preparation. You may also want to consult the New York curriculum website at *www.emsc.nysed. gov.*
5	Condense your notes and findings. You should develop a structured outline detailing specific facts. You may want to use index cards to aid yourself in memorizing important facts and concepts.
6	Test yourself, using the index cards. You may want to have a friend or colleague quiz you on key facts and items. Then take the second practice test on CD-ROM. Review the explanations for the questions you answered incorrectly.
7	Study any areas you consider to be your weaknesses by using your study materials, references, and notes. You may want to retake the tests on CD-ROM.

NYSTCE

Multi-Subject Content Specialty Test

Review

English Language Arts

Reading and Vocabulary Skills

Reading Comprehension

The Writing Process

Listening and Speaking Processes

Literature

Language is an intensely complex system that allows us to create and express meaning through socially shared conventions. What is amazing about language is that children generally master their native language within their first four years of life, well before they enter elementary school, even though their teachers (in this case, family members) generally have no special training. Once children enter elementary school, their knowledge of language continues to grow and develop through opportunities to interact with teachers and other children, as they explore the language arts skill areas.

There are four cueing systems through which we organize language, making written language possible. The first cueing system is semantics, or the meaning system of language. Children, early on, are taught that the speech stream needs to convey meaning. Likewise, text needs to be meaningful. If some words in a passage are unknown, the child will know that some words make sense in the context of the passage and other words do not. The second cue is syntax, or the structural system of language. Again, if a child gets stuck while reading, some words are semantically appropriate but can be ruled out because of syntactic constraints. The third cue, according to this view, is phonological, or letter–sound, information. The phonological cue can confirm predictions that are made based on semantics and syntax. The fourth cueing system is the pragmatic system, or the social and cultural restraints placed on the use of language, along with differences in pronunciation.

Reading Development and Vocabulary Skills

0001   Understand the foundations of reading development.

For example:
*   demonstrating knowledge of the developmental progression from prereading to conventional literacy, with individual variations, and analyzing how literacy develops in multiple contexts through reading, writing, and oral language experiences
*   defining phonological awareness and phonemic awareness, and analyzing their role in reading development
*   demonstrating knowledge of concepts about print (e.g., book-handling skills, awareness that print carries meaning, recognition of directionality, ability to track print, ability to recognize and name letters)
*   demonstrating knowledge of the alphabetic principle and analyzing how emergent readers use this principle to master letter–sound correspondence and to decode simple words
*   demonstrating knowledge of a variety of word identification strategies, including use of phonics, use of semantic and syntactic cues, context clues, syllabication, analysis of word structure (e.g., roots, prefixes, suffixes), and sight-word recognition
*   analyzing factors that affect a reader's ability to construct meaning from texts (e.g., word recognition, reading fluency, vocabulary development, context clues, visual cues, prior knowledge and experience)

Literacy can be defined as a child's ability to read and write in order to function adequately in society. A child's literacy skills begin to develop in infancy and continue to expand throughout the school years. An infant's response to a parent's singing, a toddler's ability to choose a book and ask to have it read to her, and a preschooler's interest in attempting to write his name on a birthday card are all examples of literacy development. Research has shown that early, frequent exposure to printed words, both in the real world and through being read to on a regular basis, will likely enhance a child's literacy acquisition.

As the child enters school, formal reading instruction begins. How children should be taught to read is a subject that stirs up intense feeling. Basically, it boils down to a discussion about starting points, and how to proceed with instruction. The two approaches are the skills-based approach, and the meaning-based approach.

In 1967, Jeanne Chall, a Harvard professor, was investigating successful practices in early childhood reading instruction. She wrote a book called *Learning to Read: The Great Debate*. In the book, she stated that the programs that stressed systematic phonics instruction were better at getting young children, and especially poor young children, to read. This pronouncement sparked a great deal of conversation about how small children should be taught, what they should be taught, and where instruction should begin.

Phonics is a method of teaching beginners to read and pronounce words by teaching them the <u>phonetic</u> value of letters, letter groups, and syllables. Because English has an alphabetical writing system, an understanding of the letter–sound relationship may prove helpful to the beginning reader. However, the suggestion of this view of initial reading instruction is that these relationships should be taught in isolation, in a highly sequenced manner, followed by reading words that represent the regularities of English in print. The children are asked to read decodable texts, by sounding out words. Typically, this approach uses reading programs that offer stories with controlled vocabulary made up of letter–sound relationships and words with which children are already familiar. Thus, children might be asked to read a passage such as, "The bug is in the pan. The bug ran and ran." Writing instruction follows in the same vein; children are asked to write decodable words, and fill in the blanks with decodable words in decodable sentences in workbooks, on the assumption that, once the children progress past this initial reading instruction timeframe, meaning will follow. This type of instruction was widely used in the late 1960s and 1970s. Today, it is still being promoted. The flaw in this kind of instruction is that many English words, including the highest frequency word of all, *the*, are not phonetically regular. Also, comprehension of text is limited, because there is not a great deal to comprehend if the text is, for example, "The bug is in the pan. The bug ran and ran." The assumption is that textual meaning will become apparent in time. Furthermore, it must be stressed that teaching phonics is not the same as teaching reading. Also, reading and spelling require much more than just phonics; spelling strategies and word-analysis skills are equally important. Nor does asking children to memorize phonics rules ensure application of those rules, and, even if it did, the word the child is attempting to decode is frequently an exception to the stated rule. Another point: teaching children how to use phonics is different from teaching them about phonics. In summary, the skills-based approach begins reading instruction with a study of single letters, letter sounds, blends and digraphs, blends and digraph sounds, and vowels and vowel sounds in isolation in a highly sequenced manner. The children read and write decodable words, with a great emphasis on reading each word accurately, as opposed to reading to comprehend the text as a whole.

The other side of the great reading debate is the meaning-based approach to reading. This approach grew out of the work of Dr. Kenneth Goodman, who was a leader in the development of the psycholinguistic perspective, which suggests that, to derive meaning from text, readers rely more on the structure and meaning of language than on the graphic information from text. He and other researchers demonstrated that literacy development parallels language development. One of Goodman's contributions to the field was a process called miscue analysis, which begins with a child reading a selection orally, and an examiner noting variations of the oral reading from the printed text. Each variation is called a miscue and is analyzed for type of variation. Previously, preservice teachers were urged to read and reread texts with young children until the child could read every word in the text perfectly. Goodman suggested, however, that only miscues that altered meaning needed to be corrected, while other, unimportant miscues could be ignored.

Goodman also developed a reading model that became known as the whole-language approach. It stands in sharp contrast to the emphasis on phonics that is promoted in the skills-based approach to reading. The meaning-based approach to reading emphasizes comprehension and meaning in texts.

Children focus on the wholeness of words, sentences, paragraphs, and entire books, seeking meaning through context. Whole-language advocates stress the importance of children's reading high-quality children's literature and extending the meaning of the literature through conversation, projects, and writing. Instead of fill-in-the-blank workbooks, children are encouraged to write journals, letters, and lists, and to participate in writing workshops. Word-recognition skills, including phonics, are taught in the context of reading and writing, and are taught as those things relate to the text in hand. Children are taught the four cueing systems, and are taught to ask themselves, "Does it look right? Does it sound right? Does it make sense?" The children are taught that the reason people read books is to make meaning. Thus, the focus of this approach is on both comprehension and making connections. Its flaw is that it makes heavy instructional demands on the teacher. With a skilled teacher, it's a joy to watch. Today, many classrooms are places where young children enjoy learning to read and write in a balanced reading instructional program. Research into best practice strongly suggests that the teaching of reading requires solid skill instruction, including several techniques for decoding unknown words, including, but not limited to, phonics instruction embedded in interesting and engaging reading and writing experiences with whole, authentic literature-based texts to facilitate the construction of meaning. In other words, this approach to instruction combines the best skill instruction and the whole-language approach to teach both skills and meaning and to meet the reading needs of individual children.

Fast Facts
Children are taught to ask themselves, "Does it look right? Does it sound right? Does it make sense?"

Vocabulary building is a skill that needs to be worked on daily in the classroom. One of the goals of this type of instruction is to assist children in becoming skillful in rapid word recognition. Research suggests that fluent word identification needs to be present before a child can readily comprehend text. If a child needs to painstakingly analyze many of the words in a text, the memory and attention needed for comprehension are absorbed by word analysis, and the pleasure of a good story is lost.

Typically, children who are just beginning to read decode each word as they read it. Through repeated exposure to the same words, instant-recognition vocabulary grows. It is particularly important that developing readers learn to recognize those words that occur very frequently in print. A computer analysis of books in print revealed that 100 words make up approximately 50 percent of the words read. This percentage was for all books, not just children's literature. Although game-like activities and writing seem to have some impact on developing word recognition, the single best way to develop this necessary, effortless recognition is to encourage children to read, and to provide class time for reading text that is totally the child's choice. Reading and rereading rather easy text seems to be particularly effective.

In addition to working on placing some words into readily available memory, there is sound research suggesting that students can use context clues to help identify unknown words. This body of research further suggests that instruction can help improve students' use of such clues. Frequently, three kinds of context clues are discussed. First, semantic clues require a child to think about the meanings of words, and what is already known about the topic being read. For example, when reading a story about bats, good teachers help children to activate prior knowledge about bats, and to develop an expectation that the selection may contain words associated with bats, such as *swoop*, *wings*, *mammal*, and *nocturnal*. This discussion might help a child gain a sense of what might be reasonable in a sentence. The word order in a sentence might also provide clues. For example, in the sentence, "Bats can _____," the order of the words in the sentence indicates that the missing word must be a verb. Furthermore, the illustrations in the book can often help with the identification of a word. Still, context clues are often not specific enough to predict the exact word. However, when context clues are combined with other clues such as phonics and word-part clues, accurate word identification is usually possible.

Another strategy is to pay attention to letter groups, as there are many groups of letters that frequently occur within words. These clusters of letters can be specifically taught. Common prefixes, suffixes, and inflectional endings should be pointed out to students. Being able to rapidly and accurately associate sounds with a cluster of letters leads to more rapid, efficient word identification.

As young readers build an increasing store of words that they can recognize with little effort, they use the words they know to help them recognize words that are unfamiliar. For example, a child who has seen the word *bat* many times and who knows the sound associated with the consonant *r* will probably have little difficulty recognizing the word *rat*.

The best practice for helping students to gain skill in word-recognition is real reading and writing activities. As children read and reread texts of their own choice, they have many opportunities to successfully decode a word, and realize that each time the letter combination b-a-t is in the selection, it's read as *bat*. With each exposure to that word, the child reads the word more easily. A child who writes a sentence with that word as part of the sentence is developing a greater sensitivity to meaning or context clues. The child attempting to spell that word is reviewing and applying what he knows about letter–sound associations.

Reading Comprehension

0002   Understand skills and strategies involved in reading comprehension.

For example:
- demonstrating knowledge of literal comprehension skills (e.g., the ability to identify the sequence of events in a text, the ability to identify explicitly stated main ideas, details, and cause-and-effect patterns in a text)
- demonstrating knowledge of inferential comprehension skills (e.g., the ability to draw conclusions or generalizations from a text, the ability to infer ideas, details, and cause-and-effect relationships that are not explicitly stated in a text)
- demonstrating knowledge of evaluative comprehension skills (e.g., the ability to distinguish between facts and opinions in a text, the ability to detect faulty reasoning in a text, the ability to detect bias and propaganda in a text)

Fast Facts

Vocabulary building is a skill that needs to be addressed daily in the classroom.

- applying knowledge of strategies to use before, during, and after reading to enhance comprehension (e.g., developing and activating prior knowledge, connecting texts to personal experience, previewing a text, making predictions about a text, using K-W-L charts and other graphic organizers, taking notes on a text, discussing a text)
- demonstrating knowledge of methods for helping readers monitor their own comprehension as they read (e.g., think-alouds, self-questioning strategies)
- demonstrating knowledge of various methods for assessing comprehension of a text (e.g., questioning the reader, having the reader give an oral or written retelling, asking the reader to identify the theme(s) or to paraphrase or summarize the main idea)

0003 Understand and apply reading skills and strategies for various purposes (including information and understanding, critical analysis and evaluation, literary response, and social interaction).

For example:
- recognizing how to vary reading strategies for different texts and purposes (e.g., skimming, scanning, in-depth reading, rereading) and for different types and genres of written communication (e.g., fiction, nonfiction, poetry)
- applying knowledge of techniques for gathering, interpreting, and synthesizing information when reading a variety of printed texts and electronic sources
- recognizing how to analyze and assess a writer's credibility or objectivity when reading printed and electronic texts
- analyzing and interpreting information from texts containing tables, charts, graphs, maps, and other illustrations
- demonstrating knowledge of strategies to promote literary response skills (e.g., connecting the text to personal experience and prior knowledge, citing evidence from a text to support an interpretation, using reading logs or guided reading techniques)
- identifying effective ways of modeling independent reading for enjoyment and encouraging participation in a community of readers (e.g., book clubs, literature circles)

Helping students read for understanding is the central goal of reading instruction. Comprehension is a complex process involving the text, the reader, the situation, and the purpose for reading. There are a number of factors that come into play as a child attempts to comprehend a passage. First, students cannot understand texts if they cannot read the words. Thus, a teacher who is interested in improving students' comprehension skills needs to teach them to decode well. In addition, children need time during the school day to read texts that are easy for them to read, and have to have time to discuss what has been read. Children need to read and reread easy texts often enough that decoding becomes rapid, easy, and accurate.

It has been noted frequently in the literature that children who comprehend well have bigger vocabularies than children who struggle with reading. In part, this is true because their knowledge of vocabulary develops through contact with new words as they read text that is rich in new words. However, it has also been suggested that simply teaching vocabulary in isolation does not automatically enhance comprehension.

Reading comprehension can be affected by prior knowledge, with many demonstrations that readers who possess rich prior knowledge about the topic of a reading often understand the reading better than classmates with less prior knowledge. Prior knowledge also affects interest. Generally, students like to read about somewhat familiar topics. This is an area in which the skill and interest of the teacher can play a significant role. An able teacher can make a previously unfamiliar topic seem familiar through pre-reading activities during which prior knowledge is activated, new prior knowledge is formed, and interest is stirred up. A good teacher will set a clear purpose for reading, and ask the students to gain an overview of the text before reading, make predictions about the upcoming text, and then read selectively based on their predictions. Best practice suggests that children should be encouraged to generate questions about ideas in text while reading. Successful teachers encourage children to construct mental images representing ideas in text, or to construct actual images from text that lends itself to such an activity. A successful teacher will help readers to process text containing new factual information through reading strategies, helping children to relate that new information to their prior knowledge. A potent mechanism for doing this is elaborative interrogation, wherein the teacher poses "why?" questions, encouraging children to question the author and check the answers through text verification. It is through conversation that children are able to compare their predictions and expectations about text content to what was read. It is through these conversations that children see the need to revise their prior knowledge when compelling new ideas that conflict with prior knowledge are encountered. As part of these ongoing conversations, teachers will become alert to students who are applying errant world knowledge as they read and will be able to encourage use of appropriate knowledge. These conversations lead children to figure out the meanings of unfamiliar vocabulary based on context clues, the opinions of others, and sometimes through the use of appropriate source materials such as glossaries, dictionaries, or an appropriate selection in another text. After reading activities, able teachers encourage children to revisit the text—to reread and make notes and paraphrase—to remember important points, interpret the text, evaluate its quality, and review important points. Children should also be encouraged to think about how ideas encountered in the text might be used in the future. As children gain competence, they enjoy showing what they know.

As a follow-up to the reading of a fictional selection, children should be encouraged to analyze the story using the story-grammar components of setting, characters, problems encountered by characters, attempts at solution to the problem, successful solution, and ending. It has been noted in the literature that even primary-level students, when asked to use comprehension strategies and monitoring, have benefited greatly from it.

As children's comprehension grows more sophisticated, they move from merely attempting to comprehend what is in the text to reading more critically. This means that they grow in understanding that any single text provides but one portrayal of the facts. With skillful instruction, children come to read not only what a text says; they also learn to attend to how that text portrays the subject matter. They recognize the various ways in which every text is the unique creation of a unique author, and they also learn to compare and contrast the treatment of the same subject matter in a number of texts. Teachers help students grow in comprehension through lessons. At first, teachers are happy if children are able to demonstrate their comprehension of what a text says by being able to engage in some after-reading activity that involves restating what was contained in the text in some authentic way. The next level is to have the children ponder what a text does: to describe an author's purpose, to recognize the elements of the text and how the text was assembled. Finally, some children can attain the skill set needed to successfully engage in text interpretation, to be able to detect and articulate tone and persuasive elements, to discuss point of view, and to recognize bias. Over time, and with good instruction, children learn to infer unstated meanings based on social conventions, shared knowledge, shared experience, or shared values. They make sense of text by recognizing implications and drawing conclusions, and they move past the point of believing the content of a selection simply because it was in print.

Another piece of the comprehension puzzle is that children need to be taught to monitor their own comprehension, and to decide when they need to exert more effort, or to apply a strategy to make sense of a text. The goal of comprehension instruction is for the children to reach a level at which the application of strategies becomes automatic.

In summary, comprehension is maximized only when readers are fluent in all the processes of skilled reading, from the decoding of words to the articulation and easy, appropriate application of the comprehension strategies used by good readers. Teachers need to teach predicting, questioning, seeking clarification, relating to background knowledge, constructing mental images, and summarizing. The teaching of comprehension strategies has to be conceived as a long-term developmental process, and the teaching of all reading strategies is more successful if they are taught and used by all of the teachers on a staff. In addition, teachers need to allow time for in-school reading, and recognize that good texts are comprehended on a deep level only through rereading and meaty discussions.

Fast Facts

Comprehension is maximized only when readers are fluent in all the processes of skilled reading.

The Writing Process

0004 Understand processes for generating, developing, revising, editing, and presenting/ publishing written texts.

For example:

- applying knowledge of prewriting strategies (e.g., brainstorming, prioritizing, and selecting topics including clustering and other graphic organizers)
- identifying effective techniques of note taking, outlining, and drafting
- revising written texts to improve unity and logical organization (e.g., formulating topic sentences, reordering paragraphs or sentences, adding transition words and phrases, eliminating distracting sentences)
- editing written work to ensure conformity to conventions of standard English usage (e.g., eliminating misplaced or dangling modifiers, eliminating sentence fragments, correcting errors in subject-verb agreement and pronoun-antecedent agreement)
- editing and proofreading written work to correct misspellings and eliminate errors in punctuation and capitalization
- applying knowledge of the uses of technology to plan, create, revise, edit, and present/publish written texts and multimedia works

0005 **Understand and apply writing skills and strategies for various purposes (including information and understanding, critical analysis and evaluation, literary response and personal expression, and social interaction).**

For example:
- analyzing factors a writer should consider when writing for a variety of audiences and purposes (e.g., informative, persuasive, expressive), including factors related to selection of topic and mode of written expression
- recognizing how to incorporate graphic representations (e.g., diagrams, graphs, time lines) into writing for various purposes
- applying knowledge of skills involved in writing a research paper (e.g., generating ideas and questions, posing problems, evaluating and summarizing data from a variety of print and nonprint sources)
- identifying techniques for expressing point of view, using logical organization, and avoiding bias in writing for critical analysis, evaluation, or persuasion
- demonstrating knowledge of strategies for writing a response to a literary selection by referring to the text, to other works, and to personal experience
- demonstrating awareness of voice in writing for personal expression and social interaction

Since the early 1970s, Dr. Donald Graves, a professor of education at the University of New Hampshire, has been working in classrooms trying to understand why writing seems to be so difficult to master for so many children. Through conversation with many working teachers, children, their parents, university students, and working writers, and via many keen-eyed observations in classrooms, he developed an approach to writing instruction called *process writing*.

His notion was simple: let's teach children to write the way real writers write. What do writers do? Well, to begin with, they tend to write about what they want to write about. Then they may read about the subject, talk about the subject, take notes, or generally fool around with the topic before they compose. Then they may write a draft, knowing up-front that they are not done at this point. They may share the draft with others, and end up writing all over it. They may also go over every sentence, thinking about word choice, and looking for vague spots, or spots where the piece falls off the subject. They may revise the draft again, share it again, revise it again, and so on, until they are satisfied with the product. Then they publish it. Often, they receive feedback before and after the piece is published, which may lead to a new writing effort. Some writers save scraps of writing in a journal. They may save a turn of phrase, a comment overheard on a bus, a new word, good quotes, or an interesting topic.

Doesn't this sound like a process a child might find helpful? Today, it seems a bit obvious. In the 1970s, 1980s, and even into the 1990s it seemed revolutionary. However, it was well received because teachers were pleased with the way students benefited from this kind of instruction. At the same time, in many schools computers were becoming readily available to students, and many teachers were finding that writing instruction and computers were a very happy marriage. Also, there were several excellent books available about helping children to write well. Donald Graves wrote *Writing: Teachers and Children at Work* and *A Fresh Look at Writing*. Lucy Calkins wrote *The Art of Teaching Writing*, and Nancy Atwell contributed *In the Middle: Writing, Reading, and Learning with Adolescents*. All of these and others offered support for this new way to augment children's efforts toward learning to write.

Nancy Atwell was particularly skilled in describing how a literacy-rich environment ought to be established and fostered. Children need to be encouraged to read books for enjoyment, but to also look at the craft of the author. Children need to respond to reading in writing. A great deal of research supported the notion that reading informs the writing process, and that the act of writing informs the reading process.

Donald Graves advised children to think about events in their lives as a good starting point for discovering topics. He liked to talk about Patricia Polacco books. Almost all of her books are reports of real-life events, things that happened to her and her rotten red-haired brother. For example, *Meteor!* was the story of one summer's night when a meteor fell into the yard. It could be told like this: "It was hot. We were outside. A meteor fell, and almost hit us. It didn't." The difference between that account and the published story provides a starting point for a potentially rich discussion about the craft of the writer.

Lucy Calkins, in *The Art of Teaching Writing*, addresses the importance of expecting good writing from children, and then giving them ample time to write, and the needed instruction and encouragement to make it happen. She suggests that children keep a writing notebook where they can keep little scraps of writing that might find their way into a written piece some day. This suggestion also helps with classroom management during a writer's workshop. It gives children something to do instead of wandering around the room or announcing, "I'm done!" and ceasing to write.

Another part of the writing process is to share the writing with a classmate, and allow that peer to edit the piece. Able teachers provide guidance for this process, so that the students do not simply declare the work "good" or leave the classmate in tears because the draft is ruthlessly criticized. Neither end of the spectrum results in the growth of a student's writing ability.

Following an edit for content, the piece is edited for features such as punctuation, capitalization, and spelling. The use of computers has made the entire writing process much easier. Children learn to use a thesaurus, dictionary, and the functions of spelling and grammar. Revisions can be made more easily. One of the best results, however, is that the finished piece *looks* finished. Gone are the days when a child did his or her personal best, only to get the paper back with "messy" scrawled in red across it.

Another aspect of the process is celebration. Children are invited to share their work with the class. After a young author reads their piece, classmates ought to offer affirmations and suggestions. Able teachers ought to have children save each piece of paper generated in the writing process, and store them in a personal portfolio for review.

Listening and Speaking Processes

0006 **Understand skills and strategies involved in listening and speaking for various purposes (including information and understanding, critical analysis and evaluation, literary response and expression, and social interaction).**

For example:

- recognizing appropriate listening strategies for given contexts and purposes (e.g., interpreting and analyzing information that is presented orally, appreciating literary texts that are read aloud, understanding small-group and large-group discussions)
- analyzing factors that affect the ability to listen effectively and to construct meaning from oral messages in various listening situations (e.g., using prior knowledge, recognizing transitions, interpreting nonverbal cues, using notetaking and outlining), and applying measures of effective listening (e.g., the ability to repeat instructions, the ability to retell stories)
- analyzing how features of spoken language (e.g., word choice, rate, pitch, tone, volume) and nonverbal cues (e.g., body language, visual aids, facial expressions) affect a speaker's ability to communicate effectively in given situations
- recognizing how to vary speaking strategies for different audiences, purposes, and occasions (e.g., providing instructions, participating in group discussions, persuading or entertaining an audience, giving an oral presentation or interpretation of a literary work)
- recognizing the effective use of oral communication skills and nonverbal communication skills in situations involving people of different ages, genders, cultures, and other personal characteristics
- applying knowledge of oral language conventions appropriate to a variety of social situations (e.g., informal conversations, job interviews)

Language is an intensely complex system for creating meaning through socially shared conventions. Very young children begin to learn language by listening and responding to to the people in their life. This early listening provides a foundation for acquisition of language. Babies are active listeners. Long before they can respond in speech per se, they encourage the person talking to them to continue by waving their arms, smiling, or wriggling, for example. On the other hand, they are also capable of clear communication when they have had enough by dropping eye contact or turning away, among other examples of body language.

Although listening is used extensively in communication, it does not receive much attention at school. Studies suggest that teachers assume that listening develops naturally. One study from 1986 suggests that teachers are not apt to get much training on teaching listening. A survey of fifteen textbooks used in teacher education programs revealed that out of a total of 3,704 pages of text, only 82 pages mentioned listening.

While there is no well-defined model of listening to guide instruction, there are some suggestions. Some theorists link listening skills to reading skills. They feel that reading and listening make use of similar language comprehension processes. Listening and reading both require the use of skills in phonology, syntax, semantics, and knowledge of text structure, and seem to be controlled by the same set of cognitive processes.

However, there is an additional factor in play in listening: the recipient of the oral message can elect to listen passively, or listen actively, with active listening being the desired goal. A number of studies suggest that the teaching of listening can be efficiently taught by engaging in the kinds of activities that have been successful in developing reading, writing, and speaking proficiencies and skills such as setting a purpose for listening, giving directions, asking questions about the selection heard, and encouraging children to forge links between the new information that was just heard and the knowledge already in place. In addition, children need to be coached in the use of appropriate volume and speed when they speak, and in learning how to participate in discussions and follow the rules of polite conversation, such as staying on a topic and taking turns.

Literature

0007   Understand and apply techniques of literary analysis to works of fiction, drama, poetry, and nonfiction.

For example:
- analyzing similarities and differences between fiction and nonfiction
- demonstrating knowledge of story elements in works of fiction (e.g., plot, character, setting, theme, mood)
- applying knowledge of drama to analyze dramatic structure (e.g., introduction, rising action, climax, falling action, conclusion) and identify common dramatic devices (e.g., soliloquy, aside)
- applying knowledge of various types of nonfiction (e.g., informational texts, newspaper articles, essays, biographies, memoirs, letters, journals)
- analyzing the use of language to convey style, tone, and point of view in works of fiction and nonfiction
- recognizing the formal elements of a poetic text (e.g., meter, rhyme scheme, stanza structure, alliteration, assonance, onomatopoeia, figurative language) and analyzing their relationship to the meaning of the text

0008   Demonstrate knowledge of literature, including literature from diverse cultures and literature for children/adolescents.

For example:
- demonstrating awareness of ways in which literary texts reflect the time and place in which they were written
- demonstrating awareness of the ways in which literary works reflect and express cultural values and ideas
- recognizing major themes and characteristics of works written by well-known authors
- demonstrating knowledge of important works and authors of literature for children and adolescents
- analyzing themes and elements of traditional and contemporary literature for children and adolescents

Genre

A genre is a particular type of literature. Classifications of genre are largely arbitrary—based on conventions that apply a basic category to an author's writing. They give the reader a general expectation of what sort of book is being picked up. Teachers today are expected to share a wide range of texts with children. Charlotte Huck, Susan Hepler, Janet Hickman, and Barbara Kiefer, in their book, *Children's Literature in the Elementary School*, define children's literature as "a book a child is reading." They go on to list picture books, traditional literature, modern fantasy, realistic fiction, historical fiction, nonfiction, biography, and poetry as genres of children's literature. Most genres can be subdivided into a variety of categories, and it is possible that genres could be mixed in a single title.

Picture books are books in which the illustrations and the text work together to communicate the story. There is a huge market for picture books, and they cover many topics. It is a very good idea to share picture books with children in a number of different formats.

Sometimes, able teachers simply read the book to the child without showing any of the pictures. The story is then discussed, and the children are asked if they would like the book to be reread, this time with the pictures being shared. Typically, this technique sparks a lively conversation about why the book with its illustrations is better than hearing the words alone.

Alternatively, teachers may take the children on a picture-walk through the book, allowing them to speculate about the story before reading it to them. Then, once the book is read, the speculations can be confirmed or reassessed.

Using picture books allows teachers to discuss the elements of higher-level comprehension without the burden of reading lengthy prose, for a picture book can be discussed with an eye on many different factors: design, color, space, media choice, cultural conventions, point of view, showing vs. telling, fairness, realism, or concerns. It is a way to raise issues in a classroom community, and it's a subtle way to affirm classroom members. Nearly any lesson worth teaching is better taught with a picture book in hand. Picture books can be very useful tools in a variety of ways: nearly any concept can be both deepened and expanded by reading the appropriate picture books.

Traditional literature comprises the stories that have their roots in the oral tradition of storytelling. This genre also includes the modern versions of these old stories. It is interesting to read and share multiple versions of old stories, and to compare and contrast each version. It is also interesting to read a number of folktales and keep track of the elements that these old stories have in common. It's also interesting to encourage children to notice where these old stories show up in their day-to-day lives. Children enjoy sharing what they notice. These old stories are woven into ads, comic books, jokes, and other selections.

Modern fantasy is a genre that presents make-believe stories that are the product of the author's imagination. The point of origin for all of these stories is the imagination of the author. Often, they are so beyond the realm of everyday life that they can't possibly be true. Extraordinary events take place within the covers of these books. Fantasy allows a child to move beyond the normal, ho-hum life in the classroom, and speculate about a life that never was, and may never be. But, maybe, just maybe, wouldn't it be grand if an owl were to swoop through an open window and drop a fat letter? What if you dumped some cereal into a bowl, and a lump dropped into the bowl with a thud, and it turned out to be a dragon's egg? What if you could step through a wardrobe and be someplace completely different? Fantasy is a genre that typically sparks rather intense discussions, and provides ample opportunities to illuminate the author's craft for the child.

Historical fiction is set in the past. This type of fiction allows children to live vicariously in times and places they do not normally experience any other way. This type of fiction often has real people and real events depicted, with fiction laced around them. Historical fiction informs the study of social studies. The textbook might say, "and then the tea was dumped in the harbor." *Johnny Tremain* vividly brings the event into focus. These books often bring the emotions of the situation into sharp relief. When reading *Pink and Say*, by Patricia Polacco, children are stunned when one of the boys is summarily hanged as he enters Andersonville. *Number the Stars*, by Lois Lowry, begins a conversation about what we would be willing to give up to save a friend.

Nonfiction books have the real world as their point of origin. These books help to expand the knowledge of children when they are studying a topic; however, these books need to be evaluated for accuracy, authenticity, and inclusion of the salient facts. It is a very good idea to include the children in this process, and, when an inaccuracy is detected, it's a good idea to encourage the child or children who spotted the flaw to write to the publisher and relate their findings. Typically, the publisher writes back, thus turning a published flaw into an authentic, empowering writing experience for a child. Again, these books can be the platform for teaching higher-level comprehension skills. Children and their teachers can discuss fact vs. theory. For example, the reintroduction of wolves into Yellowstone is a topic that exists in the real world, and reading materials on the subject are readily available. The *fact* is that wolves are carnivorous predators. The *theory* part of the investigation could be a discussion of the impact that reintroducing wolves into the Yellowstone ecosystem might have. This discussion will need to be supported with documentation. The materials read will need to be evaluated in terms of the intended audience, bias, inclusion of enough information, and text structure. These books can also be powerful in creating a community of learners, as they can be used as a means of gathering information about a topic that children are working on together as part of a cooperative learning group. Since nonfiction books are written at a variety of reading levels, all children can find a book to read, and since different titles have different information, the children end up swapping and talking about the books. It makes for some touching and powerful moments in a classroom.

Biography is a genre that deals with the lives of real people. Autobiography is a genre that deals with the life of the author. These books enliven the study of social studies because, through careful research, they often include information that transforms a name in a textbook into a person that one may like to get to know better. Did you know that George Washington had false teeth carved from the finest hippopotamus ivory? Did you know that Dolley Madison was stripping wallpaper—very expensive hand-painted silk wallpaper, no less—off the walls in the residence in the White House as British warships were moving up the Potomac River? Again, these books can provide a platform for dynamic lessons about higher-level comprehension skills, especially about bias. Consider the treatment of Helen Keller. Was any information included about how feisty and forward-thinking she was?

Poetry is a genre that is difficult to define for children, except as "not-prose." Poetry is the use of words to capture something: a sight, a feeling, or perhaps a sound. Poetry needs to be chosen carefully for a child, as poetry ought to elicit a response from the child—one that connects with the experience of the poem. All children need poetry in their lives. Poetry needs to be celebrated and enjoyed as part of the classroom experience, and a literacy-rich classroom will always include a collection of poetry to read, reread, savor, and enjoy. Some children enjoy the discipline of writing in a poetic format. Reggie Routman has published a series of slim books about teaching children to write poems on their own.

In summary, today there is an overwhelming variety of children's literature to choose from. When selecting books for use in a classroom, a teacher has a number of issues to consider. Is the book accurate? Aesthetically pleasing? Engaging? Bear in mind the idea that all children deserve to see positive images of children like themselves in the books they read, as illustrations can have a powerful influence on their perceptions of the world. Children also have a need to see positive images of children who are not like themselves, as who is or is not depicted in books can have a powerful influence on their perception of the world as well. Teachers ought to provide children with literature that depicts an affirming, multicultural view, and the selection of books available should show many different kinds of protagonists. Both boys and girls, for example, should be depicted as able.

Literary Elements and Techniques

Poetry (like much prose) uses various kinds of figurative language—that is, language used in ways that are not literal. Most poems (unlike prose) employ some kind of prosody, which designates various formal elements of poetry.

Figures of speech, sometimes called rhetorical tropes, include metaphor, simile, metonymy, hyperbole, apostrophe, personification, litotes (or understatement), and oxymoron. Metaphor is the comparison of two unlike things by calling one thing by the name of another. Simile is like metaphor, but compares two things using the words "like" or "as." Metonymy substitutes one word is for another with which it is closely associated. Hyperbole is a fanciful or vivid exaggeration. In apostrophe, a speaker addresses a person who is absent or an inanimate thing or abstract idea. Similarly, personification attributes human characteristics to things or ideas. Litotes, the opposite of hyperbole, understates a thought or attribute of something. An oxymoron describes something using words with opposite meanings.

Elements of prosody, or poetic form, include rhythm, meter, and rhyme. The sound of poetry is further structured by formal techniques such as alliteration, and assonance. Rhythm means the regular alteration of stressed and unstressed syllables in a poem. Meter refers to a repeated pattern of stressed and unstressed syllables in each line of a poem (or stanza, a formal subdivision of a poem), as well as the length of lines in a poem. Rhyme means the repetition of vowel sounds at the ends of lines; rhyme scheme refers to the way rhyming sounds are patterned in a whole poem. Alliteration is the repetition of consonant sounds in a poem; assonance is the repetition of vowel sounds within lines or throughout a poem.

Elements of Fiction

A work of fiction often narrates a main series of events, known as the plot. These events may form not only the core of the work's content, but also the backbone of its structure or organization. Foreshadowing anticipates or hints at the future events or conclusion of a plot, while flashbacks are narrations of events in the past of the main narration.

A fiction's narrator is the person, or the imagined "voice," who is telling the story. A first-person narrator, or first-person point of view, is a narrator who is also actually a character in the narration; first-person narrators are only aware of events that a character would likely experience. Rarely used, a second-person narrator (or point of view) seems to describe events that the reader, or some person the narrator is addressing directly, is doing. A third-person narrator (or point of view) stands outside the action of the narration itself, and may be omniscient—that is, may know everything about the characters and events in the fiction—or limited, that is, they may only know the kinds of things the characters themselves know.

Voice is the degree of formality or informality, or of emotional involvement or distance, used by a narrator; voice is closely related to tone, which is the attitude a narrator seems to take toward his or her readers.

Characters are fictional persons. Their speech is called dialog, while what the narrator says about characters is called exposition. Round characters are main characters who are thoroughly developed; flat characters are less well developed and often serve a minor function in the plot.

Setting is the place and time in which a narrative takes place.

A text's theme is the main idea or concept it deals with, the story's "problem."

Imagery, or mimesis, means vivid description, as opposed to narration in the strict sense. Imagery fleshes out the places and things in a fictional text.

Dramatic Devices

For both practical and traditional reasons, there are certain literary terms specific to dramatic literature. For example, while novels are often subdivided into chapters and poems are subdivided into stanzas, plays are usually subdivided into acts and scenes. Plays usually contain stage directions, or instructions for actors on stage as well as for production staff; they may indicate, for example, when characters should enter and exit scenes. Certain conventions, such as the aside and the soliloquy, are traditional dramatic techniques. In the *aside*, a character speaks briefly directly to the audience; in a *soliloquy*, a character utters his thoughts aloud at length. Comic relief consists of comic scenes or lines inserted into an otherwise serious play; melodrama is a kind of popular drama with clear-cut heroes and villains; stock characters, who often appear in melodramas, are stereotyped characters.

Knowledge of Literature

Purposes of Children's Literature

Children's literature usually seeks to entertain. When literature entertains, it encourages children to master the skills of literacy and appreciate the distinctive characteristics of written texts.

Literature for children also often seeks to expand their ability to think in a narrative mode. This, in turn, helps develop the ability to understand cause and effect relationships, and thereby helps children learn to plan, evaluate, and judge.

Literature also develops ethical values by illustrating the consequences of wise and unwise actions. Similarly, children's literature seeks not only to deliver factual information to children but also to instruct them in matters of emotion, thereby fostering empathy.

Children's literature helps develop the imagination, along with spatial thinking, problem solving, and creativity.

Reading should help make children aware of literate language and textuality. While much children's literature may seek to imitate the spoken word, it should also accustom children to the special rhythms, diction, and conventions of written language.

Children's literature should make children aware of universal human experiences while also fostering broadmindedness and curiosity about the lives and cultures of others.

Literary Elements of Children's Literature

Themes in children's literature are often didactic; that is, they usually intend to teach a lesson. Common themes in children's literature are overcoming fear, learning empathy, facing new or unknown situations, learning a new skill or ability, gaining patience, and overcoming hardship.

Plots in children's fiction are usually simpler than in adult books, and rely less on flashbacks and other forms of counterintuitive sequencing. Often children's books follow a single plotline, although different plots are sometimes woven together. Mystery and suspense are used in children's book to maintain interest until the end of the narrative.

In children's books—especially those for younger children—characterization is often allegorical. Animals and fantastic characters stand for ideas or personality traits. These characters are often deliberately one-dimensional in order to make them recognizable to children as distinct personalities. Characterization in books for older children is usually more complex.

The literary style of books for young children relies on rhyme, repetition, and simple syntax. Children's books include more straightforward narration than description or authorial reflection. Again, literary style in books for older children is more like that of adult literature.

Genres of Children's Literature

Books for babies and beginning readers include toy books, which often include doors and flaps to open, special materials to be rubbed or patted, and electronic devices that play voices or sounds; an example is the popular *Pat the Bunny*. Books of nursery rhymes include easy-to-remember songs and poems; the most famous nursery rhyme books are the various editions of *Mother Goose*. Alphabet and counting books teach basic literacy and numeracy skills. Concept books list and describe the objects in an abstract class, such as animals, trees, or vehicles. Wordless books tell stories in pictures only.

Picture books for older children tell simple illustrated stories. Well-known picture books for older children include Maurice Sendak's *Where the Wild Things Are*, *Blueberries for Sal* by Robert McCloskey, *The Relatives Came* by Cynthia Rylant, and *Aunt Flossie's Hats (and Crab Cakes Later)* by Elizabeth Fitzgerald Howard.

Many children's books, including many picture books, adapt (or create anew) well-known folktales, myths, legends, and fables for children. Adaptations of Aesop, the stories collected by the Brothers Grimm and Hans Christian Andersen, and versions of *The Three Billy Goats Gruff* and *Puss in Boots* fall into this category, as do adaptations of the African-American Uncle Remus stories and the Jack stories of Appalachia. These tales usually feature magic, talking animals, a strong contrast between wise and foolish behavior, and repetition of words and events. Versions of the stories of Robin Hood and King Arthur and the Knights of the Roundtable are similar.

Fantasy literature for children includes such famous books as *Alice's Adventures in Wonderland* by Lewis Carroll, *The Wonderful Wizard of Oz* by L. Frank Baum, *The Hobbit* by J.R.R. Tolkien, and *The Lion, The Witch, and the Wardrobe* by C.S. Lewis. More recent fantastic books include *The Indian in the Cupboard* by Lynne Reid Banks, *James and the Giant Peach* by Roald Dahl, and the Harry Potter books by J.K. Rowling.

Realistic fiction for older children includes fiction with contemporary or historical settings. The stories in these texts plausibly portray life as it is lived today or in the past; realistic fiction does not usually include the adventures of supernatural beings, talking animals, or anthropomorphized objects. Realistic fiction may be concerned with the problems of growing up, elements of adult life, or the lives of important historical figures. Important examples of texts in this genre include *The Yearling* by Marjorie Kinnan Rawlings, *Where the Red Fern Grows* by Wilson Rawls, *My Side of the Mountain* by Jean Craighead George, *Island of the Blue Dolphins* by Scott O'Dell, *Roll of Thunder, Hear My Cry* by Mildred D. Taylor, *That Was Then, This Is Now* by S.E. Hinton, *Jacob Have I Loved* by Katherine Paterson, *The True Confessions of Charlotte Doyle* by Avi, and *Out of the Dust* by Karen Hesse.

Nonfiction books for children may be concerned with scientific, historical, or biographical matters, or they may address the problems of childhood and adolescence. Important or award-winning children's nonfiction books include *Blizzard! The Storm That Changed America* by Jim Murphy, *The Wright Brothers: How They Invented the Airplane* by Russell Freedman, *Good Queen Bess: The Story of Elizabeth I of England* by Diane Stanley and Peter Vennema, *It's Perfectly Normal: Changing Bodies, Growing Up, Sex, and Sexual Health* by Robie H. Harris, and *When Marian Sang: The True Recital of Marian Anderson* by Pam Munoz Ryan.

Poetry for children includes nursery rhymes and songs written for small children to learn and sing. Poetry written for older children is more complex than nursery rhymes, but usually simpler than adult poetry. Recent award-winning books of poetry for children include *All the Small Poems and Fourteen More* by Valerie Worth, *Joyful Noise: Poems for Two Voices* by Paul Fleischman, and *A Visit to William Blake's Inn: Poems for Innocent and Experienced Travelers* by Nancy Willard.

Evaluating Children's Literature

The physical form of children's books is much more important than that of books for adults. Books for very young children should be especially sturdy, and books for beginning readers should use a large, widely-spaced typeface. Matte-finish paper cuts glare and is easier to read.

Books selected to be read aloud to young children should deal with familiar themes and have relatively simple storylines. Often, the best books for reading aloud are picture books.

Although some children's literature is didactic, children are often bored by preachy or overly sentimental books. Narrative books for all age levels should avoid letting thematic matters, especially direct address to the reader, overwhelm plot.

Many older books can be culturally biased or otherwise condescending to some readers. Books should be avoided that insult children's cultural or social background.

There are several awards presented to outstanding children's literature. The John Newbery Medal, the oldest award for children's literature, is awarded by the Association for Library Service to Children to the most outstanding author of a children's book in the previous year. The Randolph J. Caldecott Medal is awarded for the best illustrated book of the previous year. The International Board on Books for Young People awards the annual Hans Christian Andersen Award to a living author in recognition of his or her body of work. Lists of literary award winners can be helpful in choosing books for children.

Mathematics

Objectives

0009 **Understand formal and informal reasoning processes, including logic and simple proofs, and apply problem-solving techniques and strategies in a variety of contexts.**

For example:
- using models, facts, patterns, and relationships to draw conclusions about mathematical problems or situations
- judging the validity or logic of mathematical arguments
- drawing a valid conclusion based on stated conditions and evaluating conclusions involving simple and compound sentences
- applying inductive reasoning to make mathematical conjectures
- using a variety of problem-solving strategies to model and solve problems, and evaluating the appropriateness of a problem-solving strategy (e.g., estimation, mental math, working backward, pattern recognition) in a given situation
- analyzing the usefulness of a specific model or mental math procedure for exploring a given mathematical, scientific, or technological idea or problem

0010 **Use mathematical terminology and symbols to interpret, represent, and communicate mathematical ideas and information.**

For example:
- using mathematical notation to represent a given relationship
- using appropriate models, diagrams, and symbols to represent mathematical concepts
- using appropriate vocabulary to express given mathematical ideas and relationships
- relating the language of ordinary experiences to mathematical language and symbols
- translating among graphic, numeric, symbolic, and verbal representations of mathematical relationships and concepts
- using mathematical representations to model and interpret physical, social, and mathematical phenomena

0011 **Understand skills and concepts related to number and numeration, and apply these concepts to real-world situations.**

For example:
- selecting the appropriate computational and operational method to solve a given mathematical problem
- demonstrating an understanding of the commutative, distributive, and associative properties
- using ratios, proportions, and percents to model and solve problems
- comparing and ordering fractions, decimals, and percents
- solving problems using equivalent forms of numbers (e.g., integer, fraction, decimal, percent, exponential and scientific notation), and problems involving number theory (e.g., primes, factors, multiples)
- analyzing the number properties used in operational algorithms (e.g., multiplication, long division)
- applying number properties to manipulate and simplify algebraic expressions

0012 **Understand patterns and apply the principles and properties of linear algebraic relations and functions.**

For example:
- recognizing and describing mathematical relationships
- using a variety of representations (e.g., manipulatives, figures, numbers, calculators) to recognize and extend patterns
- analyzing mathematical relationships and patterns using tables, verbal rules, equations, and graphs
- deriving an algebraic expression or function to represent a relationship or pattern from the physical or social world
- using algebraic functions to describe given graphs, to plot points, and to determine slopes
- performing algebraic operations to solve equations and inequalities
- analyzing how changing one variable changes the other variable for linear and nonlinear functions

0013 **Understand the principles and properties of geometry and trigonometry, and apply them to model and solve problems.**

For example:
- identifying relationships among two- and three-dimensional geometric shapes
- applying knowledge of basic geometric figures to solve real-world problems involving more complex patterns (e.g., area and perimeter of composite figures)
- applying the concepts of similarity and congruence to model and solve problems
- applying inductive and deductive reasoning to solve problems in geometry
- using coordinate geometry to represent and analyze properties of geometric figures
- applying transformations (e.g., reflections, rotations, dilations) and symmetry to analyze properties of geometric figures

0014 **Understand concepts, principles, skills, and procedures related to the customary and metric systems of measurement.**

For example:
- demonstrating knowledge of fundamental units of customary and metric measurement
- selecting an appropriate unit to express measures of length, area, capacity, weight, volume, time, temperature, and angle
- estimating and converting measurements using standard and nonstandard measurement units within customary and metric systems
- developing and using formulas to determine the perimeter and area of two-dimensional shapes and the surface area and volume of three-dimensional shapes
- solving measurement problems involving derived measurements (e.g., velocity, density)
- applying the Pythagorean theorem and right triangle trigonometry to solve measurement problems

0015 **Understand concepts and skills related to data analysis, probability, and statistics, and apply this understanding to evaluate and interpret data and to solve problems.**

For example:
- demonstrating the ability to collect, organize, and analyze data using appropriate graphic and nongraphic representations
- displaying and interpreting data in a variety of different formats (e.g., frequency histograms, tables, pie charts, box-and-whisker plots, stem-and-leaf plots, scatterplots)
- computing probabilities using a variety of methods (e.g., ratio and proportion, tree diagrams, tables of data, area models)
- using simulations (e.g., spinners, multisided dice, random number generators) to estimate probabilities
- applying measures of central tendency (mean, median, mode) and spread (e.g., range, percentiles, variance) to analyze data in graphic or nongraphic form
- formulating and designing statistical experiments to collect, analyze, and interpret data
- identifying patterns and trends in data and making predictions based on those trends

Mathematical Reasoning Processes

Mathematical reasoning includes analyzing problem situations, making conjectures, organizing information, and selecting strategies to solve problems; evaluating solutions to problems; constructing arguments and judging the validity or logic of arguments; and using logical reasoning to draw and justify conclusions from given information.

Problem-solvers must rely on both formal and informal *reasoning processes*. A key informal process relies on *reasonableness*. Consider this problem:

> Center Town Middle School has an enrollment of 640 students. One day, 28 students were absent. What percent of the total number of students were absent?

Even if someone forgot how to compute percents, some possible answers could be rejected instantly: 28 is a "small-but-not-tiny" chunk of 640, so answers like 1%, 18%, and 25% are *unreasonable*.

There are also formal reasoning processes, such as *deductive reasoning*. Deductive reasoning is reasoning from the general to the specific, and is supported by deductive logic. Here is an example of deductive reasoning:

> All ducks have wings (a general assertion). Donald is a duck; therefore Donald has wings (a specific proposition).

With *inductive reasoning*, a general rule is inferred from specific observations (which may be limited). Moving from the statement "All boys in this classroom are wearing jeans" (a specific but limited observation) to "All boys wear jeans" (a general assertion) is an example of inductive reasoning. Note that conclusions arrived at via deductive and inductive reasoning are not necessarily true.

Problem Solving

The ability to render some real-life quandaries into mathematical or logical problems—workable via established procedures—is a key to finding solutions. Because each quandary will be unique, so too will be your problem-solving plan of attack. Still, many real-world problems that lend themselves to mathematical solutions are likely to require one of the following strategies.

1. **Guess and check** (not the same as "wild guessing"). With this problem-solving strategy, make your best guess, and then check the answer to see whether it's right. Even if the guess doesn't immediately provide the

solution, it may help to get you closer to it so that you can continue to work on it. An example:

Three persons' ages add up to 72, and each person is one year older than the last person. What are their ages?

Because the three ages must add up to 72, it is reasonable to take one-third of 72 (24) as your starting point. Of course, even though 24 + 24 + 24 gives a sum of 72, those numbers don't match the information ("Each person is one year older...") So, you might guess that the ages are 24, 25, and 26. You check that guess by addition, and you see that the sum of 75 is too high. Lowering your guesses by one each, you try 23, 24, and 25, which indeed add up to 72, giving you the solution. There are many variations of the guess and check method.

2. **Making a sketch or a picture** can help to clarify a problem. Consider this problem:

Mr. Rosenberg plans to put a four-foot-wide concrete sidewalk around his backyard pool. The pool is rectangular, with dimensions 12' by 24'. The cost of the concrete is $1.28 per square foot. How much concrete is required for the job?

If you have exceptional visualization abilities, no sketch is needed. For most of us, however, a drawing like the one shown below may be helpful in solving this and many other real-life problems.

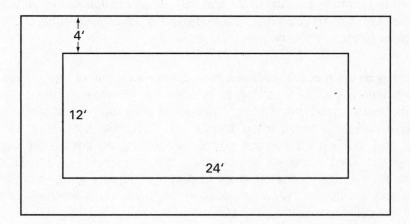

3. **Make a table or a chart.** Sometimes, *organizing* the information from a problem makes it easier to find the solution; tables and charts can be helpful.

4. **Making a list**, like making a table or chart, can help to organize information, and perhaps provide or at least hint at a solution. The strategy would work well for solving this problem: "How many different outcomes are there if you roll two regular six-sided dice?"

5. **Act it out.** Sometimes, literally "doing" a problem, with physical objects, your bodies, and so forth, can help produce a solution. A classic problem that could be solved in this manner is the following: "If five strangers meet, and if everyone shakes everyone else's hand once, how many total handshakes will there be?"

6. **Look for patterns.** This technique encourages you to ask, "What's happening here?" Spotting a pattern would be helpful in solving a problem such as:

   Nevin's weekly savings account balance for 15 weeks are as follows: $125, $135, $148, $72, $85, $96, $105, $50, $64, $74, $87, $42, $51, $60, $70. If the pattern holds, (approximately) what might Nevin's balance be the next week?

7. **Working a simpler problem** means finding the solution to a different but simpler problem, hoping that you will spot a way to solve the harder one. *Estimating* can be thought of as working a simpler problem. If you need to know the product of 23 and 184, and no calculator or pencil and paper are handy, you could estimate the product by getting the exact answer to the simpler problem, 20×200.

8. **Writing an open math sentence** (an equation with one or more variables, or "unknowns"), then solving it, is often an effective strategy. This is sometimes called "translating" a problem into mathematics. Consider this problem: "Tiana earned grades of 77%, 86%, 90%, and 83% on her first four weekly science quizzes. Assuming all grades are equally weighted, what score will she need on the fifth week's quiz in order to have an average (or mean) score of 88%?" Using the given information, you can set up the following equation, which, when solved, will answer the question:

$$\frac{(77 + 86 + 90 + 83 + x)}{5} = 88$$

9. **Work backward.** Consider this problem: "If you add 12 to some number, then multiply the sum by 4, you will get 60. What is the number?" You can find a solution by *starting at the end*, with 60. The problem tells you that the 60 came from multiplying a sum by 4. When multiplied by 4, 15 equals 60, so 15 must be the sum referred to. And if 15 is the sum of 12 and something else, the "something else" can only be 3.

There are of course hybrid approaches. You can mix and match problem-solving strategies wherever you think they are appropriate. In general, attention to *reasonableness* may be most crucial to problem-solving success, especially in real-life situations.

Mathematical Communication and Mathematical Terminology, Symbols, and Representations

While a review of even basic mathematical terminology and symbolism could fill a book, there are some key points to keep in mind:

Mathematics is, for the most part, a science of precision. When working with math symbols and terminology, meticulousness is in order. For example, "less than" does not mean the same thing as "not greater than." The following two equations are *not* equivalent (both entire sides of the first equation should be divided by 6.)

$$6m + 2 = 18$$

$$\frac{6m}{6} + 2 = \frac{18}{6}$$

All of this matters, especially in real-life problem situations.

Certain mathematical concepts and terms are frequently misunderstood. Here are a few of the "repeat offenders":

Use care with *hundreds vs. hundredths*, *thousands vs. thousandths*, and so forth. Remember that the "th" at the end of the word indicates a fraction. "Three hundred" means 300, whereas "three hundredths" means 0.03.

Negative numbers are those less than zero. Fractions less than zero are negative numbers, too.

The *absolute value* of a number can be thought of as its distance from zero on a number line.

Counting numbers can be shown by the set (1, 2, 3, 4, . . .). Notice that 0 is not a counting number.

Whole numbers are the counting numbers, plus 0 (0, 1, 2, . . .).

Integers are all of the whole numbers and their negative counterparts (. . . –2, –1, 0, 1, 2, . . .). Note that negative and positive fractions are not considered integers (unless they are equivalent to whole numbers or their negative counterparts).

Factors are any of the numbers or symbols in mathematics that, when multiplied together, form a product. (The whole number factors of 12 are 1, 2, 3, 4, 6, and 12.) A number with exactly two whole number factors (1 and the number itself) is a *prime number*. The first few primes are 2, 3, 5, 7, 11, 13, and 17. Most other whole numbers are *composite numbers*, because they are *composed* of several whole number factors (1 is neither prime nor composite; it has only one whole number factor).

The *multiples* of any whole number are what are produced when the number is multiplied by counting numbers. The multiples of 7 are 7, 14, 21, 28, and so on. Every whole number has an infinite number of multiples.

Recall that *decimal numbers* are simply certain fractions written in special notation. All decimal numbers are actually fractions whose denominators are powers of 10 (10, 100, 1000, etc.) 0.033, for instance, can be thought of as the fraction $\frac{33}{1000}$.

There is an agreed-upon order of operations for simplifying complex expressions.

First you compute any multiplication or division, left to right. Then you compute any addition or subtraction, also left-to-right. (If an expression contains any parentheses, all computation within the parentheses should be completed first.) Treat exponential expressions ("powers") as multiplication. Thus, the expression $3 + 7 \times 4 - 2$ equals 29. (Multiply 7 by 4 *before* doing the addition and subtraction.)

Exponential notation is a way to show repeated multiplication more simply. $2 \times 2 \times 2$, for instance, can be shown as 2^3, and is equal to 8. (Note: 2^3 does *not* mean 2×3.)

Scientific notation provides a method for showing numbers using exponents (although it is most useful for very large and very small numbers.) A number is in scientific notation when it is shown as a number between 1 and 10 to a power of 10. Thus, the number 75,000 in scientific notation is shown as 7.5×10^4.

Addends (or *addenda*) can be thought of as "parts of addition problems." When addends are combined, they produce *sums*. Likewise, *factors* can be seen as "parts of multiplication problems." When factors are multiplied, they produce *products*. When two numbers are divided, one into the other, the result is a *quotient*.

Equations are not the same as mathematical *expressions*. $12 + 4 = 16$ and $2x + 7 = 12$ are equations. $(144 - 18)$ and $13y^2$ are expressions. Notice that expressions are "lacking a verb," so to speak (you don't say "is equal to" or "equals" when reading expressions). Inequalities are very much like equations, but "greater than" or "less than" are added, such as in $x \leq 7$.

> **Fast Facts**
>
> **Careful use of mathematical terms and ideas is essential to communicating mathematically.**

A *trend* is a pattern over time.

Careful use of mathematical terms and ideas such as those noted above is essential to communicating mathematically.

The ability to convert among various mathematical and logical representations (graphic, numeric, symbolic, verbal) is an important skill, and, as with problem solving, precision and care are keys to quality conversions. Consider this number line, which might represent ages of students who are eligible for a particular scholarship:

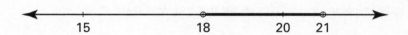

Are 21-year-old students eligible? No, because the conventional notation used on the number line shows a *circle* around the point at 21. That means that 21 is *not* included in the set. Converting the graphic representation to symbolism gives $18 < x < 21$.

Number Skills

Key properties of whole numbers (and some related terms) include the following:

The Commutative Property for Addition and Multiplication states that the order in which addends are added or factors are multiplied does not determine the sum or product. (6×9 gives the same product as 9×6, for instance.) Division and subtraction are not commutative.

The Associative Property for Addition and Multiplication states that "associating" three or more addends or factors in a different fashion will not change the sum or product. For example, (3 + 7) + 5 gives the same sum as 3 + (7 + 5). Division and subtraction are not associative.

The *Distributive Property of Multiplication over Addition* is shown hereafter in simple notation form:

$$a(b + c) = (a \times b) + (a \times c)$$

An illustration of the Distributive Property is this: multiplying 6 by 47 will give the same result as multiplying 6 by 40, multiplying 6 times 7, then *adding* the products. That is, $6 \times (47) = (6 \times 40) + (6 \times 7)$.

Some pairs of operations are considered to be *inverse*. Addition and subtraction are inverse operations, as are multiplication and division. The operations can be thought of as "undoing" one another: Multiplying 4 by 9 gives 36; dividing 36 by 9 "gives back" 4.

The *Multiplicative Identity Property of One* states that any number multiplied by 1 remains the same. ($34 \times 1 = 34$, for instance.) The number 1 is called the *Multiplicative Identity*.

The *Property of Reciprocals* states that any number (except for zero) multiplied by its reciprocal gives 1. (The *reciprocal* of a number is 1 divided by that number.)

Remember that dividing by zero is considered to have no meaning; avoid doing it when computing or solving equations and inequalities.

The *Additive Identity Property of Zero* states that adding zero to any number will not change the number (87 + 0 = 87, for instance). Zero is called the *Additive Identity*.

Division is *partitive* when you know the total and the number of parts or groups but you don't how many are in each part. Consider: "You have 7 containers of bolts and a total of 98 bolts. How many bolts are in each container (assuming the same number in each)?" Arriving at the answer is an example of partitive division.

With *measurement division*, the number of groups is not known. Using the example above, if you knew that there were 14 bolts per container, and that there were 98 bolts altogether, finding the number of containers would require measurement division.

Rational Numbers, Fractions, and Decimals

A property of real numbers is *The Density Property*. It states that, given any two real numbers, there is always another real number between them. (Think of the number line: No matter how close two points are, there is always a point between them.)

Rational numbers are those that can be written as fractions. (This includes integers; 12, for instance, can be written as $\frac{12}{1}$.)

Decimals (or "decimal fractions"), which come to an end when represented exactly, are *terminating decimals* (2.125, for instance). *Repeating decimals* are those in which the digits repeat a pattern endlessly (3.333333 . . . , for example). To use shorthand notation to show repeating decimals, you can write the "repeating_block" just once, putting a bar over it. The example above, for instance, can be shown as $3.\overline{3}$. (Both terminating and repeating decimals are rational numbers.)

Some numbers are real numbers, but cannot be accurately represented by fractions. The ratio of the length of the circumference of any circle to its diameter, or π, for instance, is irrational. There are useful approximations of π, such as 3.14159, but π cannot be "pinned down" in either fraction or decimal notation.

Fractions, decimal numbers, ratios, and percents can be thought of as different ways of representing values, and any given rational number can be shown any of those ways. It is useful to be able to convert from one to the other. The following are some conversion tips:

The practical method for changing a fraction into a decimal is by dividing the numerator by the denominator. For example, $\frac{1}{4}$ becomes 0.25 when 1 is divided by 4, as follows:

$$
\begin{array}{r}
.25 \\
4\overline{)1.00} \\
\underline{8} \\
20 \\
\underline{20} \\
0
\end{array}
$$

Naturally, this can be done longhand or with a calculator. (If the decimal number includes a whole number, as with $2\frac{3}{5}$, you can ignore the whole number when doing the division.) The decimal number may terminate or repeat. Converting a simple fraction to a decimal number will never result in an irrational number.

To convert a non-repeating decimal number to a fraction in lowest terms, simply write the decimal as a fraction with the denominator a power of ten, and then reduce to lowest terms. For example, 0.125 can be written as $\frac{125}{1000}$, which reduces to $\frac{1}{8}$.

Any decimal number can be converted to a percent by shifting the decimal point two places to the right and adding the percent symbol. 0.135, for instance, becomes 13.5%. (If the number before the percent symbol is a whole number, there is no need to show the decimal point.)

A percent can be converted to a decimal number by shifting the decimal point two places to the left and dropping the percent symbol: 98% becomes 0.98 as a decimal.

A percent can be converted to a fraction simply by putting the percent (without the percent symbol) over 100, then reducing. In this way 20% can be shown as $\frac{20}{100}$, which reduces to $\frac{1}{5}$.

Ratio notation is simply an alternative method for showing fractions. For example, $\frac{2}{5}$ can be rewritten as "2 to 5." Ratio notation is commonly used when you want to emphasize the relationship of one number to another. Ratios are often shown as numbers with a colon between them; 2:5 is the same ratio as 2 to 5 and $\frac{2}{5}$.

To illustrate all of the above equivalencies and conversions at once, consider the fraction $\frac{19}{20}$. Shown as a ratio, it's 19 to 20, or 19:20. As a decimal, you have 0.95; as a percent, 95%.

The rules for performing operations on rational numbers (fractions) parallel in many ways the computational rules for integers. Just as adding –3 and –11 gives –14, adding $-\frac{1}{9}$ and $-\frac{5}{9}$ gives $-\frac{6}{9}$ (or $-\frac{2}{3}$ in reduced form.)

Algebraic Concepts and Methods

An important skill is the ability to represent real problems in algebraic form, and the concept of the *variable* is key. A variable is simply a symbol that represents an unknown value. Most typically x is the letter used, although any letter can be used. By "translating" real problems to algebraic form containing one or more variables (often as equations or inequalities), solutions to many problems can be found mathematically.

Understanding the relationships among values, and being able to accurately represent those relationships symbolically is another key to algebraic problem solving. Consider the ages of two sisters. If you don't know the age of the younger sister, but know that the older sister is three years older, you can show the information symbolically as follows: The age of the younger sister can be shown as x, and the age of the older sister as $x + 3$. If you are told that the sum of the sisters' ages is, say, 25, you can represent that information via an equation:

$$x + (x + 3) = 25$$

which can be read as "the age of the younger sister plus the age of the older sister totals 25." This sort of translation skill is crucial for using algebra for problem solving.

Some helpful *translation* tips include the following: The word *is* often suggests an equal sign; *of* may suggest multiplication, as does *product*. *Sum* refers to addition; *difference* suggests subtraction; and a *quotient* is obtained after dividing. The key when translating is to make sure that the equation accurately matches the information and relationships given in the word problem.

Operations with algebraic expressions are governed by various rules and conventions. For instance, only *like* algebraic terms can be added or subtracted to produce simpler expressions. For example, $2x^3$ and $3x^3$ can be added together to get $5x^3$, because the terms are like terms; they both have a base of x^3. You cannot add, say, $7m^3$ and $6m^2$; m^3 and m^2 are unlike bases. (Note: To *evaluate* an algebraic expression means to simplify it using conventional rules.)

When multiplying exponential terms together, the constant terms are multiplied, but the exponents of terms with the same variable bases are *added* together, which is somewhat counterintuitive. For example, $4w^2$ multiplied by $8w^3$ gives $32w^5$ (not $32w^6$, as one might guess).

When like algebraic terms are divided, exponents are subtracted. For example,

$$\frac{2x^7}{5x^3}$$

becomes

$$\frac{2x^4}{5}$$

In algebra, you frequently need to multiply two *binomials* together. Binomials are algebraic expressions of two terms. The FOIL method is one way to multiply binomials. FOIL stands for "first, outer, inner, last": Multiply the first terms in the parentheses, then the outermost terms, then the innermost terms, then the last terms, and then add the products together. For example, to multiply $(x + 3)$ and $(2x - 5)$, you multiply x by $2x$ (the first terms), x by -5 (outer terms), 3 by $2x$ (inner terms), and 3 by -5 (last terms). The four products ($2x^2$, $-5x$, $6x$, and -15) add up to $2x^2 + x - 15$. If the polynomials to be multiplied have more than two terms (*trinomials*, for instance), make sure that *each* term of the first polynomial is multiplied by *each* term of the second.

The opposite of polynomial multiplication is factoring. Factoring a polynomial means rewriting it as the product of factors (often two binomials). The trinomial $x^2 - 11x + 28$, for instance, can be factored into $(x - 4)(x - 7)$. (You can check this by "FOILing" the binomials.)

When attempting to factor polynomials, it is sometimes necessary to factor out any factor that might be common to all terms first. The two terms in $5x^2 - 10$, for example, both contain the factor 5. This means that the expression can be rewritten as $5(x^2 - 2)$.

Factoring is useful when solving some equations, especially if one side of the equation is set equal to zero. Consider $2x^2 - x - 1 = 2$. It can be rewritten as $2x^2 - x - 3 = 0$. This allows the left side to be factored into $(2x - 3)(x + 1)$, giving equation solutions of $\frac{3}{2}$ and -1.

Consider all of the information above as the following problem is first "translated" into an equation, then solved.

> Three teachers who are retiring are said to have 78 years of experience among them. You don't know how many years of experience Teacher A has, but you know that Teacher B has twice as many as A, and Teacher C has three more years of experience than B. How many years of experience does each have?

You can start by calling Teacher A's years of experience x. You then consider the relationship to the other two teachers: You can call Teacher B's years of experience $2x$, which allows you to call Teacher C's years of experience $(2x + 3)$. You know that the teachers' years of experience add up to 78, allowing you to write:

$$x + 2x + (2x + 3) = 78$$

Using the rules for solving such an equation, you find that $x = 15$, meaning that the teachers' years of experience are, respectively, 15, 30, and 33 years.

Geometry

A fundamental concept of geometry is the notion of a *point*. A point is a specific location, taking up no space, having no area, and frequently represented by a dot. A point is considered one-dimensional.

Through any two points there is exactly one straight line; straight lines are one-dimensional. Planes (think of flat surfaces without edges) are two-dimensional. From these foundational ideas you can move to some other important geometric terms and ideas.

A segment is any portion of a line between two points on the line. It has a definite start and a definite end. The notation for a segment extending from point A to point B is $\overline{AB}$. A ray is like a a straight segment, except it extends forever in one direction. The notation for a ray originating at point *X* (an *endpoint*) through point *Y* is $\overrightarrow{XY}$.

When two rays share their endpoints, an *angle* is formed. A *degree* is a unit of measure of the angle created. If a circle is divided into 360 even slices, each slice has an angle measure of 1 degree. If an angle has exactly 90 degrees it is called a *right* angle. Angles of less than 90 degrees are *acute* angles. Angles greater than 90 degrees and less than 180 degrees are *obtuse* angles. If two angles have the same size (regardless of how long their rays might be drawn) they are *congruent*. Congruence is shown this way: $\angle m \cong \angle n$ (read "angle *m* is congruent to angle *n*").

A polygon is a closed plane figure bounded by straight lines or a closed figure on a sphere bounded by arcs of great circles. In a plane, three-sided polygons are *triangles*, four-sided polygons are *quadrilaterals*, five sides make *pentagons*, six sides are *hexagons*, and eight-sided polygons are *octagons*. (Note that not all quadrilaterals are squares.) If two polygons (or any figures) have exactly the same size and shape, they are *congruent*. If they are the same shape, but different sizes, they are *similar*.

Polygons may have lines of symmetry, which can be thought of as imaginary fold lines which produce two congruent, mirror-image figures. Squares have four lines of symmetry, and non-square rectangles have two, as shown below. Circles have an infinite number of lines of symmetry; a few are shown on the circle.

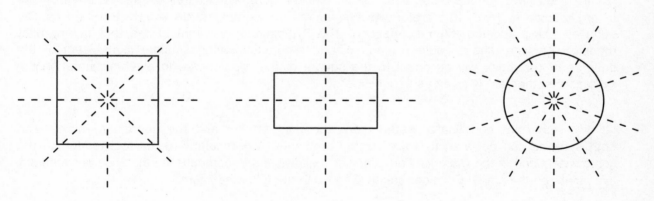

The *diameter* of a circle is a straight line segment that goes from one edge of a circle to the other side, passing through the center. The *radius* of a circle is half of its diameter (from the center to an edge). A *chord* is any segment that goes from one spot on a circle to any other spot (all diameters are chords, but not all chords are diameters).

The *perimeter* of a two-dimensional (flat) shape or object is the distance around the object.

Volume refers to how much space is inside of three dimensional, closed containers. It is useful to think of volume as how many cubic units could fit into a solid. If the container is a rectangular solid, multiplying width, length, and height together computes the volume. If all six faces (surfaces) of a rectangular solid are squares, then the object is a cube.

Parallel and perpendicular are key concepts in geometry. Consider the two parallel lines that follow, and the third line (a *transversal*), which crosses them.

Note that among the many individual angles created, there are only two angle measures: 30° (noted in the figure) and 150° (180° − 30°).

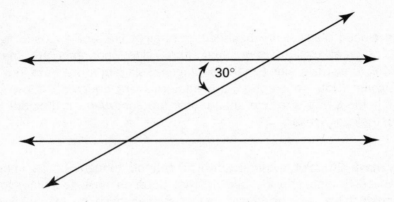

Triangles have various properties. One is that the sum of the measures of the three angles of any triangle is 180°. If, therefore, the measures of two angles are known, the third can be deduced using addition, then subtraction. The Pythagorean theorem states that in any right triangle with legs (shorter sides) a and b, and hypotenuse (longest side) c, the sum of the squares of the sides will be equal to the square of the hypotenuse. In algebraic notation the Pythagorean theorem is given as $a^2 + b^2 = c^2$.

Two important coordinate systems are the number line and the coordinate plane, and both systems can be used to solve certain problems. A particularly useful tool related to the coordinate plane is the Distance Formula, which allows you to compute the distance between any two points on the plane. Consider points C and D in the following figure.

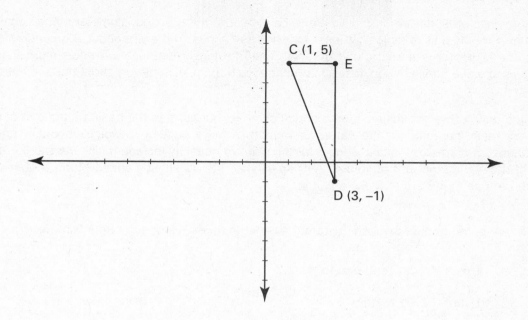

By finding the difference of the points' *x* coordinates (3 – 1, or 2) and the difference of their *y* coordinates (–1 – 5, or –6), you have found the lengths of the sides of triangle CED (2 units and 6 units—you can ignore the negative sign on the 6). You can now use the Pythagorean theorem to find the length of the hypotenuse of triangle CED, which is the same as the length from point C to D ($2^2 + 6^2 =$ 40, and the square root of 40 is approximately 6.3). Here is the distance formula in algebraic form:

$$d = \sqrt{(x_2 - x_1)^2 + (y_2 - y_1)^2}$$

Measurement

Measurement includes estimating and converting measurements within the customary and metric systems; applying procedures for using measurement to describe and compare phenomena; identifying appropriate measurement instruments, units, and procedures for measurement problems involving length, area, angles, volume, mass, time, money, and temperature; and using a variety of materials, models, and methods to explore concepts and solve problems involving measurement.

Here are some key measurement terms and ideas:

Customary units are generally the same as *U.S. units*. Customary units of length include inches, feet, yards, and miles. Customary units of weight include ounces, pounds, and tons. Customary units of capacity (or volume) include teaspoons, tablespoons, cups, pints, quarts, and gallons.

Metric units of length include millimeters, centimeters, meters, and kilometers. The centimeter is the basic metric unit of length, at least for short distances. There are about 2.5 centimeters to 1 inch. The kilometer is a metric unit of length used for longer distances. It takes more than 1.5 kilometers to make a mile. A very fast adult runner could run a kilometer in about three minutes.

Metric units of weight include grams and kilograms. The gram is the basic metric unit of mass (which for many purposes is the same as *weight*). A large paper clip weighs about 1 gram. It takes about 28 grams to make 1 ounce. Metric units of capacity include milliliters and liters. The liter is the basic metric unit of volume (or capacity). A liter is slightly smaller than a quart, so it takes more than four liters to make a gallon.

Here are some frequently used customary-to-metric ratios. Values are approximate.

1 inch = 2.54 centimeters

1 yard = 0.91 meters

1 mile = 1.61 kilometers

1 ounce = 28.35 grams

1 pound = 2.2 kilograms

1 quart = 0.95 liters

Metric-to-customary conversions can be found by taking the reciprocals of each of the factors noted above. For instance, 1 kilometer = 0.62 mile (computed by dividing 1 by 1.61).

An important step in solving problems involving measurement is to decide which area you are in: Generally, such problems will fall under one of these categories: length, area, angles, volume, mass, time, money, and temperature. Solving measurement problems will likely have you calling on your knowledge in several other areas of mathematics, especially algebra. The following is one example measurement problem that requires knowledge of several math topics:

> Sophie's Carpet Store charges $19.40 per square yard for the type of carpeting you'd like (padding and labor included). How much will you pay to carpet your 9-foot by 12-foot room?

One way to find the solution is to convert the room dimensions to yards (3 yards by 4 yards), then multiply to get 12 square yards. Finally, multiply 12 by the price of $19.40 per square yard, for a total price of $232.80.

Statistics and Probability

Measures of central tendency of a set of values include *mean*, *median*, and *mode*. The mean is found by adding all the values, then dividing the sum by the number of values. The median of a set is the middle number when the values are in numerical order. (If there is an even number of values, and therefore no middle value, the mean of the middle two values gives the median.) The mode of a set is the value occurring most often. (Not all sets of values have a single mode; some sets have more than one.) Consider the following set.

6   8   14   5   6   5   5

The mean, median, and mode of the set are 7, 6, and 5, respectively. (Note: The mean is often referred to as the average, but all three measures are averages of sorts.)

Probability theory provides models for chance variations. The *probability* of any event occurring is equal to the number of desired outcomes divided by the number of all possible events. Thus, the probability of blindly pulling a green ball out of a hat (in this case the desired outcome) if the hat contains two green and five yellow balls, is $\frac{2}{7}$ (about 29%). *Odds* are related to probability, but are different. The odds that any given event *will* occur is the ratio of the probability that the event will occur to the probability that the event *will not* occur (typically expressed as a ratio). In the example above, the odds that a green ball will be drawn are 2:5.

Statistics is the branch of mathematics that involves collecting, analyzing, and interpreting data, organizing data to describe them usefully, and drawing conclusions and making decisions. Statistics builds on probability, and typically studies "populations," meaning quantifiable groups of things. Trends and patterns not otherwise noticed may be revealed via statistics.

One key statistical concept is that of *standard deviation*. The standard deviation of a set of values tells how "tightly" all of the values are clustered around the mean of the set. When values are tightly clustered near the mean, the standard deviation is small. If values are widespread the standard deviation is large. Here is one way to find the standard deviation of a set. Consider the set used earlier:

6   8   14   5   6   5   5

First find the mean (7). Next, find the difference of each value in the set and the mean (ignoring negative signs). This gives 1, 1, 7, 2, 1, 2, and 2. Now, you square each of those values, giving 1, 1, 49, 4, 1, 4, and 4. You next take the sum of those squares (64) and divide the sum by the number of values ($\frac{64}{7} \approx 9.14$). Finally, you take the square root of 9.14, giving a standard deviation of 3.02. Think of 3.02 as the amount that the values in the set "typically" vary from the center.

Science and Technology

Scientific knowledge is a body of statements of varying degrees of certainty—some most unsure, some nearly sure, but none absolutely certain . . . Now, we scientists are used to this, and we take it for granted that it is perfectly consistent to be unsure, that it is possible to live and not know.

Richard P. Feynman (1918–1988), Nobel Prize in Physics, 1965

Science education has as its goal the training of a scientifically literate public that fully participates in the economic, political, and cultural functions of our society. Scientifically literate individuals, students and teachers alike, must have knowledge that is connected and useful. The New York science and technology curriculum, both for the preparation of pre-service teachers and for K–12 instruction, is guided by this principle.

An operational definition of the scientifically literate individual is one who uses scientific knowledge, constructs new scientific knowledge, and reflects on scientific knowledge. Such individuals have specific science content knowledge, they build upon that knowledge through their experiences and activities, and they can evaluate objectively and critically the value and limitations of that knowledge.

Principles and Processes of Scientific Investigations

Happy is he who gets to know the reasons for things.

Virgil (70–19 BCE), Roman poet

0016 Understand and apply the principles and processes of scientific inquiry and investigation.

For example:

- formulating hypotheses based on reasoning and preliminary results or information
- evaluating the soundness and feasibility of a proposed scientific investigation
- applying mathematical rules or formulas (including basic statistics) to analyze given experimental or observational data
- interpreting data presented in one or more graphs, charts, or tables to determine patterns or relationships
- evaluating the validity of a scientific conclusion in a given situation
- applying procedures for the safe and appropriate use of equipment and the care and humane treatment of animals in the laboratory

Tools of Science

From the pencil and field notebook to modern instruments in the laboratory, science involves the tools of observation, measurement, and computational analysis. The microscope and telescope each extend the range of human observation beyond human physiology. The spectroscope separates visible light into its component colors, and the spectrophotometer measures the selective absorption of those colors as a function of some property of a solution, solid, or gas. Mathematics is a tool to evaluate the results of our observations, to organize large quantities of data into averages, ranges, and statistical probabilities.

All measurements are limited by the fundamental uncertainty of the measuring device. The concept of significant figures is derived from the simple assumption that calculations on measurements cannot generate results that are more precise than the measurements themselves. If we divide one pie into three pieces the calculator might report that each piece is 0.33333333 (depending on the number of digits on the calculator display). We know from experience that there will be crumbs left in the pan and that no amount of care in dividing the pieces will result in the level of accuracy the calculation suggests. Every measuring device is presumed to be accurate to the smallest of the subdivisions marked, and every measurement with such a device should include one additional estimated digit. Measurements made with a ruler whose smallest divisions are one centimeter apart should be recorded to the tenth of a centimeter, the smallest measured digit plus one estimated digit. When scientists read the results of measurements made by others they therefore presume that the recorded values include a final digit that is an estimate based on the inherent accuracy of the instrument or device.

Technology

Compared to the goose quill, the modern mechanical pencil is a dramatic advancement in the technology of written communication. However, neither replaces the critical, analytical, and creative act of authorship. Many tools are available to assist in the observation, collection of data, analysis, and presentation of scientific information, yet none replace the role of the investigator who must formulate meaningful questions that can be answered using the tools of science. It is through the application of technology that we have the tools upon which all of modern science is based. We make some of these tools available in our classrooms to give students the opportunity to participate firsthand in the process of inquiry and discovery. The technology we employ in this context must facilitate student learning, remove barriers to understanding, and not create new barriers to delay and obscure the scientific concepts that we want to teach.

Scientific process skills, including the proper and accurate use of laboratory equipment, are an important component of science education. Instruction is necessary to guide the effective use of each measurement or observational tool: rulers, microscopes, balances, laboratory glassware, and so forth. As students develop these skills, they move from simple observations and confirmatory activities to using these tools to find answers to questions that they develop themselves.

Health and Safety

Through active, hands-on activities, science instruction is made a richer and more meaningful experience. From simple observations and activities at early grades, through detailed controlled experiments at higher grades, students who do science to learn science understand science better. While students are engaged in the process of discovery and exploration, the teacher must be engaged in protecting the health and safety of these students. The hazards vary with the discipline, and thoughtful planning and management of the activities will significantly reduce the risks to students. In all cases, students must utilize appropriate personal hygiene (hand washing) and wear personal protective equipment (goggles, gloves) while engaged in laboratory or field activities. Substitution of less hazardous materials whenever possible is a high priority. For example, in the physical sciences, replace mercury thermometers with alcohol or electronic, replace glass beakers and graduated cylinders with durable polyethylene, and eliminate or reduce the use of hazardous chemicals. In the earth sciences, rocks and minerals used in class should not contain inherently hazardous materials, students should not be allowed to taste the minerals, and reagents like HCl used for identification of carbonate minerals should be dispensed from spill-proof plastic containers. In the life sciences, special care should be given to topics such as safe practices for sharps, the safe handling of living organisms, and the care and use of microscopes. Experiments or activities involving the collection or culture of human cells or fluids should be discouraged, and proper sterilization procedures followed to prevent the growth or spread of disease agents. When they are possible, outdoor, museum, and other field activities can bring a valuable enrichment to the science curriculum in all disciplines. They also bring additional responsibilities for the safe planning and implementation of activities that increase student learning while maintaining the health and safety of the students.

Experimental Design

It is a capital mistake to theorise before one has data. Insensibly one begins to twist facts to suit theories instead of theories to suit facts.

Sherlock Holmes, the fictional creation of Arthur Conan Doyle (1859–1930), British physician and novelist

When a bat bites Gilligan, first mate of TV's ill-fated *S.S. Minnow*, he is convinced that he will turn into a vampire. Seemingly, no amount of reassurance by the Professor will convince him otherwise because, he claims, he saw the movie three times and it always came out the same way. We trust the results of experiments, both formal and informal, to help us understand our surroundings. Unfortunately, without proper control of the variables and a sound experimental design, our observations may lead us to entirely wrong-headed or incorrect conclusions.

Scientific Method

The scientific method is not a specific six-step method that is rigorously followed whenever a question arises that can be answered using the knowledge and techniques of science. Rather, it is a process of observation and analysis that is used to develop a reliable, consistent, and non-arbitrary representation and understanding of our world. We can use the scientific method (observation and description, formulation of hypotheses, prediction based on hypotheses, and tests of predictions) for many, but not all questions. The approach is best applied to situations in which the experimenter can control the variables, eliminating or accounting for all extraneous factors, and perform repeated independent tests wherein only one variable is changed at a time.

Controlling Variables

The science fair project is a common tool for instruction in the scientific method. Many formal and informal sources, often Web based, provide lists of suggested science fair topics, but not all are experiments. For the youngest students it is appropriate and useful for the focus to be upon models and demonstrations, for example the solar system model, volcano, or clay cross-section of an egg. Later the students should move to true experiments where the focus is on identifying a testable hypothesis, and controlling of all experimental variables but the one of interest. Many projects may be elevated from model or demonstration to experiment. A proposal to demonstrate how windmills work can be made an experiment when the student adds quantitative measurements designed to measure one variable while varying only one other and while holding all other variables constant. For example, using an electric fan, the number of rotations per minute can be measured as a function of the fan setting (low, medium, or high). However, while keeping the fan setting constant, several different experiments could vary any one of the following variables: number of fins, size of fins, or shape of fins while in each case measuring the rotational speed.

Collecting and Presenting Data

The male has more teeth than the female in mankind, and sheep and goats, and swine. This has not been observed in other animals. Those persons which have the greatest number of teeth are the longest lived; those which have them widely separated, smaller, and more scattered, are generally more short lived.

Aristotle (384–322 BCE), Greek philosopher

Scientifically literate individuals have detailed and accurate content knowledge that is the basis of their scientific knowledge. They do not strive to recall every detail of that knowledge, but build conceptual frameworks upon which prior knowledge, as well as new learning, is added. From this framework of facts, concepts, and theories the scientifically literate individual can reconstruct forgotten facts, and use this information to answer new questions not previously considered. The scientifically literate individual is a lifelong learner who asks questions that can be answered using scientific knowledge and techniques.

Science is based upon experimentation, but not all knowledge is derived daily from first principles. The scientifically literate individual is informed by existing knowledge, and is knowledgeable about the sources, accuracy, and value of each source. Not every source is equally reliable, accurate, or valid. Classroom teachers are advised to use trusted educational sites.

Scientifically literate individuals must be able to evaluate critically the information and evidence they collect, and the conclusions or theories to which that information and evidence leads. Such analysis incorporates an understanding of the limitations to knowledge in general, and the limitations of all measurements and information based on the quality of the experimental design. The literate individual can evaluate claims for scientific merit, identify conflicting evidence and weigh the value and credibility of conflicting information. They can also recognize that not every question can be answered using scientific knowledge, valuing the contributions of other cultures and other ways of knowing, including art, philosophy, and theology.

Scientific information is communicated to nonscientific audiences in order to inform, guide policy and influence the practices that affect all of society. This information is presented through text, tables, charts, figures, pictures, models, and other representations that require interpretation and analysis. Scientifically literate individuals can read and interpret these representations, and select appropriate tools to present the information they gather.

Physical Science

All of physics is either impossible or trivial. It is impossible until you understand it, and then it becomes trivial.

Ernest Rutherford (1871–1937), Physicist, Nobel Prize for Chemistry, 1908

0017 Understand and apply concepts, principles, and theories pertaining to the physical setting (including earth science, chemistry, and physics).

For example:
- analyzing interactions among the earth, the moon, and the sun (e.g., seasonal changes, the phases of the moon)
- analyzing the effects of interactions among components of air, water, and land (e.g., weather, volcanism, erosion)
- distinguishing between physical and chemical properties of matter and between physical and chemical changes in matter
- distinguishing among forms of energy and identifying the transformations of energy observed in everyday life
- analyzing the effects of forces on objects in given situations
- inferring the physical science principle (e.g., effects of common forces, conservation of energy) illustrated in a given situation

Matter and Energy

Broadly speaking, our experiences with the world involve interactions with and between matter and energy. The physical sciences give us a clearer understanding and appreciation of our surroundings and the way we interact with and affect those surroundings. Matter can be described and distinguished by its chemical and physical properties. Physical properties, such as color and density, are termed *intrinsic* when they do not change as the amount of the matter changes. Properties like mass or volume do vary when matter is added or removed, and these are termed "extrinsic properties." Mass is the amount of matter in an object, which is sometimes measured using a lever arm balance. Weight, although sometimes incorrectly used interchangeably with mass, is a measure of the force of gravity experienced by an object, often determined using a spring scale. An electronic scale may display an object's mass in grams, but it is dependent on gravity for its operation. Such a device is only accurate after using a calibration mass to adjust the electronics for the unique local gravitational force. While we may say an object is "weightless" as it floats inside the space shuttle, it is still affected by the gravitational forces from both the Earth and Sun, which keep it in orbit around each. The force of gravity is proportional to the product of the masses of the two objects under consideration divided by the square of the distance between them. Earth, being larger and more massive than Mars, has proportionally higher gravitational forces. This is the basis of the observation in H. G. Wells' *The War of the Worlds* that the Martian invaders were "the most sluggish things I ever saw crawl."

Density, the ratio of mass to volume, is an intrinsic property that depends on the matter, but not the amount of matter. Volume is defined as the amount of space an object occupies. The density of a 5-ton cube of pure copper is the same as that of a small copper penny. However, the modern penny is a thin shell of copper over a zinc plug, and the density of this coin is significantly lower than that of the older pure copper coin. Density is related to buoyancy. Objects sink, in liquids or gases alike, if they are denser than the material that surrounds them. Archimedes' principle, also related to density, states that an object is buoyed up by a force equal to the mass of the material the object displaces. Thus, a 160-lb concrete canoe will easily float in water if the volume of the submerged portion is equal to the volume of 20 gallons of water (water is approximately 8 lbs/gal × 20 gal = 160 lbs). Density is not the same as viscosity, a measure of thickness or flowability. The strength of intermolecular forces between molecules determines, for example, that molasses is slow in January, or that hydrogen bromide is a gas in any season.

All matter is composed of atoms, or combinations of atoms selected from among the more than one hundred elements. The atom is the smallest particle of an element that retains the properties of the element; similarly, the molecule is the smallest particle of a compound. Molecules cannot be separated into smaller particles (atoms or smaller) without a chemical change disrupting the chemical bonds that bind the molecule together. Physical separations, through the use of filter paper, centrifuge, or magnet for example, do not affect chemical bonds. The scientific concept of a cycle, in this case without a time dependence, is evident in the fundamental makeup of matter and reflected in the structure of the periodic table. Mendeleev is credited with the development of the modern periodic table, in part for his predicting the existence of then-unknown elements based on the repeating trends in reactivity and physical properties. The concepts associated with atoms and molecules are not found in the elementary benchmarks, but they should be well understood by the elementary teacher nonetheless, as they provide the basis of all our understanding of matter and chemical change.

Energy is loosely scientifically defined as the ability to do work. Kinetic energy is the energy of motion ($KE = 1/2mv^2$), where m is the mass and v the velocity of an object. Chemical energy is stored in the bonds of our food, held for later conversion to kinetic energy and heat in our bodies. Potential energy is held in an icicle hanging off the roof ($PE = mgh$) where m is mass, g is the gravitational force constant, and h is the height. When the icicle falls, its potential energy is converted to kinetic energy, and then to sound energy as it hits the pavement, and additional kinetic energy as the fragments skitter off. At the elementary level, students need to be able to identify the types of energy involved in various phenomena and identify the conversions between types. In the popular Rube Goldberg competitions, students use a number of sequential energy conversions to perform a simple task like breaking a balloon or flipping a pancake. Energy is conserved in each of these normal processes, converted to less useful forms (e.g., heat) but not created or destroyed.

Similarly, matter is never created or destroyed in a normal chemical reaction. Nuclear fusion is an obvious exception to both rules, following Einstein's equation $E = mc^2$; however, these reactions are generally not allowed in the classroom or school laboratory.

Students gain useful experience with energy conversions as they study simple electrical circuits and chemical dry cells. The dry cell produces electrical energy from chemical potential energy. The size of the dry cell is proportional to the amount of starting material, and thus the available current, but not the electromotive force or voltage, which is an intrinsic property. The D cell produces the same 1.5-volt potential as the AAA cell; the difference is in how long they can maintain the flow of current in the circuit. The battery is dead when one or more of the starting materials has been depleted, or when the essential electrolytic fluid leaks or dries out. The measured cell voltage depends on the oxidation and reduction potentials and of the half-reactions involved and on the concentration of each chemical species. When a cell reaches equilibrium, the measured cell potential and free energy of the cell both reach zero.

Seldom do we find chemical reactants present in the precise quantities to match the stoichiometric ratio indicated by the chemical equation defining a reaction. In a battery, or any reaction for that matter, one of the chemicals will be depleted before the others. The concept of a limiting reactant is important in chemistry, whereby one reactant is consumed before the other, similar to the summer BBQ where hot dogs are in packages of ten, but the buns are in packages of eight. In contrast, how quickly a battery drains is linked to the rates of chemical reactions (kinetics), dependent on temperature, concentration, and the presence of a catalyst. Many chemical reactions involve multiple steps, where one step, the rate-limiting step, controls the rate of the entire process. This is much like the sister in the family who is always the last one to get in the car when everyone else is in a hurry.

Simple dry cells do not pose a serious safety hazard—always an issue in hands-on activities—and are thus good for student experiments. A series connection linking dry cells in a chain increases the overall voltage, and thus the brightness of the bulb, a parallel connection with batteries placed in the circuit (like rungs in a ladder) increases the effective size of the cell but the voltage remains the same.

Changes in Matter

Scientific theories have their utility in providing a unified explanation for diverse and varied observations. Atomic theory, which views atoms and molecules as the fundamental building blocks of all matter, would be modified or abandoned if it didn't also explain other observations. Snow tracked into the kitchen quickly melts before either evaporating or being absorbed into someone's socks, which then must be hung by the fire to dry. In either of these changes the fundamental particles of water are the same, an assembly of three atoms held by covalent (shared electron) bonds in a bent molecular geometry associated with polar molecules. New attractions are possible between polar water molecules and the ions formed when some compounds are dissolved in solution. The relative strength of the new attractions to the water overcomes the attractions within the pure solid, allowing the solid to dissolve and in some cases dissociate in solution. Insoluble compounds do not dissolve because the strength of the attractions within the solid exceeds those available between the molecules and/or ions and the solvent.

Phase changes are also explained using atomic theory. Evaporation from a liquid occurs when individual molecules gain sufficient energy to break free from the intermolecular attractions in the liquid phase. The stronger the intermolecular attractions, the lower the vapor pressure and the higher the boiling point. The boiling point is the temperature at which the vapor pressure of molecules leaving solution equals the atmospheric pressure. Lowering the atmospheric pressure above a liquid makes it easier for the highest energy liquid molecules to escape, thus the boiling point is lower. Cooking while camping at high altitudes requires more time and, thus, more fuel because food cooks slower as a result of the lowered boiling temperature.

All matter has a temperature above the theoretical value of absolute zero because all matter is in continual motion. In a balloon filled with nitrogen gas, some molecules are moving relatively fast, others relatively slowly. The temperature of the gas is a measure of this motion, a measure of the average kinetic energy of the particles. Molecules are very small and fast moving, and there are vast empty spaces between them. The average speed of nitrogen molecules at 25°C is over 500 meters per second, whereas the lighter hydrogen molecules have an average speed in excess of 1,900 meters per second. One cubic centimeter of air at room temperature and normal pressure contains roughly 24,500,000,000,000,000,000 molecules (2.45×10^{19} molecules). The same quantity of water would contain roughly 3.34×10^{22} water molecules, while the same one cubic centimeter of copper would contain roughly 8.5×10^{22} copper atoms. The differences between these numbers are not nearly as large as the numbers themselves, yet the differences are readily observable. Gases have significant empty spaces between the molecules and thus can be compressed, whereas liquids and solids have less or no compressibility, respectively. If air enters the lines of hydraulic brake systems, the pedal depresses easily as the trapped gas compresses instead of having the non-compressible liquid transfer the motion into braking power.

While the atoms and molecules of all materials are in constant motion (vibrational energy), those in gases and liquids are also free to move about their own axes (rotational energy), and about the container (translational energy). Increasing the temperature of a solid imparts additional energy, which increases the vibrational energy. Once any particular atom or molecule gains sufficient energy to break free of the intermolecular attractions to the bulk solid or liquid it will slip or fly away (melt or evaporate, respectively). Hotter atoms require more space in which to vibrate. For this reason wagon wheel rims are heated in the forge to expand the metal before slipping the rim onto the wheel, basketballs left outside on a cold night don't bounce well, and in thermometers the expansion of alcohol or mercury is used to indicate temperature.

Motion

The motion of atoms and molecules is essential to our understanding of matter at the molecular level, but we have many examples of motion readily available on the macroscopic level in the world around us. Many an idle moment can be passed with a young child timing small athletic feats: for example, "How long will it take you to run to that tree and back?" or "The time to beat is 8.65 seconds; who can do it faster?" These experiences provide an informal experience with measurements of motion that serve as the basis for more scientific descriptions of speed, direction and changes of speed.

We can use time and motion to evaluate other chemical and physical phenomena. The periodic motion of a pendulum can be timed to determine the period, and experiments devised to explore the effect of pendulum mass, string length or amount of initial deflection. Hook's law can be studied by timing the vibrations of a spring. Chemical kinetics can be studied by timing reactions and observing changes in absorbance, conductivity, or pH. The growth rates of seedlings can be studied as a function of soil, water and light conditions. Such activities provide a natural framework to teach the concepts of scientific exploration, control of variables, collection, and presentation of data.

Waves and Vibrations

Waves are one mechanism of energy transport from one location to another. We experience waves directly in the forms of light, sound and water, and indirectly through radio and TV, wireless networks, and X-rays. Waves are periodic in their nature, and the concept of periodicity (cycles) is one of the key interdisciplinary concepts that include the motions of planets, the properties of elements, life cycles of plants and animals, and many other events. Energy is transmitted through a material in a translational wave when in water. For example, particles of water move perpendicular to the direction of energy travel. A wave with greater energy has greater amplitude. AM radio refers to amplitude modulation of the radio signal, where the carrier wave amplitude is modified by adding the amplitudes of the voice or music waves to create a cumulative and more complex wave form. The receiver must subtract from this complex waveform the simple sinusoidal waveform of the carrier to leave the voice or music.

Compressional waves, like sound, are characterized by having the media move along the same axis as the direction of energy travel. The speed of sound waves is dependent on the medium through which it travels, faster in denser materials like railroad track, and faster in water than through air, yet faster in warm air than colder air. Cold air is denser, but the gas molecules in warm air move faster and more quickly convey the sound energy. Sound cannot travel in a vacuum (referring to the absence of all matter in a given space) because, as a compressional wave, it needs to have particles to compress as it travels.

Light is energy, and darkness is the absence of that energy. A shadow is not "cast" by an object, but rather the stream of light energy is blocked by the object, leaving an area of darkness. A black light behaves like any other, giving off light energy, yet at frequencies too high and wavelengths too short for our eyes to see (thus the light appears black to us). Some objects held beneath a black light absorb the energy from the ultraviolet light, and reemit this light at slightly lower wavelengths that our eyes can see, giving them the appearance that they glow in the dark. Laundry soaps with whiteners and brighteners contain additives that do something similar, converting portions of the invisible UV radiation from the Sun into lower frequency near-UV and additional visible light to make your "whites whiter." Since deer are more sensitive to near-UV wavelengths than humans, hunters are careful to launder their camouflage hunting clothes with soaps that do not contain such whiteners.

White light comprises all the visible wavelengths. Color is a property that light already has. White light passing through a prism, raindrop, or spectroscope can be separated into its constituent colors. An object appears red because it, or the dye molecules it contains, reflects the red wavelengths constituent in the white light that strike it. If a red shirt is illuminated by a blue light the shirt will appear black because there is no red light for it to reflect. Blue paint reflects blue light from a white source, and yellow paint reflects yellow. Mixing the paints gives a material that reflects blue and yellow light, and our eye sees the mixture as green. A blue filter placed before a white light allows only the blue light to pass, absorbing all other wavelengths. A red shirt, when viewed through a blue filter, will appear black because the shirt can only reflect red light, but the filter can only pass blue light. The phosphors of our TV screen are in sets of red, green, and blue, which when illuminated together release white light.

Earth and Space Science

One had to be a Newton to notice that the Moon is falling, when everyone sees that it doesn't fall.

Paul Valéry (1871–1945), French poet and philosopher

Geosphere

Scientifically literate individuals have an understanding and appreciation for the world around them. Rocks hold an early fascination, both for their utility: as objects for throwing, skipping; and also for their beauty, texture, and diversity. Physical landforms vary considerably across the face of the Earth, revealed to the observant and thoughtful eye in road cuts, and the scenic viewpoints everywhere. On a small scale, each puddle, rivulet, and mass of sand and gravel in a yard or parking lot reveals the same actions of erosion, deposition, and graded sorting of material by size and mass that are at work on a global scale to form and reform our physical environment. The scientifically literate individual continually constructs new knowledge by study of the geosphere through direct observation, through photographs, models and samples, and through graphical representations (maps). The geosphere is the source for many natural resources essential for modern life, and the recipient of pollution caused by man's activities.

Evidence of physical changes to the geosphere is abundant, and frequently newsworthy. Each landslide, earthquake, or volcanic eruption reveals something about the Earth and its structures. Fossils, preserved remnants of or marks made by plants and animals that were once alive, are one source of evidence about changes in the environment over time. Finding fossils of marine organisms in what is now a desert is an opportunity to discuss scientific ways of knowing, of how science forms and tests hypotheses, and how theories develop to explain the reasons behind observations. The scientifically literate individual understands the concepts of uncertainty in measurement and the basis of scientific theories. Such an understanding may lead the teacher in an elementary classroom to refer to fossils and rocks simply as "very old," to dinosaurs as "living long ago," and to occasionally preface statements of scientific theory with the observation that "many scientists believe . . ."

Hydrosphere

With about seventy-five percent of the Earth's surface covered with water, the hydrosphere defines our planet and its environment. Most people live near the ocean, but few people live on, or have even experienced, the vast reaches of the world's oceans. Closer to our daily lives, and important because of the fresh water necessary to sustain life and commerce, are the rivers, and streams that are abundant and familiar to residents of New York. The hydrosphere includes not just the surface waters described, but the subsurface waters of aquifers, and the water vapor present in the atmosphere. Man has a significant impact on the hydrosphere through activities that contaminate, divert, and attempt to control the flow of water. These activities can benefit one part of the environment or society while harming another.

The scientific concept of cycle is also used to describe the movement of water through its various phases, and through each part of the environment. A climate chamber formed from discarded polyethylene soda bottles can easily demonstrate these changes, and when soil, plants, and small frogs are added, a nearly complete ecosystem is formed if we count the food we add for the frog each day. In this chamber the student can observe the water cycle as liquid water evaporates, then condenses again against an ice-filled chamber to fall back to the surface. Only two phases, solid and liquid, can be observed directly, since the individual molecules of water vapor are too small to be seen by the naked eye. The white cloud visible at the tip of the teakettle, like our breath when we exhale on a cold winter day and fog, are examples of condensed water vapor (liquid water). The supply of fresh water on the Earth is limited, and water is a reusable resource that must be carefully managed. With this in mind, we are grateful for the technology to treat and purify water, which has done much to extend the human lifespan and reduce disease by providing clean and reliable sources of water in some parts of the world.

Atmosphere

The atmosphere is the layer of gases held close to the Earth by gravitational forces. In size, it has been compared with the skin on an apple. The atmosphere is densest close to the surface, where gravity holds the heavier gases and the pressure is greatest. The atmosphere becomes less dense and pressure decreases exponentially as altitude increases. All weather is contained within the lowest layer of the atmosphere (troposphere) and the temperature decreases as one rises through this layer. We can often observe the top of this layer as clouds form anvil-shaped tops when they cannot rise further than the height of the cold boundary between the lowest layer (troposphere) and the overlying layer (stratosphere).

The concept of cycle reappears in the discussion of the recurring patterns of weather, and the progression of the seasons. The basis of the seasons has much more to do with the angle of light striking the Earth, and very little to do with the distance from the Sun. Classroom weather stations and weather charts are useful learning tools, and projects to build thermometers, hygrometers, and barometers are popular in classrooms.

Density variations related to temperature drive the movement of air. Heat energy warms the air and increases water evaporation, warm air expands and rises above cooler surrounding air, rising air cools and water vapor condenses forming clouds and precipitation. Cold, heavy air settles over the polar caps and flows toward the equator, generally leading to weather trends that bring cold northerly winds into New York for part of the winter. Temperature gradients and the resulting air movement are readily observed at home where the basement is cool, the upstairs warmer, and a draft is often felt when sitting near the stairway.

Space Science

The concept of cycle again finds application in the periodic movement of the Sun and planets. The size of objects, and distances between them, are difficult to represent on the same scale. The National Mall in Washington, D.C., contains a 1/10,000,000,000th-scale solar system model in which the Sun is the size of a grapefruit, and Pluto, located some 650 yards away, is the size of a poppy seed. The openness of space is mirrored at a much smaller scale by vast open spaces between atoms and between nuclei and their electrons.

A ball rolling down the aisle of a school bus appears, to observers sitting on the bus, to swerve to the right and hit the wall as the bus makes a left-hand turn. To an observer outside the bus, the ball continued its straight-line motion until acted upon by a force, often resulting from a collision with the wall. For centuries the best science available held that the Sun rose in the east and set in the west. As scientific instruments developed and improved (telescopes for example), scientists collected new information that challenged old theories. New theories are not always well received, a fact to which Galileo would attest. We now understand that the Sun is the gravitational center of the solar system, and that the planet's motions are defined by their path along an elliptical orbit defined by its speed and its continual gravitational attraction to the Sun.

Life Science

I venture to define science as a series of interconnected concepts and conceptual schemes arising from experiment and observation and fruitful of further experiments and observations. The test of a scientific theory is, I suggest, its fruitfulness.

James Bryant Conant (1893–1978), Chemist and Educator

0018   Understand and apply concepts, principles, and theories pertaining to the living environment.

For example:

- recognizing the characteristics of living things and common life processes
- analyzing processes that contribute to the continuity of life (e.g., reproduction and development, inheritance of genetic information)
- analyzing the factors that contribute to change in organisms and species over time
- comparing the ways a variety of organisms carry out basic life functions and maintain dynamic equilibrium (e.g., obtaining nutrients, maintaining water balance)
- analyzing the effects of environmental conditions (e.g., temperature, availability of water and sunlight) on living organisms and the relationships between plants and animals within a community
- inferring the life science principle (e.g., adaptation, homeostasis) illustrated in a given situation

Cells

The concept of a cell is central to our understanding of the life sciences. Cells are the simplest living unit of life, just as atoms are the building blocks of molecules, and molecules of cells. Cell theory states that all organisms are composed of cells, that all cells arise from preexisting cells, and that the cell is the basic organizational unit of all organisms. Groups of specialized cells, or tissues, may have highly specialized characteristics and functions within an organism. A single organism may comprise only a single cell, or many billions of cells, and cells themselves range in size from the micron to many centimeters in dimension. Growth in most organisms is associated with cell division and replication, in addition to enlargement of the cells.

Classification

A dichotomous key is a tool of science that allows us to organize and classify objects by their observable traits and properties. In the life sciences, classification keys are widely used, and the simplest are based on the gross anatomy of all organisms, including plants, animals, fungi, protists, and two kingdoms of bacteria. Through comparison of the number of wings or legs, habitat, and eating habits we begin, at the earliest levels, to understand patterns in nature, constructing our own understanding of the world around us, and practice the basic elements of scientific thought and discovery.

Scientific knowledge may be classified or organized by grouping similar types of knowledge into thematic concepts. Many concepts are so broad as to find application in multiple disciplines. Cycle, for example, is a powerful concept that has widespread application throughout science, useful for both explanation and prediction. Life cycles are central to the study of biology. The recurring pattern of events in the life cycle links birth, growth, reproduction, and death. The concept of a cycle is also evident in the carbon cycle, nitrogen cycle, Krebs cycle, hydrogeologic cycle, periodic table, and many other processes, including the transformations of energy needed to sustain life. The food chain represents the complex interdependency of all plants and animals on the energy from the Sun, and the recycling of nutrients from simple to complex organisms.

Heredity

The discussion of life cycles brings forward the concept that the offspring of one generation bears likeness to, but also variation from, the previous generation. Some characteristics of the individual parent are passed along, while others appear not to be. We observe the connections between the visible traits of the parents and children, connections evident in all sexually reproducing organisms. It is clear that the offspring of dogs are other dogs, which generally look much like the parent dogs. Details of how such traits are conveyed through genetics are important to understand; yet instruction in these topics is allocated to the curriculum of higher grades.

Evolution

The goal of science education is to develop a scientifically literate public. At the elementary level this involves an understanding of how physical traits promote the survival of a species, how environmental changes affect species that are not adapted to those new conditions, and the role of heredity in passing and modifying the traits of successive generations. There are ample examples available to illustrate these concepts to the elementary student. A rabbit whose coat regularly turns white before the snowfall is at a temporary disadvantage, and is therefore subject to a higher degree of predation. That rabbit may not live to produce other early-white-coated rabbits. Technology, the application of knowledge for man's benefit, includes activities that are designed to select those traits that are intended to lead to healthier, stronger, and more productive crops and animals.

While the tenets of evolution as scientific theory are widely accepted, particularly as they apply to the short-term changes and adaptations within a species, the subject continues to generate some debate. To place the discussion in its proper context, some discussion of the scientific use of terms is appropriate, because the common usage of a term may differ significantly from its scientific usage. A *scientific fact* is an observation that has been repeatedly confirmed. However, scientific facts change if new observations yield new information. Frequently, the development of new, more sophisticated or precise instruments leads to such new information. A *scientific hypothesis* is a testable statement about the natural world, and as such is the starting point for most scientific experimentation. A hypothesis can generally be proven wrong, but is seldom proven right. *Scientific theories*, like atomic theory and cell theory, are well-substantiated explanations of some aspect of the natural world. A scientific theory provides a unified explanation for many related hypotheses. While a theory is generally widely accepted (e.g., through much of human history people accepted a flat Earth circled by a moving Sun), theories remain open to revision or even replacement should a better, more logical, more comprehensive or compelling explanation be found.

Not all issues of our human experience are subject to the analysis and rigors of scientific experimentation and validation. Our understanding of art, poetry, philosophy, and religion rely on ways of thinking and understanding that are not necessarily subject to repeated validation through the controlled scientific experiment, or which may rely more on personal values or deference to authority. The scientifically literate individual will distinguish the role and value of scientific thought from other ways of knowing, while maintaining respect and appreciation for the ways of thinking and understanding practiced in disciplines outside of science.

Technology and the Principles of Engineering Design

The system of nature, of which man is a part, tends to be self-balancing, self-adjusting, self-cleansing. Not so with technology.

E. F. Schumacher, *Small Is Beautiful*, 1973

0019   Apply knowledge of technology and the principles of engineering design.

For example:
*   demonstrating an understanding of technological systems (e.g., transportation system) and the principles on which technological systems are constructed (e.g., the use of component subsystems)
*   analyzing the roles of modeling and optimization in the engineering design process
*   evaluating a proposed technological solution to a given problem or need
*   applying criteria for selecting tools, materials, and other resources to design and construct a technological product or service
*   recognizing appropriate tests of a given technological solution
*   analyzing the positive and negative effects of technology on individuals, society, and the environment

The state of New York is one of the few states that have specific learning standards, for all educational levels, on "technology" and "engineering." As an elementary teacher, you will be expected to know the content for these standards well enough to teach them. Here are brief versions of the relevant standards:

- Engineering design is an iterative process involving *modeling* and *optimization* used to develop technological solutions to problems within given constraints.

- Technological tools, materials, and other resources should be selected on the basis of safety, cost, availability, appropriateness, and environmental impact.

- Technological processes change energy, information, and material resources into more useful forms.

- Technological systems are designed to achieve specific results and produce outputs, such as products, structures, services, energy, or other systems.

- Project management is essential to ensuring that technological endeavors are profitable and that products and systems are of high quality and built safely, on schedule, and within budget.

Technological Systems

All technological systems contain the same basic components. They all start with an **input** (that is, the thing that is going into the system), and they all end with an **output**, which is the desired end-product (sometimes called the system variable). For example, on a car's cruise control (a device that allows the car to travel at a constant speed) can be thought of as the amount of gasoline being fed into the car's engine. (Before cruise control systems existed, the driver alone controlled the input with the accelerator.) The output is the speed of the car.

The means for controlling the speed is called the **process**. A simple way to accomplish the task of constant speed might be to lock the throttle in place when the driver turns on the cruise control mechanism. Doing this will keep the speed constant—if the car is moving on a flat surface. This type of system is called an **open-loop system**; it proceeds directly from input through process to output. The main disadvantage in this type of system is that lacks sensitivity to the **dynamics** of the system; it has no effective control of itself once the process has begun. The driver of such a cruise control would have to disengage the system every time it went up a hill, or she would be crawling and barreling down.

To keep the speed constant on hilly terrain, the system needs a **feedback loop**, which allows the output to communicate with the process. This type of system is called a **closed-loop** system.

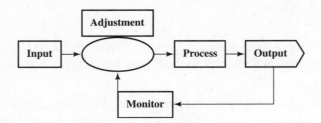

The feedback part of the system typically consists of a **monitor** and an **adjustment**. The monitor measures something about the output variable; for example, a cruise control monitor will notice when the car was slowing down (i.e., it was going up an incline). It will then feed that information back to the adjustment device, which will adjust the process accordingly without requiring additional input from the driver: this is the advantage of the closed-loop system.

The cruise control of a car is not, of course, independent of the other systems involved in the operation of a car. The ignition system and the braking system are just two of the many other systems involved. And in a highway system, each car would be just one more subcomponent.

Transportation systems, such as a city's mass transit system, consist of many subsystems, all of which contain their own feedback loops. To analyze such a system, one has to diagram it and look at all its components. To make improvements, one must look at all the processes that are connected with the piece of the system that needs improvement, then weigh the effects of any change in that piece on the system as a whole against the benefits of the proposed improvement. In this case, "the system as a whole" includes all stakeholders in that system, meaning not only riders but also motorists and anyone else who has a stake in getting a large number of people to where they want to go (e.g., store owners, employers).

Here are some questions to ask when evaluating whether a new technology system, or subsystem, is useful and cost-effective:

- *Does it fulfill its stated purpose and is there a way to measure its performance?* For example, does a new computer instructional system provide advantages over the old one (or over the traditional instructional system)? How will you know?

- *Can it integrate elements of the existing system?* For example, can a new computer instructional system use existing digital and non-digital resources?

- *Will stakeholders be able to make needed adjustments?* For example, would teachers and students using a new computer instructional system easily be able to adjust it for their own purposes?

- *What are the material costs?* This includes both labor and materials, and also labor involved in the planning and evaluation stages.

- *What are the training costs?*

- *What are the maintenance costs?*

- *Will implementation of the system be equitable, or will some stakeholders benefit more than others?* Note that, usually, one group of people will benefit more than others (e.g., a new computer instructional system might benefit special needs students more than others), so the question then becomes whether it is reasonable that one group should benefit more than others.

Systems and Ecology

Our surroundings constitute a complex, interconnected system in which the living organisms exist in relationship with the soil, water, and air, linked together through chemical and physical processes, and in states of continual change or dynamic equilibrium. *Ecosystem* is the term for all the living and nonliving things in a given environment and how they interact. Scientifically literate individuals are aware of their surroundings, the interdependence of each part, and the effects that man's activities can have on those surroundings. Mutualistic and competitive relationships also exist between the organisms in an ecosystem, defining how organisms rely upon each other, and exist in competition and conflict with each other.

Energy transformations are the driving force within an ecosystem. Many organisms obtain energy from light. For example, light drives the process of photosynthesis in green plants. Solar energy also provides necessary heat for cold-blooded animals. Organisms may also derive energy from other organisms, including other plants and/or animals. When one source of energy is depleted in an ecosystem, many organisms must shift their attention to other sources of energy. For example, a bear will eat berries, fish, or nuts depending on the season. The energy pyramid for an ecosystem illustrates these relationships and identifies those organisms that are most dependent on the other organisms in the system. Higher order organisms cannot survive for long without the other organisms beneath them in the energy pyramid. The availability of adequate food within an ecosystem can be used to explain the system's functioning, the size of an animal's territory, or the effects of over-predation of a single species upon those organisms above it in the food chain.

Ecosystems change over time, both from natural processes and from the activities of man. The scientifically literate individual will be able to identify how the environment changes, how those changes impact the organisms that live there, and recognize the differences between long-term and short-term variation. Natural succession is observed when one community replaces another, for example the colonies of fungus that grow, thrive, and then are replaced by different colonies on rodent droppings held under ideal conditions.

Science, Technology, and Society

It is unworthy of excellent men to lose hours like slaves in the labor of calculation which could be relegated to anyone else if machines were used.

Gottfried Wilhelm von Leibniz (1646–1716), German polymath

0020 **Understand the relationships among and common themes that connect mathematics, science, and technology, and the application of knowledge and skills in these disciplines to other areas of learning.**

For example:
- making connections among the common themes of mathematics, science, and technology (e.g., systems, models, magnitude and scale, equilibrium and stability, patterns of change)
- applying principles of mathematics, science, and technology to model a given situation (e.g., the movement of energy and nutrients between a food chain and the physical environment)
- applying principles of mathematics, science, and technology to explore phenomena from other areas of learning (e.g., applying statistical methodologies to examine census data)
- designing solutions to problems in the physical and social worlds using mathematical, scientific, and technological reasoning and procedures
- analyzing the effects of human activities (e.g., burning fossil fuels, clear-cutting forests) on the environment and evaluating the use of science and technology in solving problems related to these effects

Science disciplines hold to certain central values that unify them in their philosophy and methodology. Science relies on evidence collected in verifiable experiments, on conclusions validated by replication, and on theories that explain observations and that are capable of making testable predictions. Modern scientific thought traces a significant portion of its development to the work of Western European scientists, much, but far from all. It is important to recognize the contributions made by all peoples and cultures to the development of scientific knowledge. Men and women from all continents and races continue to make meaningful contributions to the advancement of science in all disciplines. Examples are readily available for enrichment and instruction from online resources.

Technology can be loosely defined as the application of science for the benefit of mankind. For both political and economic reasons not all people have the same ready access to clean, safe water supplies nor to adequate food supplies, in spite of the technological capabilities that basic science has provided. Science certainly can benefit, but it too, arguably, can harm mankind and our environment. Science gives us the knowledge and tools to understand nature's principles and that knowledge can often be applied for some useful purpose. Few would debate the benefits of the wheel and axle, the electric light, the polio vaccine, or plastic. The benefits of science and technology become more complicated to evaluate when discussing the applications of gene splicing for genetically modified foods, of cloning, of nuclear energy to replace fossil fuels, or the application of atomic energy to weapons of mass destruction. Science can tell us how to do something, not whether we should.

Scientific literacy helps us participate in the decision-making process of our society as well-informed and contributing members. Real-world decisions have social, political, and economic dimensions, and scientific information is often used to both support and refute these decisions. Understanding that the inherent nature of scientific information is unbiased, and based on experimental evidence that can be reproduced by any laboratory under the same conditions can help us all make better decisions, recognize false arguments, and participate fully as active and responsible citizens.

Interdisciplinary Science

All theoretical chemistry is really physics; and all theoretical chemists know it.

Richard P. Feynman (1918–1988), Nobel Prize in Physics, 1965

The separation of the natural sciences into life, physical, and earth sciences is relatively arbitrary. Many school curricula, and state-level science standards, are based on the cross-disciplinary integration of science based on key concepts rather than individual disciplines. The science concept of cycle is one of many concepts that find application, and can be used to understand science content, in more than one scientific discipline. This approach to science instruction is viewed as important for several reasons. It is consistent with the goals of scientific literacy and of developing science content knowledge upon which students build and extend their own understanding. Science knowledge is constantly developing and expanding in a continuous process, made more meaningful through the development of an organizing framework. Scientific concepts, which often have application in contexts outside the laboratory, help us see similarities and recognize patterns, which allow us to better function within society.

Science concepts can serve as organizers, often unifying disparate topics in the process of learning science. Examples of key interdisciplinary science concepts include: cause-effect, model, cycle, equilibrium, population, and gradient. As an example, the concept of model is among the most ubiquitous in all of science. Models are tentative schemes or structures that relate to real world objects or phenomena. Our explanations of many phenomena rely on models, descriptions of electricity, atoms, tectonics, and genetics. Like a model airplane, a scientific model will bear a certain resemblance to the real object that is useful at some level to represent, but not fully replicate, the real object. Models are used when the phenomenon or object of interest cannot be used directly. Models may be constructed to scale, but often are not, in order to emphasize some portion of the object. An artistic drawing is a model, as is a three-dimensional, cross-sectional plastic casting, or a computer-rendered animation. Each has its limitations, and its beneficial function, to extend our understanding of the object or phenomenon. Models can limit our understanding when they are treated as statements of descriptive fact or when the limitations of the physical model are confused with the characteristics of the real object or phenomenon.

Social Studies

The NYSTCE includes five test objectives. These objectives represent a broad range of integrated social sciences concepts from the content areas of history, geography, political science, and economics. Embedded within each broad objective are a number of essential social sciences concepts. A thorough understanding of each objective requires deep knowledge of the embedded concepts coupled with the ability to analyze and apply those concepts in a comparative analysis of New York, U.S., and world contemporary and historic society. For each objective an explanation of the embedded concepts is provided.

When preparing for the social studies portion of the elementary test, you should review the embedded concepts enumerated within each objective. Once you think you have a thorough understanding of each concept, you should determine whether or not you can apply your understanding within the context of New York, U.S., and world contemporary and historic contexts.

0021 **Understand major ideas, eras, themes, developments, and turning points in the history of New York State, the United States, and the world.**

For example:
- defining important conceptual terms (e.g., racism, nation-state, nationalism, feudalism) and using them to analyze general historical phenomena and specific historical events
- analyzing the social effects of major developments in human history (e.g., the agricultural revolution, the scientific revolution, the industrial revolution, the information revolution)

- understanding major political, social, economic, and geographic characteristics of ancient civilizations and the connections and interactions among these civilizations
- examining reasons for organizing periods of history in different ways and comparing alternative interpretations of key events and issues in New York State, U.S., and world history
- analyzing the effects of European contact with indigenous cultures and the effects of European settlement on New York State and the Northeast
- analyzing how the roles and contributions of individuals and groups helped shape U.S. social, political, economic, cultural, and religious life

0022 **Understand geographic concepts and phenomena and analyze the interrelationships of geography, society, and culture in the development of New York State, the United States, and the world.**

For example:
- defining important geographic terms and concepts (e.g., habitat, resource, cultural diffusion, ecology) and using them to analyze various geographic issues, problems, and phenomena
- demonstrating an understanding of the six essential elements of geography: the world in spatial terms, places and regions, physical settings, human systems, environment and society, and the use of geography
- recognizing physical characteristics of the earth's surface and the continual reshaping of it by physical processes (e.g., how weather, climate, and the water cycle influence different regions)
- analyzing the development and interaction of social, political, cultural, and religious systems in different regions of New York State, the United States, and the world
- examining ways in which economic, environmental, and cultural factors influence demographic change, and interpreting geographic relationships, such as population density and spatial distribution patterns
- analyzing the impact of human activity on the physical environment (e.g., industrial development, population growth, deforestation)

0023 **Understand concepts and phenomena related to human development and interactions (including anthropological, psychological, and sociological concepts).**

For example:
- using concepts, theories, and modes of inquiry drawn from anthropology, psychology, and sociology to examine general social phenomena and issues related to intercultural understanding
- evaluating factors that contribute to personal identity (e.g., family, group affiliations, socialization processes)
- recognizing how language, literature, the arts, media, architecture, traditions, beliefs, values, and behaviors influence and/or reflect the development and transmission of culture
- analyzing the roles and functions of social groups and institutions in the United States (e.g., ethnic groups, schools, religions) and their influence on individual and group interactions

- analyzing why individuals and groups hold different or competing points of view on issues, events, or historical developments
- understanding the processes of social and cultural change

0024   Understand economic and political principles, concepts, and systems, and relate this knowledge to historical and contemporary developments in New York State, the United States, and the world.

For example:
- defining important economic and political terms and concepts (e.g., scarcity, opportunity cost, supply and demand, productivity, power, natural rights, checks and balances) and using them to analyze general phenomena and specific issues
- analyzing the basic structure, fundamental ideas, accomplishments, and problems of the U.S. economic system
- recognizing and comparing basic characteristics of major models of economic organization (e.g., traditional, market, command) and various governmental systems (e.g., democratic, authoritarian)
- analyzing values, principles, concepts, and key features of American constitutional democracy (e.g., individual freedom, separation of powers, due process, federalism)
- comparing different perspectives regarding economic and political issues and policies in New York State and the United States (e.g., taxing and spending decisions)
- analyzing ways in which the United States has influenced other nations (e.g., in the development of democratic principles and human rights) and how other nations have influenced U.S. politics and culture

0025   Understand the roles, rights, and responsibilities of citizenship in the United States and the skills, knowledge, and attitudes necessary for successful participation in civic life.

For example:
- analyzing the personal and political rights guaranteed in the Declaration of Independence, the U.S. Constitution, the Constitution of the State of New York, and major civil rights legislation
- recognizing the core values of the U.S. democratic system (e.g., justice, honesty, the rule of law, self-discipline, due process, equality, majority rule, respect for minority rights)
- demonstrating an understanding of the U.S. election process and the roles of political parties, pressure groups, and special interests in the U.S. political system
- explaining what citizenship means in a democratic society and analyzing the ways in which citizens participate in and influence the political process in the United States (e.g., the role of public opinion and citizen action groups in shaping public policy)
- examining the rights, responsibilities, and privileges of individuals in relation to family, social group, career, community, and nation
- analyzing factors that have expanded or limited the role of the individual in U.S. political life during the twentieth century (e.g., female suffrage, Jim Crow laws, growth of presidential primaries, role of the media in political elections)

0026 **Understand and apply skills related to social studies, including gathering, organizing, mapping, evaluating, interpreting, and displaying information.**

For example:
- evaluating the appropriateness of various resources and research methods for meeting specified information needs (e.g., atlas, bibliography, almanac, database, survey, poll) and applying procedures for retrieving information using traditional resources and current technologies (e.g., CD-ROM, the Internet)
- demonstrating an understanding of concepts, tools, and technologies for mapping information about the spatial distribution of people, places, and environments (e.g., mapping grids, latitude and longitude, the advantages and limitations of different types of maps and map projections)
- analyzing information in social studies materials (e.g., identifying central themes in important historical speeches or documents, distinguishing fact from opinion, evaluating multiple points of view in policy debates)
- interpreting information presented in one or more graphic representations (e.g., graph, table, map) and translating written or graphic information from one form to the other
- summarizing the purpose or point of view of a historical narrative

History

Developing historical perspective includes knowledge of events, ideas, and people from the past. That knowledge encompasses an understanding of the diversity of race, ethnicity, social and economic status, gender, region, politics, and religion within history. Historic understanding includes the use of historical reasoning, resulting in a thorough exploration of cause-effect relationships to reach defensible historical interpretations through inquiry.

Significant knowledge of events, ideas, and people from the past results from careful analysis of cause and effect relationships in the following chronological eras: beginnings of civilization to 1620; colonization and settlement (1585–1763); revolution and the new nation (1754–1815); expansion and reform (1801–1861); Civil War and Reconstruction (1850–1877); the development of the industrial United States (1870–1900); the emergence of modern America (1890–1930); the Great Depression and World War II (1929–1945); postwar United States (1945–1970); and contemporary United States (1968–present).

Significant knowledge of historical events, ideas, and people from New York's past would result from careful analysis of cause and effect relationships in the chronological eras listed above for the United States. Included in this knowledge is an understanding of the evolution of political ideas, institutions, and practices in New York and the influence of technology, agriculture, urbanization, industry, and labor on the development of the New York economy. It is also necessary to understand the importance of family and local history.

This objective also involves the ability to analyze and interpret the past. Analysis and interpretation result from an understanding that history is logically constructed based upon conclusions resulting from careful analysis of documents, eyewitness accounts, letters, diaries, artifacts, photos, historical sites, and other primary and secondary sources.

Geography and Human Behavior

Understanding major geographic concepts involves comprehending both physical features of geography and the cultural aspects of geography. This would include knowledge of the five fundamental themes of geography, comprehension of the relationships within and between places, understanding interdependence within the local, natural, and global communities, and familiarity with global issues and events.

The five themes of geography are: place; human-environmental interaction; location; movement and connections; and regions, patterns, and processes. An understanding of these themes would include the ability to use them to analyze regions within New York, the United States, and the world to gain a perspective about interrelationships among those regions. The use of the five themes should also result in the ability to compare regions.

An understanding of the theme of location requires knowledge of both absolute and relative location. Absolute location is determined by longitude and latitude. Relative location deals with the interactions that occur between and among places. Relative location involves the interconnectedness among people because of land, water, and technology. For example, knowledge of the history of Albany includes an understanding of how its location on the Hudson has contributed to its economic development and vitality.

An understanding of the theme of human-environmental interaction involves consideration of how people rely on the environment, how we alter it, and how the environment may limit what people are able to do. For example, knowledge of the meat and grain industries in New York's history includes an understanding of how the people of New York utilized the Erie Canal to take their products to regional markets.

An understanding of the theme of location, movement, and connections involves identifying how people are connected through different forms of transportation and communication networks and how those networks have changed over time. This would include identifying channels of the movement of people, goods, and information. For example, the manufacturing industry in New York City had a profound impact on the movement patterns of ideas and people of both the New York metropolitan area and elsewhere in the state.

An understanding of the theme of regions, patterns, and processes include identifying climatic, economic, political, and cultural patterns within regions. Understanding why these patterns were created includes understanding how climatic systems, communication networks, international trade, political systems, and population changes contributed to a region's development. An understanding of regions enables a social scientist to study their uniqueness and relationship to other regions.

Understanding global issues and events includes comprehending the interconnectedness of peoples throughout the world. For example, knowledge of the relationship between world oil consumption and oil production would result in an understanding of the impact that increased demand for oil in China would have on the price of a barrel of oil, which in turn could affect the decisions of consumers of new vehicles in the United States.

Economic and Political Principles

An understanding of economics involves exploring the implications of scarcity.

Fast Facts

An understanding of economics involves exploring the implications of scarcity (the concept that wants are unlimited while resources are limited). Exploration of scarcity involves an understanding of economic principles spanning from personal finance to international trade. Economic understanding is rooted in exploring principles of choice, opportunity costs, incentives, trade, and economic systems. (For a definition of each of the economic principles see the Handy Dandy Guide [HDG] developed by the National Council on Economic Education. For brief definitions based upon this guide see the Web site: *http://ecedweb.unomaha.edu/lessons/handydandy.htm*). This exploration includes analysis of how those principles operate within the economic choices of individuals, households, businesses, and governments.

In addition, economic understanding includes knowledge of the role that price, competition, profit, inflation, economic institutions, money, and interest rates play within a market system. A complete understanding of markets includes knowledge of the role of government within an economic system, including how monetary and fiscal policy impacts the market. (These economic concepts are based upon the *National Content Standards in Economics* published by the National Council on Economic Education. A brief overview and complete list of standards can be found at *http://ncee.net/ea/standards/*).

An understanding of various political systems involves the ability to compare different political systems, their ideologies, structures, institutions, processes, and political cultures. This requires knowledge of alternative ways of organizing constitutional governments from systems of shared power to parliamentarian systems. Systems of shared power include federal systems, where sovereign states delegate powers to a central government; a federal system, where a national government shares power with state and local governments; and Unitarian systems where all power is concentrated in a centralized government.

Understanding local and state governments results from knowledge of the role of federal and state constitutions in defining the power and scope of state and local government. That knowledge should include comprehension of reserved and concurrent powers. Furthermore, an understanding of state and local government results from knowledge of the organization and responsibilities of such governments.

Understanding of the role of law in a democratic society results from a knowledge of the nature of civil, criminal, and constitutional law and how the organization of the judicial system serves to interpret and apply such laws. Essential judicial principles to know include comprehension of rights, such as the right of due process, the right to a fair and speedy trial, and the right to a hearing before a jury of one's peers. Additional judicial principles include an understanding of the protections granted in the Constitution, which include protection from self-incrimination and unlawful searches and seizures.

Understanding global interdependence begins with recognition that world regions include economic, political, historical, ecological, linguistic, and cultural regions. This understanding should include knowledge of military and economic alliances such as NATO, the G8 members, or cartels such as OPEC, and how their existence affects political and economic policies within regions. Knowledge of world regions and alliances leads to identification of issues that affect people in these areas. Common issues that affect people around the world include food production, human rights, resource use, prejudice, poverty, and trade.

A true sense of global interdependence results from an understanding of the relationship between local decisions and global issues—how individual or community actions regarding waste disposal or recycling may affect worldwide resource availability, for example. Or how fuel emissions standards affect air pollution or how fuel standards affect oil supply and gas prices.

The Responsibilities of Citizens

The social sciences portion of the NYSTCE requires comprehension of the ideals of American democracy, including a core set of values expressed in America's essential founding documents, the Declaration of Independence, the Articles of Confederation, the U.S Constitution, and the Bill of Rights. Those values include life, liberty, pursuit of happiness, common good, justice, equality, truth, diversity, popular sovereignty, and patriotism.

Furthermore, the ideals of American democracy include the following essential Constitutional principles: the rule of law, separation of powers, representative government, checks and balances, individual rights, freedom of religion, federalism, limited government, and civilian control of the military. Essential democratic principles include those principles fundamental to the American judicial system, including: the right to due process of law; the right to a fair and speedy trial, protection from unlawful search and seizure, and the right to decline to self-incriminate.

Fast Facts It is essential for citizens to be active in order to maintain a democratic society.

Comprehension of the rights and responsibilities of citizens of the United States involves understanding that it is essential for citizens to be active in order to maintain a democratic society. This activity includes participation in political activities such as voting, providing service to communities, and regulating oneself in accordance with the law.

Diversity

Understanding the role of cultural diversity in shaping New York, the United States, and the world begins with knowledge of the commonalities and differences among such groups as African-Americans, Asian-Americans, Hispanic-Americans, and Native Americans. Commonalities and differences can be found when analyzing the role of language, education, religion, culture, and struggles for equality within and among groups. Understanding the role of cultural diversity in shaping New York, the United States, and the world should include an understanding of the struggles various groups undertake to gain equality and recognition within society.

A historical perspective of the role of cultural diversity in shaping the development of New York and the United States begins by gaining a sense of the types of people who came to Colonial America and their reasons for coming. This understanding can help one gain an appreciation for the diverse peoples that eventually won their independence from Great Britain. Following those people from the east during the various migrations westward can explain how various groups of people settled what today is the American West. Studies of Old Immigration (1830–1850) and New Immigration (1900–1920) further complete the picture of the settling of America that encouraged diverse peoples to come here. Within this historical understanding one should be able to identify examples of how immigrants sought to assimilate themselves into American culture, contributions of immigrant groups to American culture, and ways that immigrants have been exploited.

Diverse cultural groups have shaped world history. Diversity has both positive and negative results—from contributing to disputes over territories, creating alliances that eventually lead to world and regional conflicts, outsourcing of jobs, and relocation of companies from the United States to foreign countries, to more positive examples such as the economic specialization that enhances choice and the modern globalization that results in economic interdependence. The impact of cultural diversity on world history can be explored by careful analysis of the following events, among others: the origin and spread of Christianity and Islam; colonialism and exploration; the beginning of World War I; and contemporary conflict in the Middle East.

Locating, Organizing, and Interpreting Social Sciences Information

The ability to understand and apply skills and procedures related to the study of social sciences involves knowledge of the use of systematic inquiry. Inquiry is essential for use in examining single social sciences topics or integrated social sciences. Being able to engage in inquiry involves the ability to acquire information from a variety of resources, and organize that information, which leads to the interpretation of that information. Inquiry involves the ability to design and conduct investigations, which in turn leads to the identification and analysis of social sciences issues.

In addition, this understanding includes knowledge about and the use of the various resources used in systematic social science inquiry. Those resources include primary and secondary sources, encyclopedias, almanacs, atlases, government documents, artifacts, and oral histories.

The Fine Arts

0027 **Understand the concepts, techniques, and materials of the visual arts; analyze works of visual art; and understand the cultural dimensions and contributions of the visual arts.**

For example:
- identifying basic elements (e.g., line, color) and principles (e.g., unity, balance) of art, and recognizing how they are used to communicate meaning in works of art
- analyzing two-dimensional and three-dimensional works of art in terms of their visual and sensory characteristics
- applying knowledge of the characteristics of various art media (e.g., two-dimensional, three-dimensional, electronic) to select a medium appropriate for a given artistic purpose or intent
- applying knowledge of basic tools and techniques for working with various materials (e.g., clay, textiles, wood)
- analyzing how works of art reflect the cultures in which they were produced (e.g., materials or techniques used, subject matter, style)
- comparing works of art of different cultures, eras, and artists in terms of characteristics such as theme, imagery, and style

0028 **Understand concepts, techniques, and materials for producing, listening to, and responding to music; analyze works of music; and understand the cultural dimensions and contributions of music.**

For example:
- comparing various types of instruments (e.g., strings, percussion, woodwind, brass, electronic) in terms of the sounds they produce
- defining and applying common musical terms (e.g., pitch, tempo)
- using basic scientific concepts to explain how music-related sound is produced, transmitted through air, and received by listeners
- relating characteristics of music (e.g., rhythm, beat) to musical effects produced
- recognizing basic technical skills that musicians must develop to produce an aesthetically acceptable performance (e.g., manual dexterity, breathing techniques, knowledge of musical notation)
- analyzing how different cultures have created music reflective of their histories and societies (e.g., call-and-response songs, ballads, work songs, folk songs)

0029 **Understand concepts, techniques, and materials related to theater and dance; analyze works of drama and dance; and understand the cultural dimensions and contributions of drama and dance.**

For example:
- comparing dramatic and theatrical forms and their characteristics (e.g., pantomime, improvisation)
- relating types of dance (e.g., ballet, folk, modern) to their characteristic forms of movement, expressive qualities, and cultural origins
- analyzing how technical aspects of performance (e.g., costumes, props, lighting) affect the message or overall impression created by a performance
- recognizing how language, voice, gesture, and movement are used to develop character and create interaction among performers in theatrical productions
- analyzing ways in which different cultures have used drama and dance (e.g., to teach moral lessons, to preserve cultural traditions, to affirm the sense of community, to entertain)

Visual Arts

Why We Create Visual Art

Visual Communication

At its most fundamental level, art—be it opera, ballet, painting, or pantomime—is a form of communication. The realm of visual art encompasses many forms of communication, including sculpture, painting and drawing, ceramics, performance art, printmaking, jewelry, fiber art, photography, and film and video. Each medium or field of specialization communicates differently than the others. Take, for instance, the difference between viewing a sculpture and a tapestry. Sculpture (in the round) requires the viewer to physically move around in space to comprehend the work, whereas a tapestry can generally be viewed from a stationary position. Sculpture is three-dimensional, encompassing height, width, and depth, whereas a tapestry is two-dimensional, encompassing only height and width. While both forms of art can have a strong visual presence, sculpture is unique in that it has the capacity to be fully physically engaging in actual space. Artists choose different disciplines and media because each method and medium has its own communicative potential.

Aesthetics

As viewers, we can be affected by visual art in ways that are difficult to define. The powerful experience of encountering, for example, a huge carved Olmec head sculpture in an outdoor garden in Villahermosa, Mexico, or contemplating a quiet, delicate Vermeer painting in The Hague, Netherlands, is sometimes termed an aesthetic moment or experience. We may try to put into words the experience of these moments—beautiful, colossal, overwhelming, transcendental—but the words often seem inadequate. What the art is communicating is perhaps hard to verbalize, but the feeling is undeniable. As viewers, we are momentarily transported so that we are no longer aware of our surroundings or ourselves. When art communicates to us in such a direct and forceful way, we consider this an aesthetic experience.

Although aesthetics has long been recognized as the branch of philosophy pertaining to beauty, it is impossible to find agreement on what is beautiful. In keeping with the root of the word, aesthetics can be understood more as a study of sensation or feeling than of beauty. This broader understanding of aesthetics has the ability to encompass the range of sensations that one can experience in viewing a work of art. Art is not always beautiful in the traditional sense of the word, and our aesthetic philosophies must be able to encompass this reality.

Current Tendencies in Visual Art

Visual art, like other forms of communication, has the capacity to convey the complexity of issues, ideas, and feelings. What generally (and traditionally) distinguishes visual art from the other disciplines in the arts is the emphasis on the visual. However, there are numerous visual artists who work entirely in sound, for example. What, then, is the factor that distinguishes visual artists from experimental sound artists, video artists from cinematographers, and performance artists from actors or dancers? The categories that distinguish one discipline from another are becoming increasingly blurred. While the traditional areas of fine art study (namely music, theatre, dance, and visual art) still exist, many artists today are what we term *interdisciplinary*. These artists are often conversant with different art disciplines while maintaining an identity in their primary field of study. The interdisciplinary crossover of art forms has opened up many exciting possibilities for music, theatre, dance, and visual art. Indeed, interdisciplinary art has the potential to capture the complexities of our present world differently than was previously possible.

Understanding Art

The Role of Visual Art in Society

From the earliest cave paintings to the most recent art installations, visual art has functioned as a form of commentary on the society from which it springs; consequently, visual art is continually changing. Over the millennia, visual art has played (and continues to play) a key role in the dissemination of aesthetic tendencies, political ideas, religious and spiritual doctrines, cultural beliefs and critiques, and societal norms and trends. Conversely, visual art has changed and adapted to these same influences. In essence, visual art has the capacity to both shape and be shaped by the society in which it exists.

Visual art has also served the vital role of empowering the artist in his or her subject matter. For example, there has been broad speculation about the functions of the animal imagery that adorns the caves of France and Spain: Some suggest that the act of representing the animals gave the creator power over the creature or the creature's soul, while others have postulated that these artistic gestures were an early form of inventory—a means to count, organize, and track the myriad animals that existed in the outside world.

The function of art as an empowering tool is as vital today as it was in past millennia. Much like the cave painters of the past, contemporary artists often use their art as a means to chart and order the complexities, wonders, and inspirations of the present-day world.

Anonymous Artists

Fast Facts The earliest examples of art known to us date back to about 40,000 BCE, and the majority of this art remains anonymous to us.

The earliest examples of art known to us date back to about 40,000 BCE, and the majority of this art remains anonymous to us. For example, all of the extant art from Egypt, of which thousands of examples survive, was created anonymously, in service to the pharaohs, gods, and society of the artists. There are instances of work crews having inscribed their names on the pyramids; however, since the form, subject matter, and imagery were determined by the dictates of that society, this seems to be more about individuals taking pride in their work than a desire for individual recognition. While this began to change during the Greek and Roman eras (wherein we begin to recognize individual artists' styles and artists more commonly signed their names), the role of the artist as an individual creator (and the subject, form, and content of art being determined by the individual artist) is a relatively recent phenomenon.

It is also important to recognize that what remains of a past society like Egypt is always incomplete. We do not have the benefit of knowing what did not survive (e.g., homes, art, and utilitarian objects of everyday life).

How We View Art

A critical aspect of understanding art requires consideration of the context in which the art has been created; indeed, by examining the specifics of an artist's milieu—geographical, political, racial, social, religious, economic, and so forth—it is possible to truly appreciate and comprehend the profound differences that occur among works of art. Moreover, the way we view art is always mitigated by all of these same factors. Throughout history, art has readily been categorized based on some of the above factors, particularly temporal, geographic, and cultural ones. For instance, we tend to distinguish pre-Colombian artifacts by time periods (classical, postclassical), regional stylistic variations (Puuc, Zapotec), and tribal or geographical distinctions (Incan, Mayan, Aztec). These categories exist as a means of organizing and distinguishing the myriad groups of people, objects, styles, and places from which visual art arises. In today's visual art world, these same categories are often incomplete or inappropriate in illuminating the distinctions between art forms: these categories alone omit or underplay the importance of specific cultural context on the work of art. Moreover, there is a long-standing tradition of Western scholars using a Eurocentric, comparative value system when examining the differences between visual arts of various cultures. This system is often biased and generally lacking in that it does not account for the contextual specifics of each culture, Some scholars have relegated or dismissed works of art as "primitive," "naïve," or simply "crude," based upon comparisons with art that is created under the aesthetic traditions of Europe. Comparing visual art from one culture to another is a rich, valuable, and worthwhile form of study, but only if cultural biases are not informing the process.

Consider the world we live in: In less than a day, one can travel to Micronesia, sub-Saharan Africa, or New Zealand. Furthermore, the Internet allows us immediate access to any person, group, country, company, or interest. Our understanding of influences in visual art has to encompass the understanding that the global network that reaches every part of the planet now influences every region of the world. In this global climate, it is not always possible to neatly categorize or even identify the influences that occur in visual art. It is possible, however, to recognize, distinguish and appreciate certain tendencies in visual art.

Concepts And Skills

Principles and Elements

In viewing and creating visual art, there are endless considerations in how to convey ideas, thoughts, and feelings in the visual realm. The elements—point, line, plane, shape, value, texture, color—and principles—balance, harmony, variety, directional thrust, focal area, and so forth—of art play an integral role in creating, viewing, and analyzing visual art. For instance, the choice of a particular color in a painting can change the whole mood of the work. Additionally, the meaning of a certain color in a work of art can change dramatically depending on the period or culture in which the work of art was created.

The color red, for instance, can simultaneously signify love, war, anger, passion, danger, warmth, death, life, and many other things depending on the cultural significance of the color, the context of the color in the work of art, and the intention of the artist. As we view and create visual art, we are constantly fine-tuning our sensibilities so that we are sensitive to the subtleties of the elements and principles of art.

Form and Meaning

As discussed previously, visual art functions as a reflection of the values, beliefs, and tendencies of an individual or society. Naturally, the *form* of art changes in relation to its function or meaning. For instance, the native carvers of Africa's Ivory Coast ascribe specific meaning to forms in the carving of their ceremonial masks. Each formal element on the mask—bulging eyes, elongated nose, perforated cheeks, and so on—serves a spiritual, cultural, and symbolic function during a ceremony, in that the mask creates a connection to the spirit world for both the performer and the tribe.

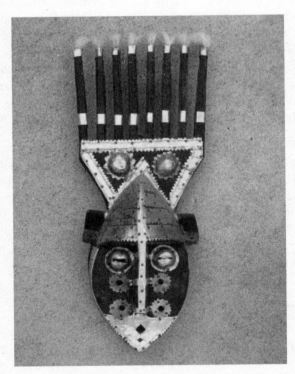

Figure 1.1   Ivory Coast Ceremonial Mask. Date unknown.

The forms on the mask, therefore, are culturally recognized, determined, and created for a specific purpose. This is very different from the view of visual art that emerged during the nineteenth century in Europe: namely, the role of form in a work of visual art was elevated to a primary level, while subject and content took an increasingly secondary role. The result of this elevation of form in visual art is what was eventually termed *formalist* art in the twentieth century in North America.

Formalism, at its peak with Post-Painterly Abstraction in the 1950s and 1960s, prided itself on its lack of meaning, symbolism, and subject matter: Simply put, it was about form or material and nothing more. It is astounding that one culture can ascribe deep, symbolic meaning to form or material while another culture can revel in its relative meaninglessness. The stark contrast between the beliefs of the Baule and the Post-Painterly Abstractionists indicates the vast differences that occur between art forms from different cultures and the importance of understanding how material associations can affect meaning in a work of art.

Deciphering Clues

Sometimes when viewing a work of art, we are unable to obtain information about the artist or the artist's intentions. In these instances, our role as viewer is akin to being a detective: We must collect as much information about the work of art as possible in order to make an educated guess about its meaning. The following mixed media drawing can be analyzed and understood based solely upon the clues we are given in the artwork.

Figure 1.2   Student work by Regina Chandler.

By considering aspects of the art principles and elements in the drawing, we are often able to learn about the artist's intentions. The first thing we may notice in the drawing is the chair, which for many reasons draws the attention of a viewer. It appears to be the closest object to the viewer; it is the largest object (relatively speaking) in the drawing, and it can lead one's eyes into the space behind it. Another noticeable feature is the viewer's relationship to the chair. The chair is drawn in extreme, slightly distorted three-point perspective. The initial point of view that the viewer confronts is one of ambiguity. In one way, the viewer is looking down the stairs and the chair appears to be falling away; in another way, the viewer is looking up the stairs and the chair is falling toward the viewer. Adding to the ambiguity in this drawing are the light source and shadows; indeed, the viewer is given at least two light sources that create shadows on the stairs and on the underside of the chair. Lastly, the viewer of this piece is confronted with the randomly collaged atmosphere of road maps. The predominant theme that seems to emerge from the drawing is one of confusion and ambiguity. One might assume that, based on these observations, the student's intention here was to play with the rules of perspective in order to create an indeterminate space and feeling. The drawing holds one's attention by virtue of its changeability. It is possible that the student had specific intentions about the choice of maps and the illusion of the chair (perhaps a memory or a symbolic reference to somewhere specific), and sometimes we are fortunate enough to learn the inspiration of an artist's work. Yet, in this particular example, one is able to piece together enough clues from the drawing to enjoy and appreciate the work without knowing all of the specifics of the artist's motivation.

Material Factors

Understanding the differences between works of art happens on many levels. As previously discussed, the aesthetic standards by which one assesses a work of art must take into account the many cultural factors that influence visual art. Equally important to aesthetic consideration is knowledge of the many tools, techniques, and materials that artists employ in their art. The number of potential materials for creating works of art has increased exponentially over the past 150 years or so. This situation can be attributed both to industrial innovations and to artists' broadening their scope to include found materials and unusual non-art objects and media. The foregrounding of materiality that occurred with the formalist artists in the twentieth century has further contributed to the recent expanse of materials for art making. The inclusion of uncommon materials in visual art has dramatically changed the criteria by which one assesses visual art; in fact, it is no longer unusual to be confronted with traditionally carved marble sculptures (Louise Bourgeois) and cast and licked chocolate sculptures (Janine Antoni) in the same gallery space. What becomes important in analyzing these diverse works is an understanding of the motivation behind the artwork. It is equally legitimate for one artist to pursue traditional carving in stone while another artist explores conceptual possibilities in cast and licked chocolate. One may be more attracted to one art form over another, but ultimately, it is critical for us to respect the diversity that contributes to the variety, richness and complexity of the art world.

Music

When preparing for this part of the exam, it is important to focus on the objectives to which music is primarily related. They include contexts for the music, concepts and skills involved in experiencing music, and the aesthetic and personal dimensions of music. These constitute a broad overview of the field of music and the musical experience.

One objective is to "understand historical, cultural, and societal contexts for the arts (visual arts, music, drama, dance) and the interrelationships among the arts." This suggests an integration of subject matter that is an opportunity for teachers and students to make connections between social studies, reading or language arts, and the fine arts. For example, when students are reading stories about the American Revolution, they should be aware that it occurred during the period known as the Classical Period in music history. Listening to a work by Haydn or Mozart and talking about how they reflected the "old world" and then comparing the work to a Colonial American tune of the time like "Chester" by William Billings is a great exercise. Similarly, the visual art of Andy Warhol, the music of the Beatles, the assassination of John F. Kennedy, and the war in Vietnam all share the same approximate time frame. In these and the virtually infinite number of other cases or combinations, the students can be asked to find contrasts and similarities or they can attempt to find ways that historical context affected art and ways that art affected and reflected history.

These examples from American History are easy for most to grasp quickly. However, the objective seeks to have teachers and students consider the role of the Arts, to include music, in history and culture beyond the American experience. Listening to music from China, Japan, Germany, Australia, or Africa when studying those cultures can enrich the experience and make it more memorable for students. It is even more valuable to experience live or videotaped performances of the music and dance of these cultures because often the music is performed in traditional costume with traditional instruments (sometimes very different from modern instruments) and seeing the costumes and the movement are an important part of understanding the culture.

According to the objective, merely experiencing the music is not enough. The students must be able to recognize the music or art as part of its historical context and then, through discussion or written exercises that emphasize higher order thinking, they must demonstrate an understanding of the music's place in the historical context and be able to note things that are common and things that are different from context to context—period to period, culture to culture, and so forth—appropriate to their age and level of development. For example, Haydn, Mozart, and Billings used simple melodies in their compositions, but Haydn and Mozart wrote mostly large works like symphonies and operas, whereas Billings wrote mostly psalms and songs. Students must be aware of these facts and then consider why more highly developed forms were preferred in the "old world" while basic psalms and songs were more common in the Colonies. The obvious answer is that colonists did not have the time or the resources to encourage or produce larger musical works. However, the discussion could go beyond that basic step depending on the sophistication of the students.

Another objective is to "understand concepts, techniques, and materials" for producing, listening to, and responding to music. Understanding concepts and techniques suggests more than an appreciation of these concepts and skills. The students ought to experience music making and be taught to listen as musicians listen. They should learn how to put their response to music into accepted music terminology.

Making music is a basic experience. Mothers sing to their babies. Children beat sticks together, make drums, and sing during their play. Adults whistle or sing along with tunes on the radio. People are naturally drawn to sound and music. It is an important part of culture, religious practice, and personal experience for all people. Some people become professional musicians, whereas others whistle, sing, or play for their own enjoyment and nothing more. It is important that students have the opportunity to experience as many forms of music making as possible. It is through the acquisition of basic skills in singing and playing instruments that people can grow in their ability to express themselves through music. As students develop skills, they are also exposed to basic musical concepts such as melody, harmony, rhythm, pitch, and timbre. Then, with experience, they come to make decisions about what is acceptable or not acceptable within a given cultural or historical context and thereby develop their own aesthetic awareness. There is only a very small segment of society that does not make music. These people would likely choose to make music if they could, but are unable as a result of a physical impairment or personal choice (e.g., a vow of silence). Music making is a natural part of human experience.

Listening is a skill that is often taken for granted. There is not a "right" way to listen. However, listening can be much more than allowing the sound to flow past the ears. It can be as basic as listening for melodies and analyzing for form and chord structure or as advanced as critiquing the interpretation on its musical and aesthetic merits. Listening with knowledge and understanding can make the experience of a musical performance much deeper and more meaningful. While music can be experienced and found satisfying, challenging, or beautiful without prior knowledge of a piece or an understanding of its form, cultural significance, and so forth, these things can enrich the experience.

Fast Facts **Music does not provide specific information, instructions, or reactions. People respond to it naturally.**

People respond to music naturally. They do not need prompting or help to respond. They just respond. However, in order to share that response, they must learn how to put their response to music into musical terminology. Some people call music a language, but it does not function as a spoken language. It does not provide specific information, instructions, or reactions. Rather, it sparks thoughts, feelings and emotions. In order to try to put the experience into words, musicians and artists have developed vocabulary and approaches to discussing music and art. This is not to say that there is only one way to respond to or to talk about music or art. However, it is easier to understand music and musicians, art and artists, if the students understand and can use the kind of vocabulary and approaches that musicians or artists use to discuss their work. This includes things as basic as melody and harmony and as profound as the aesthetic experience.

This objective is also about self-expression through and with regard to music. People cannot express themselves or effectively communicate if they do not understand the structures and rules that underlie the "language" that they are trying to use. Although music does not provide the kind of specific communication that spoken language does, it does have structures that can be considered and discussed to help students understand the music and express their responses to the music.

Part of meeting this objective is to understand and promote the aesthetic and personal dimensions related to music. The aesthetic experience is what draws people to music. That experience that everyone has had, but cannot describe because words seem clumsy when it comes to something that can be so profound and wonderful. The type of music or the period or the performer does not necessarily limit the aesthetic experience. It is equally possible to have an aesthetic experience when listening to a child sing a simple melody as it is when listening to a professional orchestra performing a Beethoven symphony. The important thing is to share that aesthetic experience. It is part of what makes music and art special.

There are many ways to encourage exploration of and growth through aesthetic responsiveness. A common experience is a crucial starting point. Have the students listen to several pieces of music and, after listening attentively, ask them to describe how each one made them feel. It is often best to write their response down before starting a discussion. Then, ask them if they can explain why each piece of music made them feel the way they indicated. Younger students will likely provide simple, straightforward emotional responses (e.g., "It made me feel happy!"), while older students should be exploring why it affected the feelings that it did and using both musical concepts (e.g., "It made me feel happy because it was in a major key.") and non-musical associations (e.g., "It made me feel happy because it sounded like a circus and I like to go to the circus."). Through this kind of sharing, along with teacher insights and reading about how other people have responded to music, students can explore and come to a deeper understanding of their personal responses to music, other art forms, and possibly the world. In addition, it should provide them with practical ways to express their responses or reactions to what they experience in life.

According to the objective, having an aesthetic experience, recognizing its value, and being able to grapple with discussing or sharing that experience are not enough. It is also important to promote and develop this part of the musical and artistic experience. Teachers and students must attempt to foster an appreciation for the arts and their ability to create meaning. The arts provide an opportunity to explore and express ideas and emotions through a unique view of life experiences. It is through the experience of music, or any art form, that people begin to transcend the mundane day-to-day experience and reach beyond to a richer life experience.

The objectives that deal with music include contexts for the music, concepts, and skills involved in experiencing music, and the aesthetic and personal dimensions of music. Music does not exist in a vacuum. The context (e.g., historical or cultural) of a piece of music is very important. Students should know and be able to discuss the context of music through integration of subject matter. Music ought to be experienced in every way possible. Students must be given opportunities to develop basic performance skills as well as listening skills and vocabulary for responding to music. And, to pull all of these together, teachers and students should develop their aesthetic awareness and help others to do the same. While music and the musical experience can be complex, it is important to remember these basic ideas. In the end, it is not whether someone is a professional musician or an avid listener, but that they know the wonders of music and the arts.

Drama

The arts are a part of the core curriculum, both in terms of New York standards and the No Child Left Behind federal mandate. Dance, music, drama, and the visual arts are essential parts of a complete education. Study of one or more art forms develops the intellect, provides unique access to meaning, and connects individuals with works of genius, multiple cultures, and contributions to history.

Drama and theatre activities benefit students' educational growth, regardless of their future career.

Fast Facts

Drama and theatre activities offer learners opportunities to experience an art form in many different ways. Whether studying a play, mounting a production, attending a performance, or engaging in creative drama in the classroom, this subject helps students to learn about themselves and their world, develop social skills, strengthen both their verbal and nonverbal communication skills, creatively problem-solve, analyze, and collaborate. Some of the benefits inherent in this instructional methodology include developing concentration skills, analyzing content, demonstrating artistic discipline, improving listening, learning to apply research, communicating information, and making and justifying artistic choices. These are important to a student's educational growth, regardless of that individual's future career. Students who have a chance to learn about and through drama are motivated; their imaginations are engaged and their work is often quite focused.

More specific aesthetic benefits also are acquired. By participating in these activities, students learn about dramatic process and product. They acquire knowledge of theatre artists and their responsibilities. They engage in making artistic choices and learn about the personal discipline that the arts demand. Furthermore, students develop personal aesthetics that are based on informed judgments. They develop insight into cultures and communities, and better understand how this art form is manifest in both their artistic and their everyday lives.

Drama means "to do, act." Drama/theatre is an experiential way to connect to content. Students are engaged physically, mentally, and emotionally. In today's classroom, infusing these techniques into the curriculum allows for hands-on learning that is meaningful and lasting. Young people can learn not only about drama/theatre but also through the art form if it is partnered with another subject. Using these techniques helps children to understand both artistic and paired subject content.

Drama offers multiple approaches to gaining knowledge. Whether a student's preferred learning style is visual (verbal), visual (nonverbal), aural, or tactile/kinesthetic, infusing lessons with drama/theatre expands ways of knowing, especially because of the variety of activities available. Multiple approaches to knowledge acquisition and retention help to insure that all children learn. It should be no surprise, then, that in addition to students who regularly achieve in their studies, even those who generally are less successful may thrive in classrooms where drama/theatre is a regular part of their learning environment. Teaching and learning through and with dramatic art is a unique and effective approach to instruction at all educational levels and with students of varying degrees of academic achievement.

Educators teaching elementary school age children will find that understanding child drama and the continuum of activities that defines it will help them to determine what type of activity is best to use at any given time. While the following comparison helps to distinguish the two major components of this progression, it is important to recognize that one is not better than the other; they are simply different in composition and purpose. Creative drama, children's theatre, and the activities between them offer ample opportunities for integration and demonstrate that the arts are powerful partners for learning.

At one end of the drama/theatre spectrum is creative drama. In this format, process is more important than product; the benefit to the participant is paramount. Creative drama is frequently used in classrooms because it is informal drama that can work in any setting and with any number of children. Scenery, costumes, and/or props are not required. These activities move from teacher-centered to student-centered, from shorter to longer activities and sessions, from unison play to individual play, and from simple beginning activities to more complex story work. Participants need little, if any, previous experience with this approach to curriculum. Once they are introduced to this pedagogy, however, both their interests and their skills will grow.

Here are definitions for the many types of activities that are components of creative drama.

> **Beginning Activities:** These are warm-up activities such as name games, chants, listening games, and other simple exercises designed to relax and motivate participants.

> **Games:** These are more challenging than beginning activities and often focus upon developing players' concentration, imagination, and teamwork skills. Frequently, they are played with students seated or standing in a circle.

> **Sequence Games:** The teacher takes a story or similar material and divides it into particular events or scenes, placing each on an index card. These are randomly distributed to players. When a student recognizes his/her cue being performed, that student goes next. Index cards should have the cue at the top and the new action at the bottom, preferably in a different font or color. The teacher should keep a master list, in order, of cues. This helps students if the correct sequence is interrupted or lost.

> **Pantomime:** Players use their bodies to communicate rather than their voices. Pantomime sentences and stories, creative movement exercises, and miming games are common examples.

Improvisations: These are spontaneously created performances based upon at least two of the following: who (characters), what (conflict), where (setting), when (time), and how (specifics of interpretation). Performed either in pantomime or with dialogue, improvisations should not be planned or rehearsed. Interesting episodes that emerge may be further developed through story creation. Role-playing improvisations deal with problem solving. Students are exposed to differing points of view by replaying and switching roles. Role-playing should not be confused with playing in-role, which is when the teacher enters the dramatization as a character.

Stories: A number of activities can be based upon stories and can range from simple to complex. In the former category, for example, are *noisy stories*. These are simple stories that players help to tell by making sounds or saying words associated with characters. *Story creation* activities require that players develop stories, and these activities can be stimulated by various items, including props, titles, students' own writing, or true events. *Open-ended stories* are those from which students build stories given only a beginning and then share their creations either orally, in writing, or through performance. *Story dramatization* is the most complex informal dramatic activity, as it utilizes players' previously developed skills in service to playing stories. Once proficient here, students move naturally to formal theatrical endeavors.

Several types of activities bridge the gap between creative drama and theatre for youth. These include theatre-in-education (TIE), readers' theatre, and puppetry. Each can be integrated into classroom practice.

Theatre-in-Education (TIE): Originating in Britain, Theatre-in-Education is performed by actor-teachers and students. Using material based upon curriculum or social issues, players assume roles and, through these, explore and problem-solve. TIE's structure is flexible and its focus is educational.

Puppetry: Puppets can range from simple paper bag or sock creations to elaborately constructed marionettes. Puppets can be used for creative drama and theatre activities. Likewise, puppet stages can be as simple as a desktop or table, or they can be intricately constructed with artistically designed settings and theatrical trappings.

Readers Theatre: Called Theatre of the Imagination, Readers Theatre offers performance opportunities without elaborate staging. Traditionally, this type of performance has players sitting on stools, using onstage and/or offstage focus, and employing notebooks or music stands to hold scripts. A narrator may be used and readers may or may not play multiple roles. This type of performance is wedded to literature. A common misconception, however, is that this is simply expressive reading. To truly impact an audience, Readers Theatre must be more than that. Rich characterization, suggested movement, and clear interpretation of the literature are required. In their minds' eyes, audience members complete the stage pictures suggested by the interpreters.

Children's theatre is product-oriented and audience-centered. This theatre for young people can be performed by and for children, by adults for youth, or with a combined cast of adults and young people. In addition, actors can be either amateurs or professionals. Here, dialogue is memorized, the number of characters in the play determines the cast size, and scenery and costumes are generally expected production elements.

Educators may take their students to see plays or they may wish to stage plays in their classrooms or other school facilities. In addition to the familiar format, plays for young people can also be done as participation plays and as story theatre. These last two are especially adaptable to educational venues.

Traditional Theatre: In this most commonly used form of theatre, performers and audience are separate entities. Actors use character and story to communicate and the audience responds with feedback (e.g., laughing, applauding). Typically, actors perform on a stage and are supported by others who contribute the technical elements of theatre.

Participation Theatre: Children are given opportunities to use their voices and bodies within the context of the play. They might be asked for their ideas, invited to join the actors, or given chances to contribute to the play in meaningful ways.

Story Theatre: In this format, actors can function as both characters and narrators, sometimes commenting upon their own actions in role. They can play one role or multiple parts. Scenery, if used, is minimal and costume pieces can suggest a character. Story theatre is classroom friendly and closely linked to literature.

Young people benefit from exposure to theatre, whether as participant or audience member. Opportunities abound for developing vocal skills, vocabulary, imagination, understanding of dramatic structure and types of conflict, physical skills, and empathy. Theatre offers innovative instructional options.

Theatre is not a new art form; it emerged in ancient Greece as a part of religious celebrations. The fact that theatre has evolved over centuries is a testament to its nature; it is both experimental and transitional, allowing innovative elements to be absorbed into the mainstream while continuing to look for new artistic inventions. This is not its only dichotomy.

Theatre is a profession for some and an avocation for others. It is a communal and a collective art form. Regardless of its structure, theatre engages through both visual and auditory stimulation. And because it uses live actors performing for an audience that is "in the moment" with them, it can be repeated but it will never be exactly the same.

How does theatre help students to learn? Plays reflect culture. They hold up a mirror that allows us to travel to different places and time periods, learning about the conditions, people, and viewpoints that have shaped the world of the play. They challenge learners to explore and to deepen their understanding. Theatre introduces children to some characters who are like them and to some who are not. It enriches and broadens a child's way of knowing.

Using drama in the classroom may result in a lively educational environment. Teachers should welcome the energetic chatter and movement indicating students who are learning. They should also recognize that, in this type of experience, there might not be one correct answer or interpretation. Part of the joy and challenge of using drama in the classroom is that it pushes students to think creatively and independently. If teachers view themselves as co-explorers in this process, the journey they take with their students is both productive and fun!

Dance

It has been said, "to dance is human." How true! Dance is one of the most human of endeavors. Throughout history, dance has been rich with meaning and passion. It expresses the depths of humanness across all cultures.

Fast Facts **Dance expresses the depths of humanness across all cultures.**

Dance plays important roles among the peoples of the world. There are many ways in which dance is a mirror of culture. Dance may be looked at as a social activity. Dance can also be a performing art. Dance is also a creative pursuit.

Dance as a Mirror of Culture

As far back into ancient times as written records or artwork exist, we have evidence that all cultures dance. From the earliest artwork to that of today, the dancing figure is the artistic subject of many cultures. When we consider why people draw, paint, or sculpt, we learn that they portray what is important to them, what their community or culture values. Dance is important enough to be represented in the art of most cultures from antiquity to today.

Cultural Values

When a culture values strength and power, their dance will show it. When a culture values the community over the individual, it is clear in the dance. When a culture values order and hierarchy in social structure, the dance will give evidence of the same structure. With an observant eye, one can learn a great deal about a culture by studying its dances. This section speaks to many dance-evident cultural values such as gender roles, sexuality, concepts of beauty and aesthetics, community solidarity, and creativity.

Religion

Most cultural dances are historically connected to religion. All over the world we can observe dances of devotion and worship of the deities where movements might include bowing in reverence, lifting arms to the heavens, and gestures of receiving of divine benefits. We can observe dances that tell stories of the power and conquests of deities (e.g., Egyptian, Greek, Indian, Japanese). These movements may include a wide, strong stance with fisted hands and stamping feet. It is also common to see the important stories of the gods told through dance and mime.

We can observe dances that appeal to the gods for survival. For hunting success (e.g., Native American, Inuit) movements may include pantomime of the animal and hunter and the inevitable killing of the animal. For fertile fields and lavish harvest (e.g., Hebrew, Egyptian, European) movements may include pantomime of the planting, tending, and harvesting, as well as lifting or expanding actions that suggest crop growth. For victory in war (e.g., Chinese, Roman, African) movements may include use of swords, spears, or shields and the miming of conflict and victory. In most cultures the power of the dance to cause the gods' positive response is unquestioned.

We can observe dances that ask for divine blessings on life events. For the birth of a child (e.g., African, Polynesian) the movements may include childbearing actions, cradling and "offering" the child up to the deity, and crawling, walking, and running to indicate growth of the child. For initiation into adulthood (e.g., Native American, African) the movements may include shows of strength and manhood for the male and swaying and nurturing gestures for the female. For marriage (in most cultures) movements are jubilant, reflect traditional gender roles for men and women, and may include movements that suggest sexuality and fertility. For funerals (e.g., Egyptian, Cambodian, Zimbabwean) movements may reenact the life story of the deceased and may include grieving as well as celebration of an afterlife. For many cultures, dance is the primary connection between people and their gods.

Gender Roles

How should a man move? How should a woman move? Each culture answers these questions in dance. Most often the rules are unwritten, but they are clear nonetheless. In the dances of the Polynesian culture of the Cook Islands, for example, men keep a pulsing rhythm in their bodies by taking a wide stance and pumping knees open and closed. Their movements are always strong and powerful. The women stand with feet together and sway softly from side to side with undulating hips and rippling arms. In their dances, the man and woman never touch. In fact, they often dance in separate gender groups. In the ballroom dancing of European and American cultures, the man leads the woman by holding her and guiding her. She follows his lead. They move in perfect synchrony and reflect the Western cultural ideal of a flawless heterosexual union (led by the man) that is effortless and perfect. Each culture defines gender-specific movements and speaks volumes about the roles of men and women through its dance.

Beauty and Aesthetics

All cultures define beauty in their own way. Dances clearly reflect that ideal (aesthetic) of beauty. Some African dances, for example, feature plump and fleshy women dancers who embody health, fertility, the earth, and beauty to their people. In the European traditional form of ballet, however, the skeletal ballerina is spotlighted to reflect the fragile, ethereal, romantic ideal of female beauty. Another contrast can be made between the traditional court dances of Bali and American Modern dance. In Bali, the court dances have existed for centuries. Dancers train for many years to perform with great serenity, balance, and symmetry. They embody the ideal beauty of Balinese culture. In contemporary America, modern dance can express the very different aesthetic of a driving, off-balance asymmetry. Each image mirrors a cultural definition of what is beautiful. We can all discover many different kinds of beauty through experiencing the dances of various cultures.

Dance as a Social Activity

Social dance has a relatively short history in the human race. Dance has always drawn people together as communicants in a common religion and as celebrants of community events in the context of religion. However, the practice of dance for the primary purpose of gathering people together to enjoy each other's company is only centuries old, rather than millennia-old. When we look at the history of social dance we can clearly see changes in social structure and accepted behavior through changes in the dances.

Folk Dances around the World

Folk dances are cultural dances that have remained quite stable for a long period of time. The music has remained constant and the movements have changed little over the years. Folk dances usually reflect the national traditions of various cultures. They evoke pride in people's traditions and culture by keeping alive the dances of their ancestors. Dancers swell with pride as they perform the dances of their forebears with others that share their heritage. Folk dances are usually about the group, not the specific dancer or couple. Folk dance is a solid connection to the past and a vehicle for "belonging." When one dances a dance, one belongs to the group that has danced that dance through the ages. For some cultures that are being absorbed into western society and swallowed by global culture, such as the Inuits of northern Canada, languages are gradually lost, traditional crafts are lost and ancient religion is lost, but the dances are the last to go. People cling to their dances as the last remnant of a shared past. For the Punjab Indians who immigrated to England in the past century, the dances of their Indian culture are so important to their understanding of their cultural heritage that all children study the dances and the people perform them at social gatherings. People dance their own culture's folk dances to understand who they are and where they came from. It is also valuable to learn the folk dances of other cultures. When we dance the dances of others, we learn about them and gain respect for them by "dancing in their shoes."

Social Dances of Western Cultures

Social dances of Western cultures are usually about the couple and heterosexual courtship. In contrast with folk dance, social dances usually change over time. Through several centuries in Europe and America, changes in social dance have created a fascinating mirror of changing social attitudes toward courtship and gender. When the waltz emerged in full force on the European scene in the nineteenth century, it was soundly condemned as scandalous because the couple was for the first time dancing face to face in an embrace. However, the man continued to lead the dance and the woman followed. Each new social dance has met with similar resistance as the changes in social attitudes toward gender and sexuality have initiated new ways of moving. Embraces become closer, sexual movements become more suggestive, and clothing becomes more revealing as times and social attitudes change.

It is possible to clearly track changes in the social attitude in America by looking at the social dances of various times. The Lindy Hop of the late 1920s and 1930s is a good example. The earliest swing dance, the Lindy Hop emerged from the heart of the African-American culture of Harlem. Its popularity grew and the mainstream white culture was fascinated. White Americans began to flock to Harlem to learn the Lindy Hop. In this time of great separation between the races, the Lindy Hop forged new connections between people of different skin color. Social strictures began to marginally break down.

Another example of the power of social dance to reflect changing social attitudes is the Twist. During the 1960s in America, the Twist emerged and took the social dance scene by storm. Its impact was felt in the fact that the couple did not have to synchronize their movements. In fact, the dancers no longer had to touch each other. Each one danced alone. This dance reflects an important social change in 1960s America when women's liberation and the civil rights movements announced that each person had equal rights regardless of gender or race. The Twist was a revolutionary dance that allowed the individual to pursue her/his own movement. Neither dancer leads nor follows. What a mirror of society!

Dance as a Performing Art

Dance has played another role in history, the role of performing art. In various cultures elite groups of people are designated as dancers/performers. Their occupation is to dance before audiences. There are several examples of performing styles, old and new, among various cultures.

In Japan, Kabuki emerged as a performing art from a long history in the streets. Traditionally, men play all women's roles in elaborate makeup and costume. Highly controlled, stylized movements and lavish costumes represent favorite stories and characters. The theatre art is studied for a lifetime and the popularity of top Kabuki actors/dancers can equal the level of movie stars in Japan.

In India, the Bharata Natyam is a centuries-old dance rooted in the Hindu religion. A solo female dancer who is highly trained in this intricate form of storytelling performs the Bharata Natyam. The dancer utilizes the entire body, but especially the hands and eyes, in a very colorful and expressive dance.

From South Africa comes a style of dance called Gumboots. Out of the dark and silent goldmines and the oppressive lives of the slave laborers emerges a style of dance performed by groups of men wearing miners' gumboots. The dancers leap, turn, and stamp their boots in well-grounded group formations. Their rhythmic and exuberant dance tells of solidarity within adversity and of the workers' amazing endurance.

Finally, out of Irish step-dancing traditions and American innovation comes the Riverdance phenomenon. In this vertically lifted, stylized Irish dancing, the dancers hold their arms tightly at their sides while making quick explosive movements of the legs. They balance mainly on their toes while creating lightning-fast tap rhythms with their hard-soled shoes in kaleidoscopic group patterns.

In Europe and America, the primary performance styles of dance are ballet, modern, jazz, and tap dance.

Ballet, a stylized form in which the body is elongated and extended into space, emerges from the royal courts of Renaissance Europe. Female dancers, or ballerinas, study for years to be able to dance "en pointe," on the tips of their toes. The romantic ballet literally elevates the ballerina to an otherworldly figure unhampered by gravity. Ballet has a long history as an elite form of dance that contains elements of the affectations of royalty. Modern forms of ballet, however, have stretched the limits of the traditional form to include many more movement possibilities.

Modern dance emerged around the turn of the twentieth century, primarily in America, as a reaction against the style restrictions of ballet. It is a "freer" form of dance in which the dancer explores and creates dance with very few stylistic limits. Modern, and now postmodern, dancers and choreographers use many existing movement styles and combine them in innovative ways to create new forms.

Jazz and tap dance emerged in America from a similar source. They both meld the dance styles of Europe, Africa, and various other cultures. Both grow from the fertile cross-cultural ground of nineteenth and twentieth century America to create new dance blends and hybrids. Jazz dance is a performing style that also borrows from American social dance and uses contemporary music, physical power, body-part isolations, and gravity to create strong and rhythmic dances. Tap dance uses metal taps attached to the toes and heels of dance shoes to create intricate and complex rhythms. These four western performing styles have greatly influenced each other throughout the twentieth and into the twenty-first centuries. Choreographers and dancers borrow from each other, style lines become blurred, and new blends between styles are common and exciting. Performing forms are constantly changing through time, but each has a cherished tradition.

Dance as a Creative Pursuit

Creative Problem-Solving

Arguably the earliest creative act of a human being is movement. Long before mastering poetry, visual art, or music, a child creates movement. Fundamentally, in all creative pursuits, we are practicing problem solving. Creative problem solving includes: contemplating a problem, considering various solutions, trying various solutions, choosing one solution, altering and fine-tuning the solution, and finally evaluating the solution. Development of creative problem solving skills is important in human life. All education programs profess the importance of problem solving, and the arts are no exception. The more we use creative movement in the classroom, the greater the learning potential. As students create, they learn about the world, about others, and about themselves.

The Body as the Medium

Dance is an art that requires only the human body, standard equipment for all children. No pen, paintbrush, or musical instrument is needed. As children explore the basics of movement (body, space, time, and relationship), they gain the movement vocabulary to express themselves more and more eloquently. Mastery of the body as a creative medium should be a primary goal in dance education.

Dance Content

Usually, dances are about something. They often have identifiable content. Most dances create meaning in some form, even when quite abstract. When a human being creates a dance, he or she may be expressing such diverse ideas as: community, literary conflict, properties of magnets, regular or irregular rhythms, mathematical patterns, or visual design. A dancer/ choreographer may be exploring feelings such as: alienation, comfort, precision, smooth or bumpy flow, anger, or peace. A choreographer may also be sharing experiences through dance by telling a story or by creating an environment that arises from their life experience. Students are encouraged to create meaning in dance by expressing ideas, exploring feelings, or sharing experiences learn a great deal about themselves while developing their creative problem-solving skills.

Dance in the Classroom and across the Curriculum

Why isn't there more dancing in the schools? General classroom teachers may feel inadequate to teach dance but maybe they define dance too narrowly as merely patterns of intricate steps. Dance in the elementary schools should be about creative movement. Any sensitive teacher can guide students through creative movement that builds upon classroom learning.

For example, in language arts, students can learn spelling and vocabulary words by groups spelling words with their bodies or acting out the meaning of the word. They can *embody* the concept of opposites, for example, by exploring (alone or with a partner) heavy/light, near/far, curved/angular, or symmetrical/asymmetrical. Students can also dance the character or mime the story they are studying.

Movement and math also share much ground. Creative movement studies can use repetition and rhythm to count in multiples or can use partner body sculptures to reflect symmetry and asymmetry, for example.

Science studies can include exploration of gravity, creating a group machine, demonstrating the flow of electrical currents and circuits, or moving within the properties of various types of clouds.

Social studies supply many rich ideas for creative movement, too. Some movement ideas include drawing a map of the classroom and creating a movement "journey" or exploring various occupations, transportation forms, or types of communities through creative movement. Folk dances are always a powerful means to experience other cultures.

Summary

Dance is a powerful force in human life that can express and teach about others, our world, and our selves. Dance is a mirror of culture, cultural values, religion, gender roles, and concepts of beauty. Dance is a social activity that draws people together into belonging and expresses community through folk dance and social dance. Dance is a performing art in many cultures, reflecting cultural ideals through choreography and performance. And finally, dance is a creative pursuit that uses creative problem solving to transform body movement into meaning: expressing ideas, exploring feelings, and sharing experiences. Dance is a powerful teaching tool that can bridge the disciplines of the curriculum.

Health and Fitness

The health and fitness study guide offers a perspective on the importance of maintaining a healthy mind and body as well as demonstrating how the two work in conjunction. This includes discussions of cardiovascular fitness, nutrition, team sports, and the role of athletics. Preparing your mind through study will leave you in great shape to succeed on test day.

Movement and Physical Fitness

0030 Understand basic principles and practices of personal, interpersonal, and community health and safety; and apply related knowledge and skills (e.g., decision making, problem solving) to promote personal well-being.

For example:
- identifying common health problems and explaining how they can be prevented, detected, and treated
- recognizing the basic knowledge and skills necessary to support positive health choices and behaviors
- applying decision-making and problem-solving skills and procedures in individual and group situations (e.g., situations related to personal well-being, self-esteem, and interpersonal relationships)
- recognizing basic principles of good nutrition and using them to plan a diet that accommodates nutritional needs, activity level, and optimal weight

- analyzing contemporary health-related issues (e.g., HIV, teenage pregnancy, suicide, substance abuse) in terms of their causes, effects, and significance for individuals, families, and society and evaluating strategies for their prevention
- interpreting advertising claims for health-care products and services and distinguishing between valid and invalid health information
- analyzing environmental conditions and their impact upon personal and community health and safety

0031 Understand physical education concepts and practices related to the development of personal living skills.

For example:
- recognizing sequences and characteristics of physical development throughout the various developmental levels
- demonstrating knowledge of activities that promote the development of motor skills (e.g., locomotor, manipulative, body mechanics) and perceptual awareness skills (e.g., body awareness, spatial and directional awareness)
- applying safety concepts and practices associated with physical activities (e.g., doing warm-up exercises, wearing protective equipment)
- understanding skills necessary for successful participation in given sports and activities (e.g., spatial orientation, eye-hand coordination, movement)
- analyzing ways in which participation in individual or group sports or physical activities can promote personal living skills (e.g., self-discipline, respect for self and others, resource management) and interpersonal skills (e.g., cooperation, sportsmanship, leadership, teamwork, communication)

0032 Understand health-related physical fitness concepts and practices.

For example:
- recognizing components, functions, and common disorders of the major body systems
- demonstrating knowledge of basic components of physical fitness (e.g., strength, endurance, flexibility) and applying principles of training
- applying strategies for developing a personal fitness plan based on self-assessment, goal setting, and an understanding of physiological changes that result from training
- analyzing the relationship between life-long physical activity and the prevention of illness, disease, and premature death
- applying knowledge of principles and activities for developing and maintaining cardiorespiratory endurance, muscular strength, flexibility, and levels of body composition that promote good health

Principles of Cardiovascular Fitness

Cardiovascular fitness, or aerobic capacity, is the ability of the entire body to work together efficiently—to be able to do the most amount of work with the least amount of effort. Cardiovascular fitness is composed of four basic components: strength and power; endurance;

movement speed and flexibility; and agility. Training is required to develop consistent aerobic capacity, and training is composed of several principles. To begin, a warm-up is essential. An effective warm-up will increase body temperature and blood flow, and it will guard against strains and tears to muscles, tendons, and ligaments. A good warm-up consists of stretching exercises, calisthenics, walking, and slow jogging. Although children have trouble understanding the importance of warm-up, they should get into the habit of doing it, because it will be particularly important as they grow older.

While exercising, a student must be aware of his or her body's adaptations to the demands imposed by training. Some of these adaptations are improved heart function and circulation, improved respiratory function, and improved strength and endurance. All of these lead to improved vigor and vitality. In order to effect these adaptations, the students must exert themselves to a far greater degree than their normal daily activities. This exertion is referred to as **overload**. Despite what this term suggests, it does not imply that children should work beyond healthy limits. However, it does imply that they must push themselves in order to see results. The rate of improvement and adaptation is directly related to the frequency, intensity, and duration of training.

In addition to regular training, you must gear your students' training toward those adaptations that are important to them. This is known as **specificity**. Performance improves when the training is specific to the activity being performed. That is, certain activities will have more effect on cardiovascular health than on overall muscle tone and appearance, and vice versa. Therefore, you should always try to maintain a balance in the exercise you assign.

The body thrives on activity, and therefore the axiom "use it or lose it" certainly holds true. Lack of activity can cause many problems, including flabby muscles, a weak heart, poor circulation, shortness of breath, obesity, and a degenerative weakening of the skeletal system. It is important to note, however, that when many people begin a program of exercise, they expect to see results immediately. More often than not, this is not the case. Individual response to exercise varies greatly from person to person. This can be affected by heredity, age, general cardiovascular fitness, rest and sleep habits, an individual's motivation, environmental influences, and any handicap, disease, or injury that may impede the body's adaptation to training. The sum of all these factors is an individual's potential for maximizing their own cardiovascular fitness. Unfortunately, very few people live up to this full potential.

Finally, a good program of exercise always ends with a cooling-off period. Very much like the warm-up, and just as essential, the same low-impact exercises used during a warm-up may be used to cool off after a period of intense exertion. Without cooling off, blood will pool and slow the removal of waste products. With this basic introduction in mind, let's look at some more specific forms of exercise and the positive effects they have on the body.

Aerobic Exercise

Aerobic exercise involves both muscle contraction and movement of the body. Aerobic exercise requires large amounts of oxygen and, when done regularly, will condition the cardiovascular system. Some aerobic exercises are especially suited to developing aerobic training benefits, with a minimum of skill and time involved. Examples of good aerobic activities are walking, running, swimming, rope skipping, and bicycling. These activities are especially good in the development of fitness because all of them can be done alone and with a minimum of special equipment. In order to be considered true aerobic conditioning, an activity must require a great deal of oxygen, must be continuous and rhythmic, must exercise major muscle groups and burn fat as an energy source, and must last for at least 20 minutes at an individual's target heart rate. You may determine the target heart rate by subtracting 80% of your age from 220 for adolescents; healthy younger children do not need to be restricted to an arbitrary limit on heart rate during exercise.

Interval training is also a good way to develop fitness. This type of exercise involves several different aerobic activities performed at intervals to create one exercise session. If a student learns about interval training, she will be better able to create her own fitness program.

Low-Impact Aerobics

For some people, low-impact aerobics may have some advantages over traditional, or high-impact, aerobics. Because low-impact aerobic exercise is easier to perform, it is an option for all ages and levels of fitness. It is easier to monitor heart rate, and there is less warm-up and cool-down required. Because one foot is on the ground at all times, there is less chance of injury. In all other respects, such as duration and frequency, low-impact aerobic exercise is identical to high-impact.

Anatomy and Physiology

Anatomy describes the structure, position, and size of various organs. Because our bones adapt to fill a specific need, exercise is of great benefit to the skeletal system. Bones that anchor strong muscles thicken to withstand the stress. Weight-bearing bones can develop heavy mineral deposits while supporting the body. Because joints help provide flexibility and ease of movement, it is important to know how each joint moves. Types of joints are ball and socket (shoulder and hip), hinge (knee), pivot (head of the spine), gliding (carpal and tarsal bones), angular (wrist and ankle joints), partially moveable (vertebrae), and immovable (bones of the adult cranium).

Muscles are the active movers in the body. In order to teach any physical education activity properly, the functions and physiology of the muscles must be understood. Since muscles move by shortening, or contracting, proper form should be taught so the student can get the most out of an activity. It is also important to know the location of each muscle. This knowledge will help in teaching proper form while doing all physical education activities. Understanding the concept of antagonistic muscles, along with the related information concerning flexors and extensors, is also vital to the physical educator. Imagine trying to teach the proper form of throwing a ball if you do not understand the mechanics involved. Knowledge of anatomy and physiology is also necessary to teach proper techniques used in calisthenics as well as in all physical activities. Some physical education class standbys are frequently done improperly or done when the exercise itself can cause harm. Examples of these are squat thrusts, straight-leg sit-ups, straight-leg toe touches, straight-leg push-ups for girls, and double leg lifts.

Sports and Games

Individual, dual, and team sports all have a prominent place in a successful physical education curriculum. Since one of the attributes of a quality physical education program is its carryover value, it is easy to justify the inclusion of these activities in a curriculum. Learning the rules and keeping score supplies a framework for goals and for learning how to deal with both victory and defeat. Here are examples of some sports and games that are useful to achieve the aforementioned goals:

Team Sports

- Volleyball—six players, two out of three games. Winner scores 25 points with a margin of 2.

- Basketball—five players. Most points at the end of the game wins.

- Softball—9 or 10 players. Most runs at the end of seven innings wins.

- Field hockey—11 players. Most goals wins.

- Soccer—11 players. Most goals wins.

- Flag football—9 or 11 players (can be modified to fit ability and size of the class). Six points for a touchdown, one or two for a point after, and two for a safety.

Dual Sports

- Tennis—Either doubles or singles. Four "points"—15, 30, 40, and game. Tie at forty—deuce. Winner must win by a margin of two. Remember, *love* means zero points in tennis.

- Badminton—Either doubles or singles. 15 points (doubles) or 21 (singles) by a margin of 2.

- Table tennis—Either doubles or singles. 21 points by a margin of 2.

- Shuffleboard—Either singles or doubles. 50, 75, or 100 points, determined by participants before the game begins.

Individual Sports

- Swimming—Very good for cardiovascular conditioning and can be done almost anywhere there is water.

- Track and field—Scoring varies with event.

- Bowling—Scoring is unique; good math skills are encouraged.

- Weight training—No scoring involved, but the benefits are many. Muscles are toned and strengthened through the use of weight training. Either weight machines or free weights can be used. It is important for students to learn the proper techniques and principles of weight training so they can reap the benefits while avoiding injury. When weight training, participants must consider the concept of muscular balance—this is equal strength in opposing muscle groups. All opposing groups (antagonistic muscles), i.e., triceps and biceps, hamstrings and quadriceps, need to be equal or body parts may become improperly aligned. The responsibility of the physical educator is to teach accurate information about the human body as well as teach ways to prevent injury and achieve efficiency in movement. Understanding that abdominal strength is important to lower back strength can help students create an exercise program to help avoid back injuries.

- Gymnastics—Includes tumbling. Excellent activity for developing coordination and grace. Also requires strength, which is developed by the activities done. This training can begin at a very early age with tumbling activities and progress to gymnastics.

- Golf—A fantastic carryover activity that can be taught on campus, at the golf course, or both. Requires coordination, concentration, and depth perception.

- Rhythmics—Includes ball gymnastics and other activities that may require music. Rhythmics can be taught in early elementary physical education, enabling students to develop music appreciation as well as spatial awareness.

- Dance—Can be done either individually or with a partner. Dance is especially good at developing spatial awareness and the ability to follow instructions. Dance instruction should begin in elementary school. Basic steps are walk and/or skip and are suitable to teach to first and second graders. Skip, slide, and/or run are suitable for second and third graders. The more difficult step-hop can be taught to grades 3 through 6. The ability to dance can also aid in the development of social skills and teamwork. The instructor must be careful not to teach too many steps before the dance is tried with the music. Most students enjoy dance in spite of themselves.

Adaptive Physical Education

Public Law 94-142 provides the legal definition for the term "handicapped children." It includes children who have been evaluated as being mentally impaired, deaf, speech impaired, visually handicapped, emotionally disturbed, orthopedically impaired, multi-handicapped, having learning disabilities, or having other health impairments (anemia, arthritis, etc.). PL 94-142 states that these children need special education and services. The challenge in teaching physical education to handicapped children is tailoring activities to fit each child. For example, blind or partially sighted students can participate in weight lifting, dance, and some gymnastic and tumbling activities. These students can also participate in some other activities with modifications. A beeper ball can be used for softball; a beeper can be used for archery. If a beeper is not available for archery, the teacher can put the student in position and assist in aiming. Many games and activities can be modified for the handicapped. Sometimes all it takes is a little ingenuity to change activities so that handicapped students can enjoy participating.

There are many students who are only temporarily disabled who will benefit from adaptive physical education. Examples of temporary disabilities are pregnancy, broken bones, and recovery from surgery and disease.

Movement Education

Movement education is the process by which a child is helped to develop competency in movement. It has been defined as "learning to move and moving to learn." Movement competency requires the student to manage his or her body. This body management is necessary to develop both basic and specialized activities. Basic skills are needed by the child for broad areas of activity that are related to daily living and child's play. Specialized skills are required to perform sports and have very clear techniques. Basic skills must be mastered before the child can develop specialized ones. The child controls his movement during nonlocomotor (stationary) activities, in movements across the floor or field, through space, and when suspended on an apparatus. To obtain good body management skills is to acquire, expand, and integrate elements of motor control. This is done through wide experiences in movement, based on a creative and exploratory approach. It is important that children not only manage the body with ease of movement but also realize that good posture and body mechanics are important parts of their movement patterns.

Perceptual motor competency is another consideration in body management. Perceptual motor concepts that are relevant to physical education include those that give attention to balance, coordination, lateral movement, directional movement, awareness of space, and knowledge of one's own body. Basic skills can be divided into three categories: locomotor, nonlocomotor, and manipulative skills. A movement pattern might include skills from each category.

Locomotor skills involve moving the body from place to place: walking, running, skipping, leaping, galloping, and sliding. Skills that move the body upward, such as jumping or hopping, are also locomotor skills.

Nonlocomotor skills are done in place or with very little spatial movement. Examples of nonlocomotor skills are bending and stretching, pushing and pulling, raising and lowering, twisting and turning, and shaking and bouncing.

Manipulative skills are skills used when the child handles a play object. Most manipulative skills involve using the hands and the feet, but other parts of the body may be used as well. Hand-eye and foot-eye coordination are improved with manipulative objects. Throwing, batting, kicking, and catching are important skills to be developed using balls and beanbags. Starting a child at a low level of challenge and progressing to a more difficult activity is an effective method for teaching manipulative activities. Most activities begin with individual practice and later move to partner activities. Partners should be of similar ability. When teaching throwing and catching, the teacher should emphasize skill performance, principles of opposition, weight transfer, eye focus, and follow-through. Some attention should be given to targets when throwing because students need to be able to catch and throw to different levels. Reaching is a "point-to-point" arm movement that is very common in our daily activities. In fact, reaching and grasping are typically used together to serve a number of purposes, such as eating, drinking, dressing, or cooking. The reaching/grasping task requires an "eye-hand" coordination and control of movement timing for a successful attempt.

Specialized skills are related to various sports and other physical education activities such as dance, tumbling, gymnastics, and specific games. To teach a specialized skill, the instructor must use explanation, demonstration, and drill. Demonstration can be done by other students, provided the teacher monitors the demonstration and gives cues for proper form. Drills are excellent to teach specific skills but can become tedious unless they are done in a creative manner. Using game simulations to practice skills is an effective method to maintain interest during a practice session.

Teachers must always remember to use feedback when teaching a skill or activity. Positive feedback is much more conducive to skill learning than negative feedback. Feedback means correcting with suggestions to improve. If a student continually hits the ball into the net while playing tennis, he or she is aware that something is not right. The teacher should indicate what the problem is and tell the student how to succeed in getting the ball over the net.

Movement education enables the child to make choices of activity and the method they wish to employ. Teachers can structure learning situations so the child can be challenged to develop his or her own means of movement. The child becomes the center of learning and is encouraged to be creative in carrying out the movement experience. In this method of teaching, the child is encouraged to be creative and progress according to her abilities. The teacher is not the center of learning, but suggests and stimulates the learning environment. Student-centered learning works especially well when there is a wide disparity of motor abilities. If the teacher sets standards that are too high for the less talented students, they may become discouraged and not try to perform.

Basic movement education attempts to develop the children's awareness not only of what they are doing but also how they are doing it. Each child is encouraged to succeed in his or her own way according to his or her own capacity. If children succeed at developing basic skills in elementary school, they will have a much better chance at acquiring the specialized skills required for all sports activities.

Psychological and Social Aspects of Physical Education

Physical education is a very important part of a student's elementary school education. It is not only an opportunity to "blow off steam," but it is also an arena of social interaction. One psychological aspect of physical education is the enhancement of self-esteem. Often students who have limited success in other classes can "shine" in physical education. This does not happen automatically; it is up to the teacher to create situations that enable students to gain self-esteem.

Teachers must also be careful not to damage self-esteem. An example of a potentially damaging situation occurs during the exercise of choosing members of a team. Teachers should not have captains choose the teams in front of the whole class. Nothing is more demeaning than to be the last person chosen. A better method is for the teacher to select the captains (this is also a very good way to separate the superstars: have the six best athletes be the captains). The captains then go to the sidelines and pick the teams from a class list. The teacher can then post or read the team lists after mixing up the order chosen so that no one knows who were the first and last picked.

From a developmental perspective, considerable research evidence suggests that children's participation in exercise or sports results in a number of long-term benefits, including the improvement of self-esteem, or self-confidence for social interactions; the development of sport leadership and sportsmanship; and motivation for participating in lifetime physical activities.

Health and Safety

Benefits of Diet and Exercise

One of the primary reasons for teaching physical education is to instill a willingness to exercise. To that end, it is important to understand the benefits of participating in a lifelong program of exercise and physical fitness.

Fortunately, it is not difficult to find justification for exercising and maintaining a consistently high level of fitness. The benefits of a consistent program of diet and exercise are many. Improved cardiac output, improved maximum oxygen intake, and improvement of the blood's ability to carry oxygen are just a few. Exercise also lowers the risk of heart disease by strengthening the heart muscle, lowering pulse and blood pressure, and lowering the concentration of fat in both the body and the blood. It can also improve appearance, increase range of motion, and lessen the risk of back problems associated with weak bones and osteoporosis.

Good Nutrition

Along with exercise, a knowledge of and participation in a healthy lifestyle are vital to good health and longevity. What constitutes good nutrition, the role of vitamins, elimination of risk factors, and strategies to control weight are all part of a healthy lifestyle.

Complex carbohydrates should constitute at least half the diet. This is important because these nutrients are the primary and most efficient source of energy. Examples of complex carbohydrates are vegetables, fruits, high-fiber breads, and cereals. Fiber in the diet is very important because it promotes digestion, reduces constipation, and has been shown to help reduce the risk of colon cancer. Another benefit of complex carbohydrates is that they are high in water content, which is vital to the functioning of the entire body.

Proteins should constitute about one-fifth of the diet. Protein builds and repairs the body. Sources of protein are beans, peas, lentils, peanuts, and other pod plants. Another source is red meat, which unfortunately contains a great deal of saturated fat.

There are two categories of fat: unsaturated, which is found in vegetables, and saturated, which comes from animals or vegetables. Cocoa butter, palm oil, and coconut oil are saturated fats that come from vegetables. Unsaturated vegetable fats are preferable to saturated fats because they appear to offset the rise in blood pressure that accompanies too much saturated fat. These fats may also lower cholesterol and help with weight loss. Whole milk products contain saturated fat, but the calcium found in them is vital to health. For this reason, most fat-limiting diets suggest the use of skim milk and low-fat cheese.

Research indicates a link between high-fat diets and many types of cancer. Diets high in saturated fats are also dangerous because fats cause the body to produce too much low-density lipoprotein in the system. Cholesterol, a substance found only in animals, is of two different kinds: LDL (low-density lipoproteins) and HDL (high-density lipoproteins). Some cholesterol is essential in order for the body to function properly. It is vital to the brain and is an important component in the creation of certain hormones. LDLs raise the probability of heart disease by encouraging the buildup of plaque in the arteries. HDLs do just the opposite. LDL can be controlled through proper diet, and HDL cholesterol levels can be raised by exercise. The body produces cholesterol in the liver. Excess cholesterol found in the blood of so many people usually comes from cholesterol in their diet rather than from internal production. Triglycerides are another form of fat found in the blood. It is important to monitor them because high triglycerides seem to be inversely proportional to HDLs.

Vitamins and Minerals

Vitamins are essential to good health. One must be careful, however, not to take too much of certain vitamins. Fat soluble vitamins—A, D, E, and K—will be stored in the body, and excessive amounts will cause some dangerous side effects. The remaining vitamins are water soluble and are generally excreted through the urinary system and the skin when taken in excess. A brief synopsis of the vitamins and minerals needed by the body follows:

- Vitamin A: Needed for normal vision, prevention of night blindness, healthy skin, resistance to disease, and tissue growth and repair. Found in spinach, carrots, broccoli and other dark green or yellow orange fruits and vegetables; also found in liver and plums.

- Vitamin D: Promotes absorption of calcium and phosphorus, and needed for normal growth of healthy bones, teeth, and nails. Formed by the action of the sun on the skin. Also found in halibut liver oil, herring, cod liver oil, mackerel, salmon, and tuna, and is added to many milk products.

- Vitamin E: Protects cell membranes; seems to improve elasticity in blood vessels; also may prevent formation of blood clots and protect red blood cells from damage by oxidation. Found in wheat germ oil, sunflower seeds, raw wheat germ, almonds, pecans, peanut oil, and cod liver oil.

- Thiamin/B_1: Needed for functioning of nerves, muscle growth, and fertility and for production of energy, appetite, and digestion. Found in pork, legumes, nuts, enriched and fortified whole grains, and liver.

- Riboflavin/B_2: Aids in the production of red blood cells, good vision, healthy skin and mouth tissue, and production of energy. Found in lean meat, dairy products, liver, eggs, enriched and fortified whole grains, and green leafy vegetables.

- Niacin/B_3: Promotes energy production, appetite, healthy digestive and nervous system, and healthy skin.

- Pyridoxine/B_6: Promotes red blood cell formation and growth. Found in liver, beans, pork, fish, legumes, enriched and fortified whole grains, and green leafy vegetables.

- Vitamin B_{12}: Promotes healthy nerve tissue, energy production, utilization of folic acid; also aids in the formation of healthy red blood cells. Found in dairy products, liver, meat, poultry, fish, and eggs.

- Vitamin C: Promotes healing and growth, resists infection, increases iron absorption, and aids in bone and tooth formation/repair. Found in citrus fruits, cantaloupe, potatoes, strawberries, tomatoes, and green vegetables.

- Sodium: Maintains normal water balance inside and outside cells; is a factor in blood pressure regulation and electrolyte and chemical balance. Found in salt, processed foods, bread, and bakery products.

- Potassium: Prevents muscle weakness and cramping; important for normal heart rhythm and electrolyte balance in the blood. Found in citrus fruits, leafy green vegetables, potatoes, and tomatoes.

- Zinc: Taste, appetite, healthy skin, and wound healing. Found in lean meat, liver, milk, fish, poultry, whole grain cereals, and shellfish.

- Iron: Red blood cell formation, oxygen transport to the cells; prevents nutritional anemia. Found in liver, lean meats, dried beans, peas, eggs, dark green leafy vegetables, and whole grain cereals.

- Calcium: Strong bones, teeth, nails, muscle tone; prevents osteoporosis and muscle cramping; helps the nerves function and the heart beat. Found in milk, yogurt, and other dairy products, and dark leafy vegetables.

- Phosphorus: Regulates blood chemistry and internal processes; helps build strong bones and teeth. Found in meat, fish, poultry, and dairy products.

- Magnesium: Energy production, normal heart rhythm, nerve/muscle function; prevents muscle cramps. Found in dried beans, nuts, whole grains, bananas, and leafy green vegetables.

Weight Control Strategies

Statistics show that Americans get fatter every year. Even though countless books and magazine articles are written on the subject of weight control, often the classroom is the only place a student gets reliable information about diet. For example, it is an unfortunate reality that fat people do not live as long, on average, as thin ones. Being overweight has been isolated as a risk factor in various cancers, heart disease, gall bladder problems, and kidney disease. Chronic diseases such as diabetes and high blood pressure are also aggravated by, or caused by, being overweight.

Conversely, a great many problems are presented by being underweight. Our society often places too much value on losing weight, especially for women. Ideal weight as well as a good body-fat ratio is the goal when losing weight. Exercise is the key to a good body-fat ratio. Exercise helps to keep the ratio down, thus improving cholesterol levels, and helps in preventing heart disease.

In order to lose weight, calories burned must exceed calories taken in. No matter what kind of diet is tried, this principle applies. There is no easy way to maintain a healthy weight. Here again, the key is exercise. If calorie intake is restricted too much, the body goes into starvation mode and operates by burning fewer calories. Just a 250-calorie drop per day combined with a 250-calorie burn will result in a loss of one pound a week. Crash diets, which bring about rapid weight loss, are not only unhealthy but also ineffective. Slower weight loss is more lasting. Aerobic exercise is the key to successful weight loss. Exercise speeds up metabolism and causes the body to burn calories. Timing of exercise will improve the benefits. Exercise before meals speeds up metabolism and has been shown to suppress appetite. Losing and maintaining weight is not easy. Through education, people will be better able to realize that losing weight is hard work and is a constant battle.

Another aspect of health concerns awareness and avoidance of the health risks that are present in our everyday lives. Some risk factors include being overweight, smoking, using drugs, having unprotected sex, and stress. Students should learn the consequences of using drugs, both legal and illegal, and they should learn at least one of the several ways to reduce stress that are commonly used in most elementary schools. Education is the key to minimizing the presence of these risk factors. Unfortunately, because of the presence of peer pressure and the lack of parental control, the effect of education is sometimes not enough.

Family Health

The role of the family in health education deserves special consideration. The "family" includes people who provide unconditional love, understanding, long-term commitment, and encouragement. Variations in family living patterns in our society include, for example, nuclear and extended families, single-parent families, and blended families. Children from all types of families deserve equal consideration and respect; they should get it at least in the classroom, because they often do not in the larger society.

Community Health

The health of students and their families depends not only on individual and family decisions, but on the factors involving the wider society. One of these factors is advertising, which often encourages children to make unhealthy decisions. Students as young as kindergarten and first grade can learn how to recognize advertisements (e.g., for candy or sugar-laden cereal) that might lead them to unhealthy behavior, and by third or fourth grade, they should be able to demonstrate that they are able to make health-related decisions regarding advertisements in various media.

In addition, any studies of the physical environment—in science, social studies, or other subjects—should be related to health whenever possible. Examples include the effects of pollution on health, occupational-related disease (e.g., "black lung" disease and the effects of chemicals on soldiers), and the differences in health care options available to people in different parts of the world and in different economic circumstances.

Differentiation between communicable and noncommunicable disease can be taught at the youngest grade levels. Very young children should learn to wash their hands frequently, for instance. Older children should be able to explain the transmission and prevention of communicable disease, and all children should learn which diseases cannot be transmitted through casual contact.

Family and Consumer Science and Career Development

Child Development and Care

0033 Understand concepts and practices related to child development and care and apply knowledge of family and interpersonal relationships.

For example:

- recognizing stages and characteristics of physical, cognitive, social, and emotional development during infancy, childhood, and adolescence
- demonstrating knowledge of children's physical, dietary, and hygienic needs (e.g., nutritional guidelines, dental care, proper washing procedures) and applying developmentally appropriate methods for promoting self-care during childhood
- identifying causes of common childhood accidents and health care emergencies and applying physical care and safety guidelines for caregivers of infants, toddlers, and preschool and school-age children
- analyzing factors that affect decisions about whether and when to have children and recognizing ways to prepare for the responsibilities of parenthood
- demonstrating knowledge of family structure (e.g., extended, blended, single-parent, dual-career), roles and responsibilities of family members, and the functions of families in society
- recognizing the types and characteristics of interpersonal relationships and analyzing decision-making processes related to interpersonal relationships
- examining social and cultural influences on interpersonal communication and analyzing factors affecting the formation of positive relationships in the family, workplace, and community

Choosing and Accepting the Responsibilities of Parenthood

Sometimes people, particularly young people, become parents by accident, by mistake, or simply by not thinking about or being concerned with the consequences of their actions. However, when people consciously choose to become and prepare to be parents, they reduce future pain and hardships and increase the likelihood that they will do better at that most critical job.

Not only can teachers help students think of parenting as a conscious choice, but explain the 18+ year commitment to providing a child's financial, emotional, educational, physical, and safety needs. Children need money for everything, and the family will need more space for living and growing. Parents will also give up time and energy they used to spend on themselves. In that respect, students (male in particular) may have trouble imagining the "costs" of everyday care involved. Young parents saddled with greater financial responsibilities tend to cut short their education to meet them and so get stuck in low-paying jobs. Teen mothers and their babies face greater health risks as well.

Young people face conflicting pressures to have and to postpone having children. On one hand, societal and peer expectations are to have kids, and the satisfactions and emotional rewards of parenthood are popularized. On the other, the factors cited above, plus health worries and other emotional issues weigh in against early parenting. Teachers can help students sort out the competing appeals and warnings and work toward informed and reasoned personal decisions on their own. They can begin with instruction on child development.

Knowing the Basics of Child Development

Children advance through a number of states of physical, intellectual (cognitive), social, and emotional development as they progress through infancy, childhood, and adolescence. While child psychologists and academic researchers have identified "normal" (average or typical) phases, individual variations constantly occur.

Of course, children grow in size, muscle strength, and coordination in definable stages. For instance, infants and toddlers learn to crawl, walk, jump, and climb in the first two years. They are usually toilet trained by age three and by school age can feed and dress themselves. Intellectually, they progress from sensing the world and themselves to learning words and numbers by age seven. From ages seven to eleven, they can tackle concrete problems and recognize different points of view. From early adolescence onward, they begin to master abstract thinking and complex concepts. Emotionally, babies seem to express themselves mostly by crying. Children first develop a range of emotional expressions and then learn how to control them. In the social realm, children first learn to trust others, then develop independence. Acceptable behavior and interaction skills come gradually in social settings. Moral development occurs as they are taught right and wrong; an individual conscience develops with maturation.

The forces of development are heredity and environment: genes and jeans. The parents' DNA proposes; the family, church, schools, media, and social norms dispose. All provide, in some degree, nutrition, support, protection, and instruction. All encourage, set boundaries, inspire, make rules, channel, create expectations, and shape. They succeed to the extent that they meet the children's needs and protect them from the dangers they face.

Recognizing Childhood Needs and Hazards

The amount and type of physical care a child requires changes dramatically from infancy to adolescence. Nutritionally, babies begin with breast milk/formula and move on to strained everything within a few weeks to months. Toddlers like finger food and shouldn't be given anything that would cause choking. Bathing is up to the adult, and elaborate safety precautions concerning water temperature, soap, positioning, and padding are mandatory. Gradually, children learn to feed themselves and develop strong food preferences; parents are responsible not only for hygiene but expanding menu choices beyond fat, sugar, and what is advertised on TV. Adolescents need to be taught the latest food pyramid and to avoid eating disorders from bulimia to excessive fast food. Hygiene evolves from helping young children learn to bathe themselves (and making sure they do it) to instructing teenagers in proper grooming and adult cleanliness issues.

Infants and small children get immunizations for a number of diseases from diphtheria, tetanus, and polio beginning at two months to measles and mumps at fifteen months. Parents need to be in touch with the pediatrician's office to remain current with medical research. A good home medical reference is also valuable for children and adults. Teeth brushing begins with teething. By age 3–4 children can brush on their own with adult supervision. Although permanent teeth usually come in at ages 6–7, baby teeth care is still important.

Accidents begin at home. Childproofing a house means putting plastic caps over electric outlets and putting sharp objects and toxic chemicals out of reach. The natural curiosity of children requires constant vigilance, especially as they start walking. As they grow up, parents must watch what they put in their mouth and what they climb on. Safety instruction starts with roller skates, skateboards, and bikes, and progresses to motorcycles and cars. Children can't wear protective headgear for everything, and they outgrow car seats (style and positioning change with the weight and age of the child; check current guidelines), so parents and teachers must promote a safety-first mindset (within reason) and offer do's and don'ts appropriate to the maturity level of the child. Age-adjusted limits are appreciated; scare tactics can backfire if overused.

Interpersonal Relationships

Helping students interact well with other people involves discussing the meaning of a few terms that are commonly used and misused and that carry considerable weight.

"Respect" means having a special regard for or realizing the worth of someone or something. Good relationships begin with having respect first for oneself, second for each other. Thus, a good relationship is mutual. Relationships characterized by mutual respect generate trust, an assurance that each person will not reject, betray, or hurt the other. In good relationships, people are comfortable with one another; they have rapport. When they can put themselves in the other's position, they have empathy. These relationships endure when the individuals have shared interests.

Relationships break down or fail to form when these elements are lacking or deteriorate. People and situations change, and the balance of expectations between individuals shifts. If the balance can not be (re)established, one individual has the right to walk away, especially if he/she is being exploited. Relationships also sour or fail to develop because of prejudice—an unfair or biased opinion, or stereotyping—thinking that all of one class of people (race, ethnic group, religion, gender, socioeconomic background) are alike (and usually unworthy). These forces can sometimes be met head on with education, sometimes overcome by the example of individual acts and attitudes (good deeds and civility).

Teachers can apply these principles beyond individual relationships to those forged in the community, work place, school, and family with behavior and demeanor that generates mutual trust, respect, and shared interest. Treat other people, their possessions, and things held in common (home, school, park, office) as you would like to be treated. The "golden rule" still applies in the world of young children and teenagers.

Good relationships are built with good communication. Specifically, students can be shown the link between such learnable practices as: listening to others, sharing one's own feelings and considering how others feel, using tact, not interrupting or putting other people down, keeping an open mind, sending "I" rather than "you" messages, giving feedback to check understanding, and being alert to body language and mixed messages.

Types of Families

Students today are probably more aware of (and perhaps accepting of) variations in family structure than ever before. Nonetheless, assumptions and stereotypes need exploration. The nuclear family consists of a mother, father, and children (or, more frequently, a single child) living together as a unit. Traditionally, the mother and father are married, with dad earning the paycheck and mom managing the house. More and more, these roles are either reversed or shared. When both parents "work outside the home," it is a dual-career family. When only mom or dad is part of the household, it is called a single-parent family. When a union forms between a man and woman where at least one had children from a previous relationship, a blended family is formed.

When children temporarily join the household of unrelated adults, they are part of a foster family. If they go through a process to join unrelated adults permanently, they are part of an adopted family. Of course, both of these can be nuclear, single-parent, dual-career, or blended.

Families can also include grandparents, uncles, aunts, and cousins. Whether they live in the same household or not, they form an extended family.

Whatever their structure, families exist to provide for the needs of their members. Families help children, for instance, learn to fit into society (socialization), to get along with others, and to be independent. They provide protection, safety, and thus the possibility of learning and growing. Ideally, they offer a safe haven and a network of relationships for the life of the individual.

Personal Resource Management

0034   Understand skills and procedures related to consumer economics and personal resource management.

For example:
- recognizing rights and responsibilities of consumers in various purchasing situations (e.g., rights in relation to product and service warranties and guarantees)
- demonstrating knowledge of types and characteristics of consumer fraud and applying procedures for seeking redress and registering consumer complaints
- applying knowledge of procedures for making major purchases (e.g., comparison shopping, negotiation, interpreting labels or contract terminology)
- analyzing considerations involved in selecting and maintaining housing and motor vehicles, obtaining credit and insurance, and making investments
- examining steps and considerations involved in planning and maintaining a personal or family budget and applying money management guidelines appropriate for various situations
- demonstrating knowledge of personal and family resources (e.g., time, skills, energy) and applying decision-making and goal-setting procedures for managing personal and family resources in various situations

Setting Goals

One approach to teaching students how to make decisions and manage resources is to explain the value of setting short-term and long-term goals. Goals give us a sense of direction, promote positive feelings about ourselves and our lives, and motivate us to act. Breaking even short-term goals into manageable tasks can help us avoid the procrastination trap.

Listing these tasks is the beginning of a plan. The next step is to determine the resources necessary to complete them. Human resources are our own skills, knowledge, energy, and time. Material resources are money and possessions. Community resources might include the school/public library, the Internet, and people who can help.

Of all these, time might be the most difficult to manage. Students can be taught to prioritize their activities, to schedule their week (but not every hour of every day), to combine activities, to reduce such time wasters as TV, to be flexible with backup plans, and to maintain self-control. Teachers practicing these skills when helping their students plan and make decisions can be every effective role models.

Budgeting and Managing Money

One way to begin is to have students keep a record of their spending for a week or month and list what money they have coming in from jobs or an allowance. They can then create a budget, a plan for saving and spending the money they have available. If they are not already in place, opening checking/debit/savings accounts establishes a mechanism for keeping track of money and staying on the budget. Recording expenses leads to analyzing spending. Do we really need all the things we buy? What expenses do we have regularly (car payments, activity fees)? Which ones vary (gifts, new clothes, CDs)?

For students on the verge of starting their own household, applying personal budgeting principles to a family budget can be illuminating. What are the family needs for food, clothing, and shelter? How do we balance individual and family spending needs? What are the trade-offs between short-term and long-term goals? Family budgeting is a test not only of resource management but also of interpersonal skills.

Independence and Dependence

For students, getting out on their own is liberating. Ironically, it also binds them to institutions other than the family. Young people leaving home will likely be renting an apartment or living in a dorm, alone or with others their own age. They sign rental agreements or leases that include obligations for behavior and payment, and they make security deposits to landlords and perhaps utility companies. They need to know to ask questions: Is the place safe? In good repair? Does it include furniture, utilities? Is it convenient for getting to work and/or school? If they are sharing a place, what are everyone's financial and upkeep responsibilities? Can they get along amid the daily business of living and not just on party weekends?

These same practical ties apply to buying a car. How much is the down payment? What are the monthly payments to cover the balance? Can I get a loan from the car dealer or the bank? What will the interest be? People starting out need to understand that we use credit only when necessary because of the long-term costs, which is why we shop around for the best rates. Because installment loans and credit card debts are so expensive, we strive to pay them off quickly, every month if possible.

Buying a car entails the legal obligation of having insurance. Getting rental insurance for an apartment is also a good idea, and, unlike car insurance for young drivers, is usually not expensive. Insurance payments are another fixed expense for the budget. Thus, the "independent" person acquires more ties that bind.

One way to get ahead and loosen those ties is to begin saving. We let our money make money by investing it. The simplest way to begin is with a savings account at a bank or in a payroll plan at work. Budget an amount you can put into an account before paying bills. The "extra" is easier to hold out before discretionary expenses consume it all. More ambitious investing through special funds, stocks, or life insurance requires personal counseling from a trustworthy person (family member or professional) with experience.

Consumer Economics

Buying Tactics

Merchandisers have years of experience and trained professionals dedicated to enticing us to buy things. Teachers can help students learn to be intelligent consumers by being aware of deceptive selling practices, by doing research on product choices, and by analyzing what they really need. A bargain is a product that we actually use, of a quality we need, at a price we can pay, sold by a reliable dealer. We can find bargains by comparison shopping that includes research in catalogs, on the Internet, and from objective evaluation by respected consumer publications.

For smaller everyday items, reading labels offers government-mandated information, checking unit prices provides basis for comparison, and being savvy about advertisement claims (especially celebrity endorsements) prevents mistakes. Consumers guard against impulse buys by making shopping lists and not carrying around extra cash. For larger purchase like appliances and electronics, research and time to reflect are even more important. In some cases, as with cars, prices can be negotiated. A manufacture/dealer warranty is an important part of the purchase. We have to be careful to understand just what the coverage is. A warranty is a contract, just like an apartment lease or insurance.

Rights and Responsibilities

Shopping—be it on line, through a catalog, or in a store—involves a contract as well, in that both parties have rights and obligations. For instance, consumers have a right to buy safe products, be informed about products, and choose between products that are fairly and competitively priced. Conversely, consumers have responsibilities that could be termed seller's rights. Consumers are obliged to (1) take care of merchandise they are considering (clothes we try on, produce we handle in the market, cars we test drive), (2) pay for things in good faith, saving receipts, and (3) use the product as it was intended and to specifications.

Stores and businesses are always proclaiming that they treat customers like family and want lasting relationships with them. For that dynamic to work, there must be mutual trust and respect. When there are disputes between friends and family members, the first approach is to solve them through reasoned communication. Failing that, there is the buyer-seller contract. The fourth right of consumers is redress, the right to have a wrong corrected quickly and fairly.

Consumers have a right (some say an obligation) to return products that fail. They also have a responsibility to have a sales receipt and to have read and followed the usage instructions and reviewed the warranty. First, write, call, or visit the seller stating politely the problem and whether you want the product replaced or fixed or your money refunded. If you remind the seller of your mutual interests that you sustain a relationship, you have a better chance of success. If not, you might take your problem to the Better Business Bureau, a government consumer affairs agency, or an industry consumer action and advisory panel. Small claims courts are a final resort if these levels of appeal fall short, but they have costs in fees and time and do not always provide satisfactory outcomes.

Career and Work

0035   Understand basic principles of career development; apply processes and skills for seeking and maintaining employment; and demonstrate knowledge of workplace skills, behaviors, and responsibilities.

For example:
- demonstrating knowledge of the relationship of personal interests, skills, and abilities to successful employment and recognizing the relationship between the changing nature of work and educational requirements
- recognizing factors to consider when evaluating careers and applying procedures for conducting career research
- demonstrating knowledge of steps involved in searching for a job and recognizing factors affecting the success of a job search (e.g., writing an effective letter of application, resume preparation)
- applying skills and procedures for job interviews (e.g., personal appearance and demeanor, communicating effectively during an interview)
- applying knowledge of effective communication principles, work etiquette, interpersonal skills, and techniques for handling stress or conflict in the workplace
- recognizing rights and responsibilities in relation to employment (e.g., protection from harassment and discrimination, employer's performance expectations)

Preparing for a Career

Students should be advised that if they are searching for a career, the first place to look is at themselves. What skills and interests do you have? And what are your aptitudes (abilities to learn something new)? Start listing these in categories of mental (good at math), physical (handy with tools), and social (good listener). Have people who know you add to or challenge your list. Decide, as well, how you learn best: by yourself or in groups, reading or observing, programmed instruction or trial and error, or any of many combinations. Considering these factors can help you to determine how to go about acquiring or enhancing skills.

Relating your skills, aptitudes, and interests to work possibilities might begin with career counseling with professionals who have experience and expertise in assisting people and matching them with job types. You can then consider how to continue your education/training, choosing, for instance, between vocational/technical schools, community colleges, or universities. Apprenticeships are also a route for trade occupations such as plumbing, painting, or carpentry. Keep in mind, however, that in a diverse and quickly changing world, skills training and education may be an ongoing lifetime experience.

To make sense of a complicated work world, professionals have found organizing careers into clusters helpful. The typical list of 15 clusters includes agribusiness and natural resources, business/office, communications/media, construction, environment, family and consumer services, fine arts and humanities, hospitality and recreation, health, manufacturing, marine science, marketing and distribution, personal service, public service, and transportation. Another organizing principle is interest areas, such as independent, creative thinkers (journalists, teachers, engineers); analytical investigators, (doctors, technicians, computer programmers); organizers, who work with information and numbers (accountants, bookkeepers); influencers, who lead and compete (business executives, politicians); doers, who can work with their hands and machinery (electricians, firefighters); and people-oriented helpers (nurses, counselors).

Narrowing the focus from career clusters and interest areas requires a bit of research. The library has materials and so, of course, does the Internet. Librarians and counselors can direct your search. You can also talk to family members, neighbors, and actual people working in your fields of interest (called an exploratory interview). You may get to follow them through a day of work. Better still, you can volunteer at a place of interest to get a feel for the activities, skills, and expectations of a job or career.

Searching for (Beginning) Jobs

As we all know from books and television, detectives and reporters are always looking for a place to begin an investigation: a lead. If you are looking for work, you start with a job lead or possible opening. You can sometimes find these by networking, that is, by talking to friends, neighbors, family, etc., about your search. Word gets around as more people get involved, and, in fact, more people get jobs this way than any other. Other established direct routes include: calling or writing potential employers, checking classified ads in newspapers, surfing the Internet, and asking your school counselor or placement specialist.

Once your leads develop into possibilities, you can follow up by first finding out about the prospective employer. You can possibly visit the business unofficially and talk to a few employees. Find out what you can about how they do business and what it is like to work there. When you actually apply for work, they'll expect you to have questions about them, and they'll certainly have questions about you.

Employers find out about prospective employees through application forms. You can prepare for that process by putting together a resume that describes your education, skills, work experience, and other related activities that show who you are. Resumes can be organized chronologically or by skills. Whichever format you use, don't be shy about listing your positive traits. Make sure, as well, that it is neat, easy to read, accurate, and concise enough to fit on one page. You might include, or certainly be ready to provide, references—people who can recommend you to an employer.

If you pass the paper test, you may be invited in for an interview. Before you go, review your personal information and what you know about the employer. Make a list of questions you might be asked ("Why are you the best person for this job?"). Practice for the interview with a friend or parent and get their feedback. Dress appropriately (or a little better) for the job and be neat, clean, and well groomed. Try to adopt a positive (but not cocky) attitude. Employers respond to energy and unforced enthusiasm. Listen carefully to the questions and give honest and specific answers. Body language is also important: make eye contact, offer a firm handshake, and keep good posture. Thank the interviewer at the end. Some experts believe a thank-you letter restating your interest in the job is appropriate and effective.

Resolving Issues at Work

The short answer for how to resolve conflicts and stresses at work is to avoid them. For the worker's part, that means acting professionally, regardless of occupation. Professionals respect themselves and others. They show up on time, adhere to established work rules, and cooperate with others on tasks. They follow directions, but they also take initiative and look for more responsibility. They are ready to learn new skills. They are careful with the employer's money, property, and proprietary information. They treat co-workers fairly, openly, and honestly.

Even so, conflicts can occur on the job from honest disagreements, poor communication, or even prejudice and discrimination. Conflict resolution resulting from the first two can be obtained through mediation procedures that arrive at compromises. Discrimination that results from bias/ stereotyped thinking/behavior due to age, race, gender, or disability is illegal. The employer has an obligation to provide fair treatment in the workplace. The company/institution should have mechanisms in place to deal with such situations. If they do not, community organizations and government agencies are available for redress.

Employers are also responsible for providing a safe workplace. They should want to do that because injured or sick employees are unproductive and expensive. Again, they should have mechanisms in place to handle safety issues. The government sets and enforces safety standards through the Occupational Safety and Health Administration (OSHA). Worker's compensation is often available for employees injured on the job. Employees have a safety responsibility as well: they must follow safety rules and look out for themselves and co-workers.

Another aspect of safety is coping with stress at work. Not all stress comes from obnoxious co-workers and bosses. And not all stress is bad. We experience stress during creative and particularly productive periods of work. This stress usually goes away when the challenges have passed. Good stress is linked to achievement. Bad stress is just debilitating.

Causes of stress include major life changes like a new job, a lost job, or illness in the family. Sometimes you just have too much to do in too little time. Often just talking things out with friends, family members, or work counselors/supervisors can help by itself. They can also offer ways to change workloads and responsibilities to help you cope. Sometimes, exercise, meditation, or relaxation exercises are all you need to cope with at least the symptoms of difficult situations. But don't neglect seeking professional help. Stress that cannot be cured or endured creates serious health problems. Being healthy is a responsibility you owe yourself, as well as your family and your work community.

NYSTCE

Multi-Subject Content Specialty Test

Practice Test 1

This practice test is also on CD-ROM in our special interactive NYSTCE TestWare®. It is highly recommended that you first take this exam on computer. You will then have the additional study features and benefits of enforced timed conditions and instant, accurate scoring. See page xi for guidance on how to get the most out of our NYSTCE book and software.

Test Directions For Multiple-Choice Questions

Time: 4 hours

This test contains a multiple-choice section and a section with a single written assignment. You may complete the sections of the test in the order you choose.

Each question in the first section of this booklet is a multiple-choice question with four answer choices. Read each question CAREFULLY and choose the ONE best answer. Record your answer on the answer document in the space that corresponds to the question number. Completely fill in the space that has the same letter as the answer you have chosen. *Use only a No. 2 lead pencil.*

Sample Question:

1.   Which of these cities is farthest north?

A.   Buffalo

B.   New York City

C.   Rochester

D.   Albany

The correct answer to this question is C. You would indicate that on the answer document as follows:

1.   Ⓐ Ⓑ ● Ⓓ

You should answer all questions. Even if you are unsure of an answer, it is better to guess than not to answer a question at all.

The directions for the written assignment appear later in this test.

Answer Sheet

1. Ⓐ Ⓑ Ⓒ Ⓓ	26. Ⓐ Ⓑ Ⓒ Ⓓ	51. Ⓐ Ⓑ Ⓒ Ⓓ	76. Ⓐ Ⓑ Ⓒ Ⓓ
2. Ⓐ Ⓑ Ⓒ Ⓓ	27. Ⓐ Ⓑ Ⓒ Ⓓ	52. Ⓐ Ⓑ Ⓒ Ⓓ	77. Ⓐ Ⓑ Ⓒ Ⓓ
3. Ⓐ Ⓑ Ⓒ Ⓓ	28. Ⓐ Ⓑ Ⓒ Ⓓ	53. Ⓐ Ⓑ Ⓒ Ⓓ	78. Ⓐ Ⓑ Ⓒ Ⓓ
4. Ⓐ Ⓑ Ⓒ Ⓓ	29. Ⓐ Ⓑ Ⓒ Ⓓ	54. Ⓐ Ⓑ Ⓒ Ⓓ	79. Ⓐ Ⓑ Ⓒ Ⓓ
5. Ⓐ Ⓑ Ⓒ Ⓓ	30. Ⓐ Ⓑ Ⓒ Ⓓ	55. Ⓐ Ⓑ Ⓒ Ⓓ	80. Ⓐ Ⓑ Ⓒ Ⓓ
6. Ⓐ Ⓑ Ⓒ Ⓓ	31. Ⓐ Ⓑ Ⓒ Ⓓ	56. Ⓐ Ⓑ Ⓒ Ⓓ	81. Ⓐ Ⓑ Ⓒ Ⓓ
7. Ⓐ Ⓑ Ⓒ Ⓓ	32. Ⓐ Ⓑ Ⓒ Ⓓ	57. Ⓐ Ⓑ Ⓒ Ⓓ	82. Ⓐ Ⓑ Ⓒ Ⓓ
8. Ⓐ Ⓑ Ⓒ Ⓓ	33. Ⓐ Ⓑ Ⓒ Ⓓ	58. Ⓐ Ⓑ Ⓒ Ⓓ	83. Ⓐ Ⓑ Ⓒ Ⓓ
9. Ⓐ Ⓑ Ⓒ Ⓓ	34. Ⓐ Ⓑ Ⓒ Ⓓ	59. Ⓐ Ⓑ Ⓒ Ⓓ	84. Ⓐ Ⓑ Ⓒ Ⓓ
10. Ⓐ Ⓑ Ⓒ Ⓓ	35. Ⓐ Ⓑ Ⓒ Ⓓ	60. Ⓐ Ⓑ Ⓒ Ⓓ	85. Ⓐ Ⓑ Ⓒ Ⓓ
11. Ⓐ Ⓑ Ⓒ Ⓓ	36. Ⓐ Ⓑ Ⓒ Ⓓ	61. Ⓐ Ⓑ Ⓒ Ⓓ	86. Ⓐ Ⓑ Ⓒ Ⓓ
12. Ⓐ Ⓑ Ⓒ Ⓓ	37. Ⓐ Ⓑ Ⓒ Ⓓ	62. Ⓐ Ⓑ Ⓒ Ⓓ	87. Ⓐ Ⓑ Ⓒ Ⓓ
13. Ⓐ Ⓑ Ⓒ Ⓓ	38. Ⓐ Ⓑ Ⓒ Ⓓ	63. Ⓐ Ⓑ Ⓒ Ⓓ	88. Ⓐ Ⓑ Ⓒ Ⓓ
14. Ⓐ Ⓑ Ⓒ Ⓓ	39. Ⓐ Ⓑ Ⓒ Ⓓ	64. Ⓐ Ⓑ Ⓒ Ⓓ	89. Ⓐ Ⓑ Ⓒ Ⓓ
15. Ⓐ Ⓑ Ⓒ Ⓓ	40. Ⓐ Ⓑ Ⓒ Ⓓ	65. Ⓐ Ⓑ Ⓒ Ⓓ	90. Ⓐ Ⓑ Ⓒ Ⓓ
16. Ⓐ Ⓑ Ⓒ Ⓓ	41. Ⓐ Ⓑ Ⓒ Ⓓ	66. Ⓐ Ⓑ Ⓒ Ⓓ	
17. Ⓐ Ⓑ Ⓒ Ⓓ	42. Ⓐ Ⓑ Ⓒ Ⓓ	67. Ⓐ Ⓑ Ⓒ Ⓓ	
18. Ⓐ Ⓑ Ⓒ Ⓓ	43. Ⓐ Ⓑ Ⓒ Ⓓ	68. Ⓐ Ⓑ Ⓒ Ⓓ	
19. Ⓐ Ⓑ Ⓒ Ⓓ	44. Ⓐ Ⓑ Ⓒ Ⓓ	69. Ⓐ Ⓑ Ⓒ Ⓓ	
20. Ⓐ Ⓑ Ⓒ Ⓓ	45. Ⓐ Ⓑ Ⓒ Ⓓ	70. Ⓐ Ⓑ Ⓒ Ⓓ	
21. Ⓐ Ⓑ Ⓒ Ⓓ	46. Ⓐ Ⓑ Ⓒ Ⓓ	71. Ⓐ Ⓑ Ⓒ Ⓓ	
22. Ⓐ Ⓑ Ⓒ Ⓓ	47. Ⓐ Ⓑ Ⓒ Ⓓ	72. Ⓐ Ⓑ Ⓒ Ⓓ	
23. Ⓐ Ⓑ Ⓒ Ⓓ	48. Ⓐ Ⓑ Ⓒ Ⓓ	73. Ⓐ Ⓑ Ⓒ Ⓓ	
24. Ⓐ Ⓑ Ⓒ Ⓓ	49. Ⓐ Ⓑ Ⓒ Ⓓ	74. Ⓐ Ⓑ Ⓒ Ⓓ	
25. Ⓐ Ⓑ Ⓒ Ⓓ	50. Ⓐ Ⓑ Ⓒ Ⓓ	75. Ⓐ Ⓑ Ⓒ Ⓓ	

Practice Test 1

1. The United States Constitution defines the powers of the United States Congress and the states. The U.S. Constitution reserves powers to the states in the 10th Amendment, while Article I, Section 8 of the U.S. Constitution delegates powers to the federal government. Some powers are shared concurrently between the states and federal government. Which of the following powers are concurrent powers?

    I. Lay and collect taxes
    II. Regulate commerce
    III. Establish post offices
    IV. Borrow money

    A. I and II only

    B. II and III only

    C. III and IV only

    D. I and IV only

2. The Pacific Northwest receives the greatest annual precipitation in the United States. Which of the following statements best identifies the reason that this occurs?

    A. The jet stream moving south from Canada is responsible for pushing storms through the region.

    B. The region's mountains along the coast cause air masses to rise and cool, thereby reducing their moisture-carrying capacity.

    C. Numerous storms originating in Asia build in intensity as they move across the Pacific Ocean and then dump their precipitation upon reaching land.

    D. The ocean breezes push moisture-laden clouds and fog into the coastal region, producing humid, moist conditions that result in precipitation.

Read the passage below; then answer the two questions that follow.

Mrs. Gitler teaches 26 third graders in a large inner-city school. About one-third of her students participate in the ESL program at the school. Mrs. Gitler suspects that some of the students' parents are unable to read or write in English. Four of the students receive services from the learning resource teacher. At the beginning of the year, none of the students read above 2.0 grade level, and some of the students did not know all the letters of the alphabet.

3. Which of the following describes the instructional strategy that is most likely to improve the reading levels of Mrs. Gitler's students?

   A. An intensive phonics program that includes drill and practice work on basic sight words.

   B. An emergent literacy program emphasizing pattern books and journal writing using invented spelling.

   C. An instructional program that closely follows the third-grade basal reader.

   D. All the students should participate in the school's ESL program and receive services from the learning resource center.

4. Mrs. Gitler is selecting books for the classroom library. In addition to student interest, which of the following would be the most important considerations?

   A. The books should have a reading level that matches the students' independent reading ability.

   B. All books should have a reading level that is challenging to the students.

   C. The books should include separate word lists for student practice.

   D. A classroom library is not appropriate for students at such a low reading level.

5. The distance from Tami's house to Ken's house is 3 miles. The distance from Ken's house to The Soda Depot is 2 miles. Which of the following statements are true?

   I. The greatest possible distance between Tami's house and The Soda Depot is five miles.

   II. The greatest possible distance between Tami's house and The Soda Depot is six miles.

   III. The shortest possible distance between Tami's house and The Soda Depot is one mile.

   IV. The shortest possible distance between Tami's house and The Soda Depot is two miles.

   A. I and III only

   B. I and IV only

   C. II and III only

   D. II and IV only

6.   Use the figure to answer the question that follows.

```
┌─────────────┐
│  75 MPH     │
│  MAXIMUM    │
│             │
│  40 MPH     │
│  MINIMUM    │
└─────────────┘
```

Which inequality describes the allowable speeds indicated by the speed limit sign?

A. $75 \leq x \leq 40$

B. $75 < x > 40$

C. $40 \leq x \leq 75$

D. $40 < x > 75$

7.   Which of the following illustrates the Distributive Property?

A.   Multiplying 23 by 16 gives the same product as multiplying 16 by 23.

B.   65, 70, and 12 can be added together in any order; the sum will always be the same.

C.   The sum of 102 and 9 is the same as the sum of 9 and 102.

D.   The product of 3 and 42 is the same as the sum of the products 3×2 and 3×40.

> **DIRECTIONS: Read the story, and then respond to the five questions that follow.**

BESSIE

I began my days as a cow. Well, a calf, to be more precise. I was born to the world a soft, tawny color, with liquid brown eyes and soft, floppy ears that begged to be touched. My days were simple. I spent all my time in the company of other bovine females, most especially my mother. She was a prized breeder, my mother; as a result it was my misfortune to be weaned earlier than most other calves.

Only hours after my weaning, a miraculous event changed the course of my life. Princess Georgette happened to be riding by on her shaggy little pony, alongside her nanny, when she heard my lows of despair and turned.

"Whatever could be making that pitiful noise?" she asked aloud.

One of the farmers called out to her, "'Tis only a wee calf, Highness. She'll not be at it long, I assure you."

"I shall see the creature at once," she ordered, pulling her pony up against the rail and dismounting.

At this point, I had moved hopefully toward the commotion, and, as I inched my tender nose out of the barn to investigate, I came face-to-face with the oddest-looking creature I had seen so far in my somewhat short existence. She had outrageous red curls rioting all over her head, and tumbling down over her shoulders. The thing I noticed most, though, was her hopelessly freckled nose, which, at that moment, was uncomfortably close to my own. So close, in fact, that I decided to remedy my discomfort, and did so by lowing rather loudly in her petulant little face. To my astonishment, she giggled with delight at my rudeness, and reached out to stroke my furry forehead. I found myself nuzzling up to her small chest. "Oh Nan, I must have it. Such a funny furry thing must be kept in my garden where I might entertain myself endlessly with it."

So that is how I became a member of the royal household.

My days fell into an odd sort of routine. I spent my mornings cropping on the lawns and shrubs until Georgette would appear, luring me into the hedge ways with a handful of cresses nipped from the kitchen. As soon as I got close enough and started to nibble, she would shriek, and startle me into a canter, at which she would chase me into the hedges until I was so thoroughly lost, I would have to low helplessly until Georgette found me.

Tragically, calves do not stay calves forever. As the seasons passed, her interest in our games began to wane. The gardeners had, at this time, gotten very tired of working around me as I lumbered through the hedges. They communicated up through the chain of command, straight to the king himself, their wish to be rid of me. He dismissed the problem with an order to have me put down.

Georgette pouted at this and stamped her foot, but her father would not budge an inch. "Now, don't get missish with me, Georgette. I've given the order, and I'll see it done as I've dictated whether you like it or not."

Georgette, during this speech, had become thoughtful. After a long pause, she proposed: "Well, if I must see my Bessie put down as you've said, mightn't I get a handbag and boots out of her at least?"

"Very well," sighed her father.

For my part, it was a stroke of luck that this conversation had taken place just on the other side of the hedge where I had been, only moments before, contently munching on the last bit of clover to be found this season. Naturally, I took exception to being discussed in such a candid manner. In fact, I could not believe my furry, floppy ears. I felt myself slipping into a sort of self-pity, and walked away. When I passed the westernmost gate, it occurred to me that I might not have to face my doom. This door, that was normally latched and guarded, stood open. I was out that gate and on the lane nearby in an instant.

I wandered aimlessly for hours, when I abruptly came upon a little clearing. A stream ran through it, past the coziest of tiny cottages. I trotted straight over to the stream and began drinking in long draughts. After several moments of such behavior, I became aware of another presence nearby. It was a small, old man, leaning toward me in a strange sort of furry robe, and balancing himself on the most incredibly gnarled staff, and holding a silver bucket that steamed and hissed, yet smelled overwhelmingly delicious.

"Hello," he said in a pleasant tone. "I'm happy you have finally arrived. I read it in *The Book*. Would you care to drink from my bucket?" he asked. . . .

8.   This is the beginning of a story. To what genre does it belong?

  A.   poetry

  B.   historical fiction

  C.   nonfiction

  D.   fantasy

9.   What is likely to happen next?

     A.   Bessie will go to a barn.

     B.   Bessie will catch frogs.

     C.   Bessie will run away.

     D.   Bessie will drink the potion, and turn into a brown-eyed girl.

10.   How did you know what might happen next?

      A.   The nanny never wanted the princess to have a pet cow in the first place.

      B.   Magical things often happen in stories that begin with a princess.

      C.   I read about dysfunctional families often.

      D.   The princess will have a new handbag and boots.

11.   How should this sort of story be introduced to children?

      A.   Complete a K-W-L to activate prior knowledge about fairy tales.

      B.   Ask the children to look up vocabulary words in a dictionary.

      C.   Read the children a nonfiction book about dairy farming.

      D.   Show a video about talking to strangers.

12.   If you were going to ask the children to finish this story as a writing activity, what would you do next?

      A.   Have them complete a worksheet about the vocabulary words.

      B.   Ask them to diagram the first sentence.

      C.   Ask them to form small groups, and talk about what might happen next.

      D.   Have them complete a Venn diagram about Bessie and a real cow.

13. Which of the following sequences best describes the development of a young child?

    A.   1. learning to trust others
             2. developing independence
             3. moral development

    B.   1. learning to trust others
             2. moral development
             3. developing independence

    C.   1. moral development
             2. learning to trust others
             3. developing independence

    D.   1. developing independence
             2. moral development
             3. learning to trust others

14. Which of the following skills are necessary for successfully implementing and following a family budget?

    I.   managing the tension between short-term and long-term goals
    II. record-keeping ability
    III. ability to predict the direction of the U.S. economy
    IV. good taste in clothing

    A.   I, II, III, and IV

    B.   I, II, and III

    C.   II and III

    D.   I and II

15. Which of the following statements about job interviews is NOT true?

    A.   You should prepare answers for questions you think you might be asked.

    B.   You should always wear a business suit.

    C.   Maintaining eye contact with the interviewer throughout is very important.

    D.   Always thank the interviewer at the end of the interview for considering you.

16. Which of the following individuals is most likely to find difficulty in establishing good interpersonal relationships outside her own community?

    A.   Consuela enjoys listening and finding out about other people.

    B.   Katy always tries to keep an open mind in social situations.

    C.   Aimee is a good verbal communicator but is not always aware of her body language.

    D.   Viveka always tries to live by the "golden rule."

DIRECTIONS: Use the information below to answer the two questions that follow.

An experiment is planned to test the effect of microwave radiation on the success of seed germination. One hundred corn seeds will be divided into four sets of twenty-five each. Seeds in Group 1 will be microwaved for one minute, seeds in Group 2 for two minutes, and seeds in Group 3 for ten minutes. Seeds in Group 4 will not be placed in the microwave. Each group of seeds will be soaked overnight and placed between the folds of water-saturated newspaper.

17. When purchasing the seeds at the store no single package contained enough seeds for the entire project, most contain about thirty seeds per package. Which of the following is an acceptable approach for testing the hypotheses?

    I.   Purchase one packet from each of four different brands of seed, one packet for each test group
    II. Purchase one packet from each of four different brands of seed and divide the seeds from each packet equally among the four test groups
    III. Purchase four packets of the same brand, one packet for each test group
    IV. Purchase four packets of the same brand, and divide the seeds from each packet equally among the four test groups.

    A.   I and II only

    B.   II and IV only

    C.   III and IV only

    D.   IV only

18. During the measurement of seed and root length, it is noted that many of the roots are not growing straight. Efforts to manually straighten the roots for measurement are only minimally successful as the roots are fragile and susceptible to breakage. Which of the following approaches is consistent with the stated hypothesis?

    A.   At the end of the experiment, straighten the roots and measure them

    B.   Use a string as a flexible measuring instrument for curved roots

    C.   Record the mass instead of length as an indicator of growth

    D.   Record only the number of seeds that have sprouted, regardless of length

19. A hot-air balloon rises when propane burners in the basket are used to heat the air inside the balloon. Which of the following statements correctly identifies the explanation for this phenomenon?

    A.   Heated gas molecules move faster inside the balloon; their force striking the inside causes the balloon to rise

    B.   Hot gas molecules are themselves larger than cool gas molecules, resulting in the expansion of the gas

    C.   The amount of empty space between gas molecules increases as the temperature of the gas increases, resulting in the expansion of the gas

    D.   The combustion of propane releases product gases that are lighter than air, which are trapped in the balloon, causing it to rise

20. What does it mean that multiplication and division are *inverse operations*?

   A. Multiplication is commutative, whereas division is not. For example: 4×2 gives the same product as 2×4, but $4 \div 2$ is not the same as $2 \div 4$.

   B. Whether multiplying or dividing a value by 1, the value remains the same. For example, 9×1 equals 9; $9 \div 1$ also equals 9.

   C. When performing complex calculations involving several operations, all multiplication must be completed before completing any division, such as in $8 \div 2 \times 4 + 7 - 1$.

   D. The operations "undo" each other. For example, multiplying 11 by 3 gives 33. Dividing 33 by 3 then takes you back to 11.

21. The floor of a rectangular room is to be covered in two different types of material. The total cost of covering the entire room is $136.00. The cost of covering the inner rectangle is $80.00. The cost of covering the shaded area is $56.00.

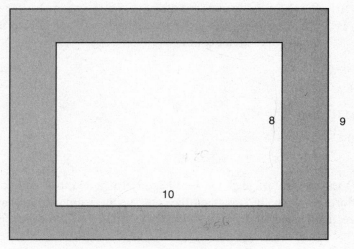

We wish to determine the cost of material per square foot used to cover the shaded area. What information given below is unnecessary for this computation?

    I. The total cost of covering the entire room.
   II. The cost of covering the inner rectangle.
  III. The cost of covering the shaded area.

   A. I only

   B. II only

   C. I and II

   D. I and III

22. The distribution of a high school chorus is depicted in the graph below. There is a total of 132 students in the chorus.

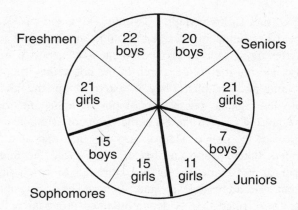

Which of the following expressions represents the percentage of freshman and sophomore girls in the chorus?

A. $\dfrac{21+15}{132} \times 100$

B. $\dfrac{21+15}{132} + 100$

C. $\dfrac{21+15}{132}$

D. $\dfrac{21+15}{100} \times 132$

23. Which of the following best describes the western, or Pacific, region of Canada comprising British Columbia and the Yukon?

A. The area contains many uninhabitable areas, including a mix of arid desert-like terrain and rugged mountain ranges that hinder rail and car transportation, resulting in minimal population settlement.

B. The area contains arid deserts and vast grasslands that are ideal for cattle farming and oil production.

C. The area contains the vast majority of Canada's natural resources and the majority of Canada's population.

D. The area contains fifty percent of Canada's population, resulting in seventy percent of Canada's manufacturing.

> **DIRECTIONS: Read the following passage and answer the question that follows:**

The police believed that Dollree Mapp was hiding a person suspected in a crime. The police went to her home in Cleveland, Ohio, knocked, and requested entry. Mapp refused. After more officers arrived on the scene, police forced their way into Mapp's house. During the police search of the house they found pornographic books, pictures, and photographs. They arrested Mapp and charged her with violating an Ohio law against possession of pornographic materials. Mapp and her attorney appealed the case to the Supreme Court of Ohio. The Ohio Supreme Court ruled in favor of the police. Mapp's case was then appealed to the Supreme Court of the United States. Mapp and her attorney asked the Supreme Court to determine whether or not evidence obtained through a search that violated the Fourth Amendment was admissible in state courts. The U.S. Supreme Court, in the case *Mapp v. Ohio*, ruled that evidence obtained in a search that violates the Fourth Amendment is not admissible. The majority opinion states, "Our decision, founded on reason and truth, gives to the individual no more than that which the Constitution guarantees him, to the police officer no less than that to which honest law enforcement is entitled, and, to the courts, that judicial integrity so necessary in the true administration of justice."

24. The excerpt above best illustrates which of the following features of judicial proceedings in the United States?

    A.   due process of law

    B.   a fair and speedy trial

    C.   judicial review

    D.   the exclusionary rule

25. Which of the following statements are true about economic activity in New York?

    I.   New York City became the financial capital of the nation in the early 20th century.
    II.   Manufacturing remains an important industry in New York State, although it has declined in recent decades.
    III. The rocky soil in many parts of New York has not impeded the state's agricultural productivity.
    IV.   The manufacturing industry is the largest employer in New York State, with the services sector a close second.

    A.   I and II only

    B.   I and III only

    C.   II and III only

    D.   II and IV only

26. Which of the following statements best defines the role of the World Trade Organization (WTO)?

    A. It resolves trade disputes and attempts to formulate policy to open world markets to free trade through monetary policy and regulation of corruption.

    B. It is an advocate for human rights and democracy by regulating child labor and providing economic aid to poor countries.

    C. It establishes alliances to regulate disputes and polices ethnic intimidation.

    D. It regulates trade within the United States in order to eliminate monopolistic trade practices.

27. The drought of the 1930s that spanned from Texas to North Dakota was caused by

    I.   overgrazing and overuse of farmland.
    II.   natural phenomena, such as below-average rainfall and wind erosion.
    III. environmental factors, such as changes in the jet stream.
    IV.   the lack of government subsidies for new irrigation technology.

    A. I and II only

    B. II and III only

    C. I and III only

    D. II and IV only

28. You have stepped into an art museum and are drawn to a painting you know nothing about. In order to appreciate the painting, it is helpful to

    I.   know all of the details of the artist's intentions and motivations.
    II.   study the clues in the artwork for potential meaning.
    III. determine the cultural significance of every visual clue in the painting.
    IV.   consider the art elements and principles in the work of art.

    A. I and II only

    B. I and III only

    C. II and IV only

    D. III and IV only

29. Which one of the following statements is most true regarding the materials of visual art?

    A. Industrial innovations in art making materials have improved art in the past 150 years.

    B. The use of uncommon materials in art making has improved art in the past 150 years.

    C. The use of unusual materials in art making has changed the standards by which we view art.

    D. Industrial innovations in art-making materials have had little influence on visual art.

30. Pitch is the relative _____ of a musical sound.

   A.   duration, or length

   B.   loudness or softness

   C.   highness or lowness

   D.   rhythm

31. This pyramid represents the pattern of progression from simple to complex activities in creative drama. Using the base of the pyramid for the simplest activities and the tip for the most complex, which of the following patterns correctly represents this progression?

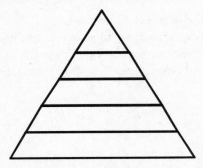

   A.   Story dramatization, story creation, improvisation, pantomime, beginning activities.

   B.   Improvisation, pantomime, beginning activities, story dramatization, story creation.

   C.   Beginning activities, improvisation, pantomime, story dramatization, story creation.

   D.   Beginning activities, pantomime, improvisation, story creation, story dramatization.

32. The primary and most efficient energy source of the body comes from

   A.   proteins.

   B.   fats.

   C.   complex carbohydrates.

   D.   simple sugars.

33. Which of the following is a locomotor skill?

   A.   bouncing

   B.   catching

   C.   throwing

   D.   leaping

34. Which is NOT a principle of aerobic conditioning?

    A.   requires oxygen

    B.   continuous and rhythmic

    C.   burns protein for energy

    D.   uses major muscle groups

35. Light is refracted when it passes across a boundary between media with different densities. This can occur between solids, liquids, gases, or result from differences within the same phase. The longer wavelengths of light are refracted less than the shorter wavelengths. Which of the following correctly places the colors of the visible spectrum in order from lowest extent of refraction to highest?

    A.   Blue/Violet – Green – Orange – Yellow – Red

    B.   Blue/Violet – Green – Yellow – Orange – Red

    C.   Red – Yellow – Green – Orange – Blue/Violet

    D.   Red – Orange – Yellow – Green – Blue/Violet

36. Around the time of World War II, the chemical industry developed several new classes of insecticide that were instrumental in protecting our soldiers from pest-borne diseases common to the tropic regions in which they were fighting. These same insecticides found widespread use at home to increase production of many agricultural crops by reducing the damage from insects like cotton weevils and grasshoppers. While farmers continued to use the same levels of insecticide, over time it was found that the insect population was increasing. Identify the best explanation for this observation:

    A.   Insecticides, like most chemicals, lose their potency when stored.

    B.   The insect population was increasing to reach the carrying capacity of a given ecosystem.

    C.   The initial doses of pesticide were too low to effectively kill the insects.

    D.   Insects with a tolerance to insecticide survived the initial doses and lived to produce insecticide-resistant offspring.

37. Under the right conditions of temperature and pressure, any type of rock can be transformed into another type of rock in a process called the Rock Cycle. Which of the following processes is not a part of the Rock Cycle?

    A.   the drifting and encroachment of sand at the edge of a desert

    B.   the melting of rock beneath the surface to form magma

    C.   the erosion of sedimentary rocks to form sand

    D.   the eruption of a cinder cone volcano

38. If a teacher is interested in improving the comprehension skills of students, that teacher should
    I.   teach students to decode well.
    II. allow time during the day to read and reread selections.
    III. discuss the selections after reading to clarify meaning and make connections.
    IV. tell jokes.

    A.   I and II only

    B.   I, II, and IV

    C.   I, II, and III

    D.   I, II, III, and IV

39. Dr. Kenneth Goodman developed the notion of miscue analysis. This is a system for examining how a child's oral reading of a passage varies from _____.

    A.   singing the same passage

    B.   encoding the passage from a dictation

    C.   the printed text

    D.   diagrams of the sentences

40. Which of the following describes the best practice in writing instruction?

    A.   Instruct students in writing, and give them time to write.

    B.   Have students complete worksheets about writing.

    C.   Have students copy famous speeches. (Have the students, in groups, convert the story into a script, and perform it in a reader's theatre format.)

    D.   Have the children create a mural of the story so far, and label all of the characters.

41. Listening is a process students used to extract meaning out of oral speech. Activities teachers can engage in to assist students in becoming more effective listeners include:

    I.   clearly setting a purpose for listening.
    II. allow children to relax by chewing gum during listening.
    III. asking questions about the selection.
    IV. encouraging students to forge links between the new information and knowledge already in place.

    A.   I and II

    B.   II, III, and IV

    C.   I, III, and IV

    D.   I, II, III, and IV

42. Why should children be taught to use graphic organizers as a method of organizing data during an inquiry?

    A.   It discourages the practice of copying paragraphs out of the source book.

    B.   It helps children to see similarities and differences across sources.

    C.   Graphic organizers look good to parents.

    D.   It provides the students an opportunity to use a word processor.

43. Why should children be encouraged to figure out the structure and the features of the text they are attempting to comprehend and remember?

    I.   It helps the students to understand the way the author organized the material to be presented.
    II. It helps the students to really look at the features of the text.
    III. Talking about the structure of the text provides an opportunity for the teacher to point out the most salient features to the students.
    IV. The discussions may help the child make connections between the new material in the chapter and what is already known about the topic.

    A.   I and III

    B.   II and IV

    C.   I and IV

    D.   I, II, III, and IV

44. Which one of the following is a responsibility of a consumer after making a purchase?

    A.   save the receipt

    B.   compare the product purchased to other products of its kind

    C.   keep a record of how the product is used

    D.   tell friends about how well the product works

45. Which one of the following statements regarding stress on the job is most true?

    A.   You should consult a medical professional if you feel stress on the job.

    B.   Stress is never good for you.

    C.   Talking about stress with co-workers or supervisors is rarely a good way to deal with stress.

    D.   Stress is often present during creative and productive work.

46. Lara likes interacting with other people, but she is nevertheless uncomfortable in unusual situations. She does well in math and science but does not particularly like those subjects. In other subjects, what interests her the most is working on group research projects with other students she likes. Her favorite subject is art, for which she has a flair but no extraordinary talent. Which one of the following is most likely to be a career interest area for her?

   A.   analytical investigator

   B.   influencer

   C.   people-oriented helper

   D.   independent, creative thinker

47. Dance can be a mirror of culture. Which of the following is not an illustration of this statement?

   A.   Women in the Cook Islands dance with their feet together and sway while the men take a wide stance and flap their knees.

   B.   Movement basics include body, space, time, and relationship.

   C.   In Africa, the birth of a child is an occasion for a dance that asks for divine blessings.

   D.   The court dancers of Bali study for many years to achieve the balance, beauty, and serenity of their dance.

Use the image below to answer the two questions that follow.

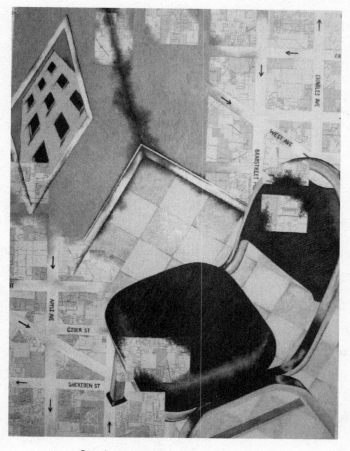

Student work by Sara Goodrich

48. As seen in the figure, the technique of gluing imagery to a two-dimensional surface is referred to as

A. montage.

B. frottage.

C. collage.

D. assemblage.

49. In the above image, the chair is the focal point of the drawing. Why?

A. It is large, frontal, and drawn in high contrast.

B. It is highly simplified and minimally detailed.

C. It is asymmetrically balanced in the drawing.

D. It is drawn in three-point perspective.

50. In order to achieve lasting weight loss, students should

    A.   enter a commercial diet program.

    B.   combine permanent dietary changes with exercise.

    C.   cut calories to below 600 per day.

    D.   exercise for two hours a day.

51. Which of the following vitamins is not fat soluble?

    A.   Vitamin D

    B.   Vitamin C

    C.   Vitamin E

    D.   Vitamin K

52. Of the following, which test does NOT measure muscular strength and endurance in children?

    A.   Pull-ups

    B.   Flexed arm hang

    C.   Grip strength test

    D.   Sit-and-reach test

DIRECTIONS: Use the passages below, adapted from Herodotus's *Histories*, to answer the question that follows.

Passage A: I think, too, that those Egyptians who dwell below the lake of Moiris and especially in that region which is called the Delta, if that land continues to grow in height according to this proportion and to increase similarly in extent, will suffer for all remaining time, from the Nile not overflowing their land, that same thing which they themselves said that the Hellenes would at some time suffer: for hearing that the whole land of the Hellenes has rain and is not watered by rivers as theirs is, they said that the Hellenes would at some time be disappointed of a great hope and would suffer the ills of famine. This saying means that if the god shall not send them rain, but shall allow drought to prevail for a long time, the Hellenes will be destroyed by hunger; for they have in fact no other supply of water to save them except from Zeus alone. This has been rightly said by the Egyptians with reference to the Hellenes: but now let me tell how matters are with the Egyptians themselves in their turn.

Passage B: If, in accordance with what I before said, their land below Memphis (for this is that which is increasing) shall continue to increase in height according to the same proportion as in the past time, assuredly those Egyptians who dwell here will suffer famine, if their land shall not have rain nor the river be able to go over their fields. It is certain however that now they gather in fruit from the earth with less labour than any other men and also with less than the other Egyptians; for they have no labour in breaking up furrows with a plough nor in hoeing nor in any other of those labours which other men have about a crop; but when the river has come up of itself and watered their fields and after watering has left them again, then each man sows his own field and turns into it swine, and when he has trodden the seed into the ground by means of the swine, after that he waits for the harvest, and when he has threshed the corn by means of the swine, then he gathers it in.

53. Which of the following best states the main issues being discussed in the above passages?

A. Ancient Egyptians were so dependent upon the Nile River that one's location determined one's prosperity.

B. The Nile River was so important to the prosperity of ancient Egyptians that it determined where many Egyptians settled.

C. Egyptians who depend upon the Nile River for irrigation will not suffer from famine as those who depend upon rain.

D. Egyptians settling in the Delta were dependent upon religion because irrigation from rain was more unpredictable than the Nile.

54. Which of the following would be considered a primary source in researching the factors that influenced U.S. involvement in the Korean War?

    I. The personal correspondence of a military man stationed with the 5th Regimental Combat Team (RCT) in Korea.
    II. A biography of Harry S. Truman by David McCullough, published in 1993.
    III. A journal article about the beginning of the Korean War by a noted scholar.
    IV. An interview with Secretary of Defense George Marshall.

A. I and II only

B. II and IV only

C. II and III only

D. I and IV only

55. Which of the following was not a major Native American tribe that resided in New York State before the 1700s?

A. the Oneida

B. the Huron

C. the Lenni-Lenape

D. the Wappinger

56. Which of the following best describes a major difference between a state government and the federal government?

   A. State governments have more responsibility for public education than the federal government.

   B. State governments are more dependent upon the personal income tax for revenue than the federal government.

   C. State governments are more dependent upon the system of checks and balances than the federal government.

   D. State governments are subject to term limits, where as federal government representatives serve unlimited terms.

57. Which equation could be used to answer the following question?

   Together, a pen and a pencil cost $2.59 (ignoring tax). The pen cost $1.79 more than the pencil. What was the cost of the pencil?

   A. $x = (2.59 - 1.79) \times 2$

   B. $2.59 = x - 1.79$

   C. $2.59 = x + (x + 1.79)$

   D. $x = 2.59 - 1.79$

58. Matt earned the following scores on his first six weekly mathematics tests: 91%, 89%, 82%, 95%, 86%, and 79%.

   He had hoped for an average (mean) of 90% at this point, which would just barely give him an A– in math class on his first report card. How many more total percentage points should Matt have earned over the course of those six weeks to qualify for an A–?

   A. 87

   B. 3

   C. 90

   D. 18

59. Ms. Williams plans to buy carpeting for her living room floor. The room is a rectangle measuring 14 feet by 20 feet. She wants no carpet seams on her floor, even if that means that some carpeting will go to waste. The carpeting she wants comes in 16-foot-wide rolls. What is the minimum amount of carpeting that will have to be wasted if Ms. Williams insists upon her no-seams requirement?

   A. 40 square feet

   B. 60 square feet

   C. 80 square feet

   D. 100 square feet

60. Use the figure to answer the question that follows.

Consider this sequence of calculator keystrokes:

$$\boxed{1}\ \boxed{8}\ \boxed{2}\ \boxed{\times}\ \boxed{1}\ \boxed{.}\ \boxed{0}\ \boxed{3}\ \boxed{\times}\ \boxed{1}\ \boxed{.}\ \boxed{0}\ \boxed{4}\ \boxed{=}$$

That sequence would be useful for finding which of the following values?

A.   The total distance an automobile travels if it covers 182 miles one day, but only 1.03 and 1.04 miles over the next two days.

B.   The amount of money in a savings account after the original deposit of $182 earns 3% and then 4% simple annual interest over two years.

C.   The total distance an automobile travels if it covers 182 miles one day, 103 miles the next day, and 104 miles the third day.

D.   The amount of money in a savings account after the original deposit of $182 grows by $1.03 and $1.04 in interest over two days.

DIRECTIONS: The following two questions are based upon this excerpt from Jules Verne's 1870 work *From the Earth to the Moon and Round the Moon* pp. 39–40 (Dodd, Mead & Company, 1962), where plans are made to construct a cannon 900 feet long to shoot a projectile to the Moon.

The problem before us is how to communicate an initial force of 12,000 yards per second to a shell of 108 inches in diameter, weighing 20,000 pounds. Now when a projectile is launched into space, what happens to it? It is acted upon by three independent forces: the resistance of the air, the attraction of the earth, and the force of impulsion with which it is endowed. Let us examine these three forces. The resistance of the air is of little importance. The atmosphere of the earth does not exceed forty miles. Now, with the given rapidity, the projectile will have traversed this in five seconds, and the period is too brief for the resistance of the medium to be regarded otherwise than as insignificant. Proceeding, then, to the attraction of the earth, that is, the weight of the shell, we know that this weight will diminish in the inverse ratio of the square of the distance. When a body left to itself falls to the surface of the earth, it falls five feet in the first second: and if the same body were removed 257,542 miles farther off, in other words, to the distance of the moon, its fall would be reduced to about half a line in the first second.

61. Propelling such a large projectile requires a massive force. The "initial force of 12,000 yards per second" is really a reference to the projectile's initial speed. The calculation of force required to move an object with a mass of 20,000 pounds from rest to a speed of 12,000 yards per second in a time span of 0.05 seconds is reflected in which of the following:

A. $20,000 \times (12,000 / 0.05)$

B. $20,000 \times 12,000 \times 0.05$

C. $(20,000 \times 9.8) / (20,000 \times 0.05)$

D. $(20,000 / 9.8) \times (12,000 / 0.05)$

62. The acceleration due to gravity is generally accepted as 9.8 m/sec^2 for objects near the Earth's surface, and the Earth's radius is approximately 4,000 miles. Given that the proposed projectile weighs 20,000 lbs at the surface, what would be the approximate mass at a distance of 8,000 miles from the surface of the Earth?

   A. 20,000 lbs / 2

   B. 20,000 lbs / 4

   C. 20,000 lbs / 8

   D. 20,000 lbs / 16

Read the passage below; then answer the two questions that follow.

The fourth-grade students in Ms. Alvarez's class are studying Native Americans. Ms. Alvarez wants to strengthen her students' ability to work independently. She also wants to provide opportunities for the students to use a variety of print and media resources during this unit of study. Ms. Alvarez plans to begin the unit by leading the class in a brainstorming session to formulate questions to guide their research about Native Americans.

63. Which of the following criteria should guide Ms. Alvarez as she leads the brainstorming session?

   A. The questions should emphasize the factual content presented in the available print materials.

   B. The questions should emphasize higher order thinking skills, such as comparison, analysis, and evaluation.

   C. The questions should reflect the interest of the students.

   D. The questions should include all of the fourth-grade objectives for this unit.

64. Ms. Alvarez has collected a variety of print and media resources for the students to use in their research. Which of the following would probably be the best way to motivate students to research the questions they have prepared?

   A. The teacher should assign two to three questions to each student so that all the questions are covered.

   B. The teacher should allow individual students to select the questions they would like to research.

   C. The teacher should select three key questions and assign them to all the students.

   D. The teacher should assign one topic to each student, then provide the students with additional information.

> **Read the statement below; then answer the question that follows.**

Mr. Drake is a first-grade teacher who is using the whole-language method while teaching about animals.

65. Before reading a story to the students, Mr. Drake tells the students what he is expecting them to learn from reading the story. What is his reason for doing this?

   A.   The students should know why the instructor chose this text over any other.

   B.   It is important for teachers to share personal ideas with their students in order to foster an environment of confidence and understanding.

   C.   Mr. Drake wants to verify that all students are on-task before he begins the story.

   D.   Mr. Drake is modeling a vital pre-reading skill in order to teach it to the young readers.

66. Dance can reflect the religion of a culture by
   I.   offering adoration and worship to the deity.
   II.   appealing to the deity for survival in war.
   III. asking the deity for success in the hunt.
   IV.   miming the actions of planting and harvesting crops.

   A.   I and II only

   B.   I and III only

   C.   II, III, and IV only

   D.   I, II, III, and IV

67. Which of the following do the dances of Waltz, Lindy Hop, and Twist have in common?

   A.   They became popular in the nineteenth century.

   B.   They are forms of "swing" dance.

   C.   They reflect changes in social attitudes of their time.

   D.   They are danced by couples touching each other.

68. Harmony results when a melody is accompanied by
   I.   a rhythm instrument.
   II.   a guitar.
   III. another instrument or singer playing or singing the melody.
   IV.   another instrument playing chords.

   A.   I and II only

   B.   I and III only

   C.   II and III only

   D.   II and IV only

69. Which of the following is NOT a characteristic of cholesterol?

    A.   Cholesterol plays a role in the function of the brain.

    B.   Cholesterol is a component in the creation of certain hormones.

    C.   Cholesterol is produced in the liver.

    D.   Excess cholesterol found in the blood of many people usually comes from internal production.

70. A table tennis game is scored to

    A.   15 points.

    B.   15 points, with a margin of two.

    C.   21 points, with a margin of two.

    D.   21 points.

71. To complete an effective aerobic workout, exercise should be performed at an individual's target heart rate for a minimum of

    A.   15 minutes.

    B.   20 minutes.

    C.   30 minutes.

    D.   45 minutes.

72. Use the figure to answer the question that follows.

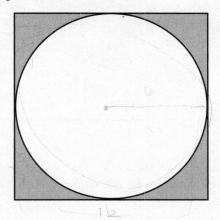

What is the approximate area of the shaded region, given that:
   a. the radius of the circle is 6 units
   b. the square inscribes the circle

A. 106 square units

B. 31 square units

C. 77 square units

D. 125 square units

73. How many lines of symmetry do all non-square rectangles have?

A. 0

B. 2

C. 4

D. 8

74. Use the figure to answer the question that follows.

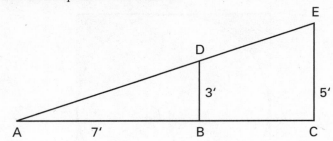

The figure above is a sketch of a ramp. Given that the two ramp supports (DB and EC) are perpendicular to the ground, and the dimensions of the various parts are as noted, what is the approximate distance from point B to point C?

A. 4.7 feet

B. 4.5 feet

C. 4.3 feet

D. 4.1 feet

75. Bemus School is conducting a lottery to raise funds for new band uniforms. Exactly 1000 tickets will be printed and sold. Only one ticket stub will be drawn from a drum to determine the single winner of a big-screen television. All tickets have equal chances of winning. The first 700 tickets are sold to 700 different individuals. The remaining 300 tickets are sold to Mr. Greenfield.

Given the information above, which of the following statements are true?

    I.   It is impossible to tell in advance who will win.
    II.   Mr. Greenfield will probably win.
    III.   Someone other than Mr. Greenfield will probably win.
    IV.   The likelihood that Mr. Greenfield will win is the same as the likelihood that someone else will win.

A. I and II only

B. I and III only

C. II and IV only

D. III and IV only

76. The literary technique of foreshadowing is often used

A. in novels, short stories and drama to manifest the characters' emotions by reflecting them in the natural world.

B. in novels, short stories, and drama to hint at future developments in the plot.

C. in lyric poetry to manifest the speaker's emotions by reflecting them in the natural world.

D. in myths and ballads to hint at future developments in the plot.

77. The novel *The Adventures of Huckleberry Finn*, by Mark Twain, has been a subject of controversy because

    A. it contains graphic descriptions of violence considered unsuitable for young readers.

    B. it challenges attitudes toward race in America.

    C. it portrays a hostile relationship between a young boy and an escaping slave.

    D. it was thought to have influenced the outcome of the Civil War.

78. The Japanese form of poetry called haiku is known for its

    A. brevity and concision.

    B. elaborate and flowery description.

    C. logic and directness of statement.

    D. humor and lifelike detail.

79. Hamlet's "To Be or Not to Be" speech, in the play by William Shakespeare, is an example of the dramatic technique known as

    A. aside.

    B. dialog.

    C. soliloquy.

    D. comic relief.

80. Identify the incorrect statement from the following:

    A. Heredity is the study of how traits are passed from parent to offspring.

    B. The chemical molecule that carries an organism's genetic makeup is called DNA.

    C. Sections of the DNA molecule that determine specific traits are called chromosomes.

    D. The genetic makeup of an organism is altered through bioengineering.

81. Which of the following sources of energy is nonrenewable?

    A. hydrogen-cell

    B. geothermal

    C. nuclear

    D. hydroelectric

82. The needle on the dial points most nearly to which reading?

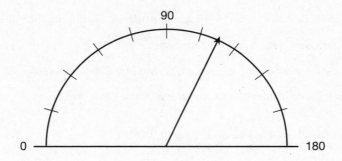

A. 108

B. 128

C. 114

D. 117

83. How many ten thousands are there in one million?

A. 100

B. 10

C. 1,000

D. 10,000

84. An owner of twin Siamese cats knows the following data:

    I.   Cost of a can of cat food
    II.   Volume of a can of cat food
    III.   Number of cans of cat food eaten each day by one cat
    IV.   The weight of the cat food in one can

Which of the data above can be used to determine the cost of cat food for 7 days for the 2 cats?

A. I and II only.

B. I and III only.

C. I and IV only.

D. III and IV only.

85. Use the figure to answer the question that follows.

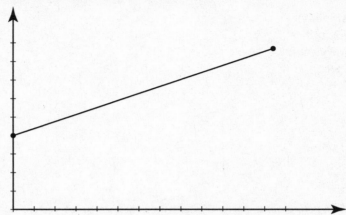

Which of the following situations might the graph illustrate?
   I.   The varying speed of an experienced runner over the course of a 26-mile race.
   II. The number of households a census taker still has to visit over the course of a week.
   III. The value of a savings account over time, assuming steady growth.
   IV. The changing height of a sunflower over several months.

A. I and II only

B. III and IV only

C. II, III, and IV only

D. I, III, and IV only

86. When a member of the House of Representatives helps a citizen from his or her district receive federal aid to which that citizen is entitled, the representative's action is referred to as

A. casework.

B. pork barrel legislation.

C. lobbying.

D. logrolling.

87. Which of the following types of pollution or atmospheric phenomena are correctly matched with their underlying causes?
   I.   global warming – carbon dioxide and methane
   II. acid rain – sulfur dioxide and nitrogen dioxide
   III. ozone depletion – chlorofluorocarbons and sunlight
   IV. aurora borealis – solar flares and magnetism

A. I and II only

B. II and III only

C. I and IV only

D. I, II, III, and IV

88. Which of the following characteristics of a sound wave is associated with its pitch?

      I.   Amplitude
     II.   Frequency
   III.   Wavelength
   IV.   Speed

   A.   I only

   B.   II only

   C.   II, III, and IV only

   D.   IV only

89. Which of the following statements correctly describes each group of vertebrates?

      I.   Amphibians are cold-blooded, spending part of their life cycle in water and part on land.
     II.   Reptiles are generally warm-blooded, having scales that cover their skin.
   III.   Fish are cold-blooded, breathing with gills, and covered by scales.
   IV.   Mammals are warm-blooded with milk glands and hair.

   A.   I and IV only

   B.   I, III, and IV only

   C.   IV only

   D.   I, II, III, and IV

90. Which of the following statements is NOT true?

   A.   Infectious diseases are caused by viruses, bacteria, or protists.

   B.   Cancers and hereditary diseases can be infectious.

   C.   Environmental hazards can cause disease.

   D.   The immune system protects the body from disease.

Directions for the Written Assignment

This section of the test consists of a written assignment. You are to prepare a written response of about 150–300 words on the assigned topic. *The assignment can be found on the next page*. You should use your time to plan, write, review, and edit your response to the assignment.

Read the assignment carefully before you begin to write. Think about how you will organize your response. You may use any blank space provided on the following pages to make notes, write an outline, or otherwise prepare your response. *However, your score will be based solely on the response you write on the lined pages of your answer document.*

Your response will be evaluated on the basis of the following criteria:

- **PURPOSE**: Fulfill the charge of the assignment

- **APPLICATION OF CONTENT**: Accurately and effectively apply the relevant knowledge and skills.

- **SUPPORT**: Support the response with appropriate examples and/or sound reasoning reflecting an understanding of the relevant knowledge and skills.

Your response will be evaluated on the criteria above, not on writing ability. However, your response must be communicated clearly enough to permit valid judgment of your knowledge and skills. The final version of your response should conform to the conventions of edited American English. This should be your original work, written in your own words, and not copied or paraphrased from some other work.

Be sure to write about the assigned topics. Please write legibly. You may not use any reference materials during the test. Remember to review what you have written and make any changes you think will improve your response.

Written Assignment

Use the information below to complete the exercise that follows.

Mrs. Whalen, a fifth-grade teacher, is assessing Demetrius, a new student to the school, for reading fluency and comprehension. She has him read the following passage aloud.

My name is Jake. That's my first name, obviously. I can't tell you my last name. It would be too dangerous. The controllers are everywhere. Everywhere. And if they knew my full name, they could find me and my friends, and then . . . well, let's just say I don't want them to find me. What they do to people who resist them is too horrible to think about.

I won't even tell you where I live. You'll just have to trust me that it is a real place, a real town. It may even be your town.

I'm writing this all down so that more people will learn the truth. Maybe then, somehow, the human race can survive until the Algonites return and rescue us, as they promised they would.

Maybe.

My life used to be normal. Normal, that is, until one Friday night at the mall. I was there with Marco, my best friend. We were playing video games and hanging out at this cool store that sells comic books and stuff. The usual.

Demetrius has trouble pronouncing nearly every word longer than two syllables: "obviously," "controllers," and "Algonites," for example. He also needs help in pronouncing the word "resist." He reads with some expression and fairly quickly, except for the words he stumbles over. When questioned about the content of the passage, he answers as follows:

Mrs. Whalen: Can you tell me something about what you were just reading?

Demetrius: There's a guy who likes video games. I think his name is Jake.

Mrs. Whalen: What can you tell me about Jake?

Demetrius: Well, he's scared. He's in trouble.

Mrs. Whalen: How do you know he's in trouble?

Demetrius: He can't give out his last name.

Mrs. Whalen: Do you have any idea what he's afraid of?

Demetrius: Not really—they're An-guh-...

Mrs. Whalen: The Algonites?

Demetrius: Yeah, them. I guess they're after the whole world.

Based on your knowledge of reading comprehension, write a response that:

• identifies two comprehension needs demonstrated by this student;

• provides evidence for the needs you identify;

• suggests two different instructional strategies to address the needs you identify; and

• explains why these strategies might be effective.

Practice Test Answer Sheets

Begin your essay on this page. If necessary, continue on the next page.

_____
_____
_____
_____
_____
_____
_____
_____
_____
_____
_____
_____
_____
_____
_____
_____
_____

Continue on the next page if necessary.

Continuation of your essay from previous page, if necessary.

Continuation of your essay from previous page, if necessary.

Continuation of your essay from previous page, if necessary.

NYSTCE

Multi-Subject Content Specialty Test

Answers:
Practice Test 1

Answer Key

1.	(D)	26.	(A)	51.	(B)	76.	(B)
2.	(B)	27.	(A)	52.	(D)	77.	(B)
3.	(B)	28.	(C)	53.	(C)	78.	(A)
4.	(A)	29.	(C)	54.	(D)	79.	(C)
5.	(A)	30.	(C)	55.	(B)	80.	(C)
6.	(C)	31.	(D)	56.	(A)	81.	(C)
7.	(D)	32.	(C)	57.	(C)	82.	(D)
8.	(D)	33.	(D)	58.	(D)	83.	(A)
9.	(D)	34.	(C)	59.	(A)	84.	(B)
10.	(B)	35.	(D)	60.	(B)	85.	(B)
11.	(A)	36.	(D)	61.	(A)	86.	(A)
12.	(C)	37.	(A)	62.	(B)	87.	(D)
13.	(A)	38.	(C)	63.	(C)	88.	(C)
14.	(D)	39.	(C)	64.	(B)	89.	(B)
15.	(B)	40.	(A)	65.	(D)	90.	(B)
16.	(C)	41.	(C)	66.	(D)		
17.	(B)	42.	(B)	67.	(C)		
18.	(D)	43.	(D)	68.	(D)		
19.	(C)	44.	(A)	69.	(D)		
20.	(D)	45.	(D)	70.	(C)		
21.	(C)	46.	(A)	71.	(B)		
22.	(A)	47.	(B)	72.	(B)		
23.	(A)	48.	(C)	73.	(B)		
24.	(D)	49.	(A)	74.	(A)		
25.	(C)	50.	(B)	75.	(B)		

Diagnostic Grid: Questions Sorted by Subarea

	SUBAREA I. LANGUAGE ARTS	QUESTION NO.
1.	Understand the foundations of reading development.	3, 39
2.	Understand skills and strategies involved in reading comprehension.	38
3.	Understand and apply reading skills and strategies for various purposes (including information and understanding, critical analysis and evaluation, literary response, and social interaction).	9, 10, 53
4.	Understand processes for generating, developing, revising, editing, and presenting/publishing written texts.	43
5.	Understand and apply writing skills and strategies for various purposes (including information and understanding, critical analysis and evaluation, literary response and personal expression, and social interaction).	12, 40
6.	Understand skills and strategies involved in listening and speaking for various purposes (including information and understanding, critical analysis and evaluation, literary response and expression, and social interaction).	41, 65
7.	Understand and apply techniques of literary analysis to works of fiction, drama, poetry, and nonfiction.	8, 76, 77, 79
8.	Demonstrate knowledge of literature, including literature from diverse cultures and literature for children/adolescents.	4, 11, 78
	SUBAREA II. MATHEMATICS	
9.	Understand formal and informal reasoning processes, including logic and simple proofs, and apply problem-solving techniques and strategies in a variety of contexts.	5, 85
10.	Use mathematical terminology and symbols to interpret, represent, and communicate mathematical ideas and information.	6, 20, 82
11.	Understand skills and concepts related to number and numeration, and apply these concepts to real-world situations.	7, 83, 84
12.	Understand patterns and apply the principles and properties of linear algebraic relations and functions.	22, 57, 60
13.	Understand the principles and properties of geometry and trigonometry, and apply them to model and solve problems.	21, 72, 73, 74
14.	Understand concepts, principles, skills, and procedures related to the customary and metric systems of measurement.	59
15.	Understand concepts and skills related to data analysis, probability, and statistics, and apply this understanding to evaluate and interpret data and to solve problems.	58, 75
	SUBAREA III. SCIENCE AND TECHNOLOGY	
16.	Understand and apply the principles and processes of scientific inquiry and investigation.	17, 18
17.	Understand and apply concepts, principles, and theories pertaining to the physical setting (including earth science, chemistry, and physics).	2, 27, 35, 37, 61, 62
18.	Understand and apply concepts, principles, and theories pertaining to the living environment.	80, 89
19.	Apply knowledge of technology and the principles of engineering design.	36, 81
20.	Understand the relationships among and common themes that connect mathematics, science, and technology and the application of knowledge and skills in these disciplines to other areas of learning.	19, 87, 88

(continued)

SUBAREA IV. SOCIAL STUDIES	QUESTION NO.
21. Understand major ideas, eras, themes, developments, and turning points in the history of New York State, the United States, and the world.	25, 54
22. Understand geographic concepts and phenomena and analyze the interrelationships of geography, society, and culture in the development of New York State, the United States, and the world.	23, 55
23. Understand concepts and phenomena related to human development and interactions (including anthropological, psychological, and sociological concepts).	13
24. Understand economic and political principles, concepts, and systems, and relate this knowledge to historical and contemporary developments in New York State, the United States, and the world.	1, 26
25. Understand the roles, rights, and the responsibilities of citizenship in the United States and the skills, knowledge, and attitudes necessary for successful participation in civic life.	24, 56, 86
26. Understand and apply skills related to social studies, including gathering, organizing, mapping, evaluating, interpreting, and displaying information.	42, 63, 64
SUBAREA V. FINE ARTS	
27. Understand the concepts, techniques, and materials of the visual arts; analyze works of visual arts; and understand the cultural dimensions and contributions of the visual arts.	28, 29, 48, 49
28. Understand concepts, techniques, and materials for producing, listening to, and responding to music; analyze works of music; and understand the cultural dimensions and contributions of music.	30, 68
29. Understand concepts, techniques, and materials related to theater and dance; analyze works of drama and dance; and understand the cultural dimensions and contributions of drama and dance.	31, 47, 66, 67
SUBAREA VI. HEALTH AND FITNESS	
30. Understand basic principles and practices of personal, interpersonal, and community health and safety; and apply related knowledge and skills (e.g., decision making, problem solving) to promote personal well-being.	32, 50, 51, 90
31. Understand physical education concepts and practices related to the development of personal living skills.	69, 71
32. Understand health-related physical fitness concepts and practices.	33, 34, 52, 70
SUBAREA VII. FAMILY AND CONSUMER SCIENCE AND CAREER DEVELOPMENT	
33. Understand concepts and practices related to child development and care and apply knowledge of family and interpersonal relationships.	16,
34. Understand skills and procedures related to consumer economics and personal resource management.	14, 44
35. Understand basic principles of career development; apply processes and skills for seeking and maintaining employment; and demonstrate knowledge of workplace skills, behaviors, and responsibilities.	15, 45, 46

Practice Test 1

Detailed Explanations of Answers

1. **D**

Both state and federal government have the power to lay and collect taxes and to borrow money. Article I, Section 8 of the Constitution establishes the powers of Congress, whereas the 10th Amendment to the Constitution (the last amendment within the Bill of Rights) sets forth the principle of reserved powers to state governments. Reading state constitutions will show that states also possess the power to lay and collect taxes.

2. **B**

The region's mountain ranges are the main reason for the high precipitation.

3. **B**

The best way to teach children to read, regardless of grade level, is to use a program of emergent literacy that includes pattern books and journal writing with invented spelling. Choice A is incorrect because, although an intensive phonics program that includes drill and practice seatwork on basic sight words may be effective with some students, it is not the most effective way to teach all students to read. Choice D is incorrect because an ESL program is intended to provide assistance to only those students who are learning English as a second language. Additionally, the learning resource teacher should provide assistance to only those students who have been identified as having a learning disability that qualifies them to receive services.

4. **A**

By selecting books for the classroom library that match students' independent reading abilities, the teacher is recognizing that students must improve their reading ability by beginning at their own level and progressing to more difficult materials. Choice B is incorrect because books that *are challenging will most likely be frustrating to at least some of the students. Choice C is incorrect because the presence or absence of separate word lists should not be a determining factor in selecting books for a classroom library. Choice D is incorrect because all children need access to a classroom library regardless of their reading abilities.*

5. **A**

Drawing a sketch with dots marking the possible locations of the two houses and The Soda Depot is a good idea. You can start with dots for the two houses, using inches for miles:

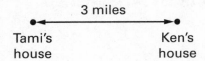

If you then draw a dot representing The Soda Depot two miles (inches) to the right of Ken's house, as in the figure that follows, you see that the greatest possible distance between Tami's house and The Soda Depot is five miles.

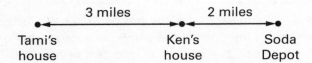

If you draw The Soda Depot dot to the left of Ken's house, as in the figure below, you see that The Soda Depot could be as close as one mile to Tami's house, but no closer. Only statements I and III, then, are true.

6. **C**

Each combined inequality can be seen as the combination of two single inequalities. Inequality A, for instance, can be seen as the combination of the following two single inequalities:

$75 \leq x$

and

$x \leq 40.$

The meaning of a single inequality is often made clearer if you transpose the statement, placing the variable on the left. That is:

$75 \leq x$

means the same thing as

$x \geq 75$.

So, combined inequality A says that x (the speeds that vehicles may drive at) is greater than or equal to 75 mph and *less than or equal to 40 mph*.

You can separate combined inequalities B and D into individual inequalities in the same way:

Combined inequality B, $75 < x > 40$, means the same as

$x > 75$

and

$x > 40$.

That means that drivers have to drive faster than 75 mph! That doesn't match what the sign says.

Combined inequality D, $40 < x > 75$ means the same as

$x > 40$

and

$x > 75$.

That's the same as combined inequality B.

The correct answer is C, $40 \leq x \leq 75$, because that combined inequality means the same as

$x \geq 40$

and

$x \leq 75$.

That is, vehicles can travel at or faster than 40 mph, but no faster than 75 mph.

7. **D** ——————————————————————————————

In simple notation form, the Distributive Property is as follows:

$a(b + c) = (a \times b) + (a \times c)$

This means that when multiplying, you may have some computational options. Consider answer D. The Distributive Property allows us to break 42 down into the convenient addends 2 and 40. You can then separately multiply each addend by 3. Thus, 3×2 equals 6, and 3×40 equals 120. We can then (courtesy of The Distributive Property) add those products together to get 126. Only answer D above is illustrative of The Distributive Property.

8. **D** ——————————————————————————————

Many of the classic stories for children exist in the realm of fantasy because of the timeless quality of such tales. Fantasy allows children to explore places and events that have never taken place, and will never take place, yet somehow contain messages that we can discuss, savor, and learn *from. Faith Ringgold, an author of books for children, has stated, "One of the things you can do so well with children is to blend fantasy and reality. Kids are ready for it; they don't have to have everything lined up and real. It's not that they don't know it's not real, they just don't care."*

9. D

After reading books that begin with a spoiled princess before doesn't it seem probable that Bessie will do just that?

10. B

Bessie's transformation is typical of books with a princess theme. Please consider some of the following titles: The Paper Bag Princess *by Robert Munsch;* The Frog Prince, Continued *by Jon Scieszka;* Princess Furball *by Charlotte Huck; and* Sleeping Ugly *by Jane Yolen.*

11. A

A K-W-L isn't just for content area lessons. "K" stands for "Know." That is, activate students' prior knowledge by asking what they already know. "W" indicates what the students "Want" to know, and "L" stands for discussing what the students "Learned" after reading the passage. Some children come to think of fairy tales as "babyish" or "girlish." This kind of discussion, laced with little chunks of stories being read aloud, helps children to recognize how delightful and charming this genre can be. It also helps them to figure out the rules of the genre, which improves their reading and writing.

12. C

This is the next step in the writing process.

13. A

The first thing children learn is to trust others. Moral development cannot occur without independence, as both independent judgment and maturation through interactions in social settings contribute to the development of a conscience.

14. D

Choice I, managing the tension between long- and short-term goals, is very important in sticking to a family budget, because family members will often have both (with children usually having the preponderance of short-term goals). This takes not only accounting ability, but also interpersonal skills to balance the needs and desires of all family members. Choice II is obviously important in keeping a budget. Choice III is a good skill to have in order to gauge how many resources the family might have in the future, but it is hardly necessary for creating and managing a budget.

15. B

When appearing for an interview, one should always wear clothing appropriate for the job, or perhaps a little dressier than required for the job; there is no one-size-fits-all prescription for how to dress for an interview. On the other hand, an interviewee should always try to figure what questions will be asked—and rehearse answers to them (choice A); should keep eye contact with the interviewer to the extent practicable (choice C); and thank the interviewer at the end of the interview (choice D).

16. C

Although verbal communication skills are very important in establishing and maintaining interpersonal relationships, being aware of—and controlling—one's body language is at least equally important. Choices A, B, and D are statements of necessary, and teachable/learnable, traits for successful social interaction.

17. B

The experiment requires a control of all variables other than the one identified in the hypothesis—exposure to microwave radiation. Seeds from different suppliers may be different; for example, one brand may be treated with a fungicide. While it is likely that item III might be acceptable, without confirming that all packages are from the same year and production run, the four packages may be significantly different from each other. The best solution is to randomly divide the available seeds equally between the four test groups. Item II allows the experiment to also compare the germination rates between the different brands, but only if the seeds from each packet are isolated within each test group, and the number of seeds large enough to create a statistically significant sample.

18. D

The hypothesis is to evaluate seed germination as a function of microwave irradiation. Recording the overall growth or length of the seed root, while interesting, is not the stated hypothesis. Item C would be a good approach if the hypothesis were to relate seed growth to some variable, as it would more accurately reflect the growth of thicker or multiple roots in a way that root length might not measure.

19. C

The gas molecules themselves do not expand in size when heated, but the spaces between them increases as the molecules move faster. The expanding hot air leaves the balloon body through the opening at the bottom. With less air in the balloon casing, the balloon is lighter. The combustion products of propane are carbon dioxide (molar mass 44 g/mol), which is heavier than air, and water (molar mass 18 g/mol), which is lighter.

20. **D**

It's true that multiplication is commutative and division isn't, but that's not relevant to them being inverse operations. Answer A doesn't address the property of being inverse.

Answer B also contains a true statement, but again, the statement is not about inverse operations.

Answer C gives a false statement. In the example shown in answer C, the order of operations tells you to compute 8 ÷ 2 first, before any multiplication.

As noted in answer D, the inverseness of two operations indeed depends upon their ability to undo each other.

21. **C**

The total area of the larger rectangle is

base × height = 12 × 9 = 108 sq. ft.

Therefore, the area of the shaded portion surrounding the inner rectangle is

108 sq. ft. – 80 sq. ft. = 28 sq. ft.

If the total cost of material used to cover the shaded area is $56 and we have 28 sq. ft., the cost per square foot is $\frac{\$56}{28 \text{ sq. ft.}}$ = $2.00 per square foot.

Answers A, B, and D are incorrect. Neither I nor II is necessary to determine the cost per square foot of the shaded area. D is incorrect because III is needed to determine the cost per sq foot.

22. **A**

In order to solve this problem we must first add the number of freshman girls to the number of sophomore girls (21 + 15). In order to find the percentage we divide this sum by the total number of students in the chorus and multiply by 100.

$$\frac{21+15}{132} \times 100 = \% \text{ of freshman and sophomore girls in chorus}$$

Answer B is incorrect; in order to find the percentage we need to multiply the fraction by 100, not divide by 100. Answers C and D are incorrect because the number of freshman and sophomore girls must be divided by the total number of students in the chorus. We then multiply by 100 to get the percent.

23. **A**

The western, or Pacific, coast of Canada is known as the Cordillera region. It includes some of the tallest and oldest trees in Canada, similar to northern California. The area is full of rugged mountains with high plateaus and desert-like areas. For more information on Canada's regions visit http://www.members.shaw.ca/kcic1/geographic.html.

24. **A**

Due process is the legal concept that every citizen is entitled to equal treatment under the law. The excerpt illustrates one aspect of due process, the exclusionary rule. But the overwhelming theme of the paragraph demonstrates judicial review.

25. **C**

I is incorrect because New York City was already the nation's financial capital in the mid-19th century. II is correct because, in spite of the decline of manufacturing in recent decades, it still employs significant numbers of people. III is correct because New York has many areas of fertile though rocky soil. IV is incorrect because the service sector employs the largest percentage of workers in New York State.

26. **A**

The main purpose of the WTO is to open world markets to all countries to promote economic development and to regulate the economic affairs between member states.

27. **A**

Overgrazing and overuse of farmland, and a lack of rainfall caused the drought of the 1930s.

28. **C**

Choice C, statements II and IV, is correct. You would want to study the clues in the artwork for potential meaning and consider the art elements and principles in the work of art. The more you know about the context in which the artist worked, the more you can appreciate the work itself. Not everything will be immediately evident, so you will want to assume the role of detective.

29. **C**

Choice C is the correct answer. The use of uncommon materials has dramatically changed the criteria by which one assesses visual art.

30. **C**

This question focuses on a specific but very basic musical concept, pitch. Answer C is the best answer and the only correct answer. Answer A refers indirectly to the basic concept of rhythm. This relates to answer D, which is totally wrong because it is another concept and not a descriptor of the concept of pitch. Answer B is wrong because it refers directly to the basic concept of dynamics.

31. D

In creative drama, activities build upon one another and establishing a foundation of skill building activities is the norm. Beginning activities are warm-ups. These are used to introduce a session and to help players become comfortable with one another. Pantomime activities are next, as these help children to develop nonverbal communication abilities and to clearly express ideas without speaking. Without these experiences, players too often rely only upon voice for sharing ideas and for characterization. As improvisations can be done with or without speaking, they follow pantomimes. When students incorporate dialogue into their improvisations, they have a better understanding of how an actor uses voice and body as artistic tools. Improvisations also help students learn to think quickly and creatively. Story creation is next. There are multiple ways of creating stories. These can be done using unison or individual play and in pantomime or with dialogue. The result can be simple or complex stories. In order to successfully engage in story creation, students should understand characterization and plot. They should be experienced at using imagination and ensemble play. Story dramatization is the most complex creative drama activity, as it incorporates skills developed at lower levels. Here, players engage in individual rather than unison play. Story dramatizations are often student-directed activities based upon original stories or stories from literature. These require an investment of time if believable characterizations are to result. Engaging in story dramatizations encourages an understanding of both drama and literature. If one were to construct a hierarchy of creative drama activities, story dramatization would be at the top.

32. C

Complex carbohydrates are the most efficient energy source for the body. While other choices provide some energy, they are not nearly as efficient as complex carbohydrates.

33. D

Leaping is the only locomotor skill listed. Bouncing (A), catching (B), and throwing (C) are manipulative movements.

34. C

A, B, and D are principles of aerobic conditioning. C is not.

35. D

Red light is refracted less, having a longer wavelength. This is the basis for our observation of a red sunrise or red sunset as light passes through more of the atmosphere than at midday. The high number of particles in a polluted or particulate-laden atmosphere leads to intense red sunsets as the more refractive blue wavelengths are refracted away from view. Differences in refraction are also the basis of TV commercials for sunglasses with yellow lenses that improve the clarity of vision. As light from an object passes through the lens of the eye, the blue wavelengths are refracted more and may be focused before reaching the retina while the longer wavelengths are focused on the retina. Multiple images within the eye leads to the perception of a blurred image. Yellow glasses that filter out the blue wavelengths eliminate one image and give the perception of sharper, clearer vision for the wearer.

36. **D**

Early doses of pesticide were strong enough to kill most of the insects. Only a few survived who, perhaps because of some genetic trait, had a slightly higher tolerance to the poison. When these pesticide-tolerant insects reproduced they passed the tolerance to their offspring. Higher doses of pesticide are initially effective, but again a few individuals survive with tolerance to that new level. Control of pest populations generally requires access to a variety of pesticides that work through different mechanisms, and which are applied in such a way as to minimize buildup of tolerance in the insect population.

37. **A**

The physical movement and accumulation of sand is not part of the rock cycle, because no transformation of rock type is involved.

38. **C**

Teaching effective comprehension is a process that takes time and practice. It seems obvious that a student cannot comprehend a text if the text cannot be decoded. It also seems obvious that, if you want students to get better at reading, they need time to read. Students also need time and input, usually in the form of conversation, to make connections between what is read and what is already known.

39. **C**

Miscue analysis is designed to assess the strategies that children use in their reading. Goodman was interested in the processes occurring during reading, and he believed that any departure from the written text could provide a picture of the underlying cognitive processes. Readers' miscues include substitutions of the written word with another, additions, omissions, and alterations to the word sequence.

40. **A**

There is a direct relationship between what is taught in school and what is learned in school. Also, if you want children to improve in writing, they need time to write.

41. **C**

Clearly setting a purpose for listening, asking questions about the selection, and encouraging students to forge links between the new information and knowledge already in place are all supported by research as effective strategies.

42. **B**

Asking children to complete a graphic organizer as they research an issue helps them keep organized, helps them see connections, and helps them pull together what they can then use in some interesting and meaningful way.

43. **D**

Children learn more from a text if the teacher helps them figure out how the book was put together. It makes the text more understandable. It also helps them to read the text critically, as part of the conversation can address the issue of what is missing in the text.

44. **A**

Of these choices, the only one that a consumer is obligated to do is to save the receipt in case the product needs to be returned. Choice B, comparing products, should really be done before a purchase; if done afterward, though, it could be useful in deciding how to make a subsequent purchase. Keeping a record of how the product (C) is not necessary, although the consumer is obligated to use the product as directed. Although some feel that telling others how a product works is a useful social good, the consumer is under no obligation to do so.

45. **D**

Not all stress in the workplace is bad: it can be present in large doses especially during high creativity—because being creative involves taking risks. For the same reason, choice A is not always true; medical professionals should be consulted only if the stress is great enough to become debilitating or otherwise injurious to one's health. And stress can actually increase creativity, so stress, at least in small enough doses, is not always bad for you (B). Talking with co-workers (choice C) is very often a good place to start if one is feeling too much stress, and sometimes even a talk with a supervisor will be productive.

46. **A**

Although Lara's favorite subject is art, the interest area to which that aptitude might apply is not listed as one of the choices. Choice B, influencer, would be an interest area for someone who likes to lead—not an enjoyable area for someone who feels shy in unusual situations. Choice D, creative thinker, probably would not apply because Lara does not seem interested in creative exploration of subjects in which she does well. There is no sign pointing against choice C, people-oriented helper, but her affinity for group-oriented research projects points much more strongly to an interest in analytic investigation.

47. **B**

The statement "Movement basics include body, space, time, and relationship" is the correct answer because this describes only the dimensions of dance movement; in no way does it speak to how dance reflects the culture of which it is part.

48. **C**

Choice C is the correct answer. This is a collage.

49. **A**

It is large, frontal, and drawn in high contrast.

50. **B**

Permanent dietary changes and exercise are the only way to produce lasting weight loss. Commercial diets (A) do not always include a program of exercise, but rather concentrate on diet. Radically reducing calorie intake (C) will cause the body to go into starvation mode and slow down digestion to conserve energy. Two hours of daily exercise (D) is not very practical and without controlling calorie intake, it would be ineffective.

51. **B**

Vitamin C is water soluble—the remaining choices are fat soluble.

52. **D**

Pull-ups (for boys) (A), flexed arm hang (for girls) (B), and the grip strength test (C), are all tests to measure muscular strength and endurance. The sit and reach test measures flexibility.

53. **C**

The Nile River's flooding was more predictable than rainfall in Greece was.

54. **D**

Both the personal correspondence of a military man stationed with the 5th RCT in Korea and an interview with Secretary of Defense George Marshall are primary sources, as they involve correspondence or testimony from individuals who were actually involved with the Korean War.

55. **B**

The Huron lived in what is now Ontario, Canada. They were enemies of the Iroquois Confederacy, which inhabited central New York State and to which the Oneida tribe belonged. The Lenni-Lenape and Wappinger tribes lived mainly in southeast New York.

56. **A**

The responsibility for public education belongs to the state governments. The federal government has often passed legislation to regulate and provide funds for public education, but the main responsibility for establishing and regulating education resides with the state governments.

57. **C**

The total price of the two items in the original problem is given as $2.59, hinting that equation B or C may be correct. (In both cases, $2.59 is shown as the sum of two values.)

Examine the right side of equation C: You note that one value is $1.79 higher than the other. That is, in equation C, x could stand for the price of the pencil, and (x + 1.79) could stand for the price of the more expensive pen. Hence, equation C is the right one. None of the others fit the information given.

58. **D**

It is helpful to compute Matt's current average. Adding up his scores, you get 522. Dividing that by 6 (the number of scores), you find that his average is 87%. Similarly, you can multiply 90 by 6 to compute the number of total points it would take to have an average of 90 (90 × 6 = 540). Matt only earned 522 points, so he was 18 shy of the A–.

59. **A**

The only way carpet from a 16-foot-wide roll will cover Ms. Williams' floor without seams is if she buys 20 feet of it. She can then trim the 16-foot width to 14 feet so that it fits her floor. Buying 20 feet of a 16-foot-wide roll means that she will have to buy 320 square feet. Her living room has an area of only 280 square feet (14 feet × 20 feet), so she'll be wasting 40 square feet (320 – 280), but no more.

60. **B**

The keystrokes indicate multiplication, and only answer B involves multiplication. Multiplication is hidden within the concept of interest. One way to compute a new savings account balance after interest has been earned is to multiply the original balance by (1 + the rate of interest). In this case, that's first 1.03, then 1.04. The keystrokes match that multiplication.

61. **A**

Force is equal to mass multiplied by acceleration (F = ma). The force needed is the product of the objects mass (20,000 lbs) and the acceleration. Acceleration is the change in speed per unit time. The projectile's acceleration is thus (12,000 yards/second – 0 yards/second) / 0.05 seconds).

62. **B**

The force of gravity is inversely proportional to the square of the distance; thus, doubling the distance reduces the gravitational force by a factor of 4. The mass reduction for this object at the top of the atmosphere, just forty miles above the surface, would be insignificant. However, experience tells us that objects are "weightless" in the space shuttle. This apparent weightlessness is a result of a balance between the forward motion of the shuttle and the gravitational attraction of the Earth. Both the shuttle and the objects in it are moving forward together at a high rate of speed, and falling together under the force of gravity. They are "weightless" only relative to each other. Were the shuttle to cease forward motion it would fall directly and precipitously to Earth under the unrelenting force of gravity.

63. **C**

The use of instructional strategies that make learning relevant to individual student interests is a powerful motivating force that facilitates learning and independent thinking. Choices A and B are both important factors to consider during a brainstorming session of this type, but both of these factors should influence the teacher only after the student interests have been included. Choice D indicates a misunderstanding of the situation described. The students are setting the objectives for the unit as they brainstorm questions.

64. **B**

Choice is an important element in motivating students to learn. Answer A is contradictory to the stated purpose of the activity. The students proposed the questions, so covering all the questions should not be a problem. Choice C is incorrect because the students have chosen what they consider to be key questions; the teacher should select different or additional key questions. Choice D is a possibility, but only if there is a specific reason why all the students should not research all the questions.

65. **D**

Comprehension is shown when the reader questions his or her intent for reading. For example, one may be reading a story to find out what terrible things may befall the main character. The rationale for choosing a book may be an interesting bit of information (A), but it is not a major topic of discussion with the students. Sharing personal information (B) creates a certain bond, but this is not directly relevant to the question. It is also important that all students are on-task before the beginning of a lesson (C), but this is a smaller part of the skill modeled in response D.

66. **D**

The correct choice is D, statements I, II, III, and IV. Dance can reflect the religion of a culture in many ways on account of its deep historical roots in religious tradition.

67. **C**

The Waltz, Lindy Hop, and the Twist each reflect changes in social attitudes of their time.

68. **D**

This question focuses on a basic musical concept, "harmony." Harmony is the performance of two or more different pitches simultaneously. Therefore, when looking at the answers provided, it is good to begin by eliminating answers that have nothing to do with pitch. A rhythm instrument is a non-pitched instrument in almost all cases, so choice I is not pitch-related and that means that answers A and B are eliminated because they both include choice I. Since two or more different pitches must be performed simultaneously to have harmony, choice III can also be eliminated because there are two performers, but not two different pitches. That eliminates answer C and leaves answer D as the best and correct answer.

69. **D**

Excess cholesterol found in the blood typically comes from cholesterol in a diet rather than internal production. Cholesterol, which is produced in the liver (C), plays a vital role in brain function (A) and is important for creating certain hormones (B).

70. **C**

Table tennis is scored to 21 and must be won by a margin of two points. In doubles play for badminton, the winner must score 15 points (A). Singles badminton is also scored to 21 points with a margin of two points needed for victory.

71. **B**

Exercising cardiovascularly for a minimum of 20 minutes per session, as part of an exercise program, will lead to effective physical results with a proper nutritional diet. Forty-five minutes (D) is an effective time period when performing a weight-lifting exercise session.

72. **B**

First, it is helpful to view the shaded area as the area of the square minus the area of the circle. With that in mind, you simply need to find the area of each simple figure, and then subtract one from the other.

You know that the radius of the circle is 6 units in length. That tells you that the diameter of the circle is 12 units. Because the circle is inscribed in the square (meaning that the circle fits inside of the square touching in as many places as possible), you see that the sides of the square are each 12 units in length. Knowing that, you compute that the area of the square is 144 square units (12 × 12).

Using the formula for finding the area of a circle (πr^2), and using 3.14 for π, you get approximately 113 square units. (3.14 × 6 × 6). Then, you subtract 113 (the area of the circle) from 144 (the area of the square) for the answer of 31.

73. **B**

If you can fold a two-dimensional figure so that one side exactly matches or folds onto the other side, the fold line is a line of symmetry. The figure below is a non-square rectangle with its two lines of symmetry shown.

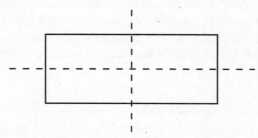

One might think that lines drawn from opposite corners are lines of symmetry, but they're not. The two halves would be the same size and shape, but wouldn't fold onto each other.

Note that the question asked about non-square rectangles. Squares (which are rectangles) have four lines of symmetry.

74. **A**

To answer the question, you must recognize that triangles ADB and AEC are similar triangles, meaning that they have the same shape. That means that the corresponding angles of the two triangles are the same, or congruent, and that corresponding sides of the two triangles are proportional. Given that, you can set up the following proportion, where x is the distance from point A to point C:

$$\frac{3}{7} = \frac{5}{x}$$

Solving the proportion by cross-multiplication, you see that the length of segment AC is about 11.7. Knowing that the length of segment AB is 7 feet, you subtract to find the length of BC (11.7 – 7 = 4.7).

75. **B**

Statement I is true because the winner could be Mr. Greenfield and it could be someone else. Statement II is not true, even though Mr. Greenfield bought many more tickets than any other individual. He still has a block of only 300; there are 700 ticket stubs in the drum that aren't his. This tells us that statement III is true.

Finally, statement IV is false. Don't confuse the true statement "all tickets have an equal chance of winning" with the false statement that "all persons have an equal chance of winning."

76. **B**

Foreshadowing is used to hint at future plot developments, not to manifest characters' or speakers' emotions. It is not used prominently in lyric poetry or in ballads.

77. **B**

B is correct. While the novel does contain some violent scenes, none of them are graphic enough to be considered unsuitable for young readers. The relationship between Huckleberry Finn and Jim, the escaping slave, is mostly warm and trusting rather than hostile; also, the book was written after the Civil War. It did challenge some attitudes toward race, however, because it portrayed close fellowship between two people of different races and showed a young white man's willingness to take risks on behalf of a black man's freedom. It also frankly uses vocabulary considered acceptable in the 19th century but considered offensive by many today.

78. **A**

A is correct. Haiku are by definition too short to contain much elaborate description. The haiku form does not emphasize logic or direct statements. And while some haiku are humorous and/or contain lifelike details, these qualities do not characterize all haiku poems.

79. **C**

The "To Be or Not to Be" speech is a soliloquy in which Hamlet utters his thoughts aloud at length. It is not an aside, since he is not speaking briefly to the audience in the midst of other action. Since Hamlet is the only one speaking, it is not a dialog, nor is it an example of comic relief, due to the speech's serious tone.

80. **C**

Genes are the sections of the DNA molecule that determine specific traits.

81. **C**

Nuclear energy is nonrenewable. Nuclear energy has potential advantages in providing large quantities of energy from a small amount of source material, but once the process of radioactive decay is nonreversible.

82. **D**

You should first count the number of spaces on the dial. There are 10 spaces. Five spaces equals 90 units, and 90 divided by 5 is 18 units. Each space is worth 18 units. The needle points to about halfway between marks 6 and 7. Thus, one half of 18, plus 6 times 18, is 117. Choice D is the correct reading.

83. **A**

You know that ten thousand contains 4 zeros, or 10^4 in place value. One million contains 10^6, or six zeros. Thus, 10^6 divided by 10^4 is 10^2 or 100. You may divide out 10,000 into one million, but that is the laborious way to solve this. Choice A is correct.

84. **B**

You are challenged to analyze which data you would need to calculate the cost of feeding 2 cats for 7 days. If you calculate the cost for one cat for 7 days, then double the answer, you will have an approximate cost for 2 cats. The total cost for one cat is the cost of a can of food, times the number of cans of food eaten each day by one cat, times 7 days.

85. **B**

One way to approach the problem is to examine each scenario for reasonableness. Regardless of a runner's mile-by-mile pace in a marathon, the runner continually increases the distance covered, and the graph will always move upward, so situation I doesn't go with the graph. The number of house-holds a census taker has left to visit decreases with each visit, so situation II doesn't fit either.

Both situations III and IV are examples of steady growth, so both match the graph. Answer B is therefore correct.

86. **A**

A is the best answer, since the term "casework" is used by political scientists to describe the activities of congressmen on behalf of individual constituents. These activities might include helping an elderly person secure social security benefits, or helping a veteran obtain medical services. Most casework is actually done by congressional staff and may take as much as a third of the staff's time. Answer B fails because pork barrel legislation is rarely if ever intended to help individual citizens. Pork barrel legislation authorizes federal spending for special projects, such as airports, roads, or dams, in the home state or district of a congressperson. It is meant to help the entire district or state. Also, there is no legal entitlement on the part of a citizen to a pork barrel project, such as there is with social security benefits. C is not the answer because lobbying is an activity directed towards members of congress, not one done by them. A lobby-ist attempts to get members of congress to support legislation that will benefit the group that the lobbyist represents. Logrolling, D, is incorrect, because it does not refer to a congressional service for constituents. It refers instead to the congressional practice of trading votes on different bills. Congressman A will vote for Congresswoman B's pork barrel project and in return B will vote for A's pork barrel project.

87. **D**

All are correctly matched.

88. **C**

The frequency of a wave is associated with pitch. Middle C has a frequency of 440 cycles per second. However, wavelength and frequency are directly related by the relationship $\nu = c \, / \, \lambda$ where ν (nu) is the frequency, c is the speed of sound, and λ (lambda) is wavelength.

89. **B** ──

Reptiles are not generally warm-blooded; all other statements are correct.

90. **B** ──

Diseases caused by viruses, bacteria, or protists that invade the body are called infectious diseases. These disease-causing organisms are collectively referred to as germs. Cancers and hereditary diseases are not infectious.

Written Assignment Answer Earning 4 Points

For Demetrius to read this text at an independent level, he needs better word identification skills and better acquaintance with the passage's genre.

If he does not know the meaning of the word "obviously," he not only misses a clue about Jake's personality, but he also goes into decoding mode, which prevents him from enjoying the text and from making connections between the text and other experiences.

Although Demetrius has two major word identification problems—decoding words phonologically and simply not having a sufficient vocabulary to read this passage—the inability I will concentrate on here is the insufficient vocabulary. Two of the words Demetrius had trouble with—"obviously" and "resist"—should be in a fifth grader's vocabulary, and they both follow somewhat unusual phonological models.

Even with better skills in this area, however, Demetrius will still have trouble with comprehension. This passage appears to be from a science fiction book, and he definitely seems unfamiliar with the genre. Thus, his first response to Mrs. Whalen's question concerning what the passage is about is Jake's affinity for video games, which may be the only thing Demetrius grasps well about the passage. When asked what else he knows about Jake, he concentrates on Jake's trouble rather than the trouble for the human race, probably because Demetrius is more accustomed to reading books in which individuals are in trouble of their own (or maybe he's just used to being "in trouble" himself).

Both strategies that Mrs. Whalen should try could be done on either an individual basis just with Demetrius or on a class-wide (or small-group) basis, depending on how many other readers in the class are at Demetrius's level. The first strategy, to increase his vocabulary, is to work with the student(s) to analyze new and unfamiliar words in all their reading. Assuming Demetrius will be worked with on an individual basis, he should read a book that is at his current instructional level (that is he can read it independently). He should make word lists of the words that he is unfamiliar with. He should define them and try to think of (or find) other words that have similar phonemes. For instance, his words and their phonemic analogies in this passage might be "obviously ↔ previously" and "resist ↔ insist." He may need help finding meanings or analogies, so Mrs. Whalen should have occasional short conferences with him to assess whether the word lists and their analogies are useful or even possible. This strategy will theoretically increase the number of words he knows and his ability to decipher unfamiliar words as well.

A second strategy is one that Mrs. Whalen would probably want to do with the whole class, and that would be to introduce the science fiction genre. Surely many students in the class will be acquainted with science fiction at least through movies and television shows, and they will be able to list a number of standard science fiction plots. Mrs. Whalen should diagram some of these plots on a board or overhead so that students will know what to expect as they read science fiction—for example, that big matters such as human survival are often at stake.

Demetrius already shows that he can make connections between what he reads and his own life, but his connections are flawed because he relies too much on his own life and too little on the text. By learning better word-recognition strategies and by recognizing conventions of the genre he is reading, he can raise his comprehension to a higher level.

Features of the Written Assignment Scoring 4

Purpose. The purpose of the assignment has been achieved. All four bullet points listed in the assignment have been addressed in an orderly way. The essay begins by stating the two comprehension needs, then gives evidence for these needs. It goes on to discuss two strategies, with reasons that the writer expects each to have a chance for success.

Application of Content. By indicating specific methods for implementing both strategies, this essay shows that the writer has an idea of how to improve reading, and how to assess whether the proposed methods are successful.

Support. Specific examples from the reading assessment are cited in describing the needs, and specific examples are given for the supposed strategies.

NYSTCE

Multi-Subject Content Specialty Test

Practice Test 2

This practice test is also on CD-ROM in our special interactive NYSTCE TestWare®. It is highly recommended that you first take this exam on computer. You will then have the additional study features and benefits of enforced timed conditions and instant, accurate scoring. See page xi for guidance on how to get the most out of our NYSTCE book and software.

Test Directions For Multiple-Choice Questions

Time: 4 hours

This test contains a multiple-choice section and a section with a single written assignment. You may complete the sections of the test in the order you choose.

Each question in the first section of this booklet is a multiple-choice question with four answer choices. Read each question CAREFULLY and choose the ONE best answer. Record your answer on the answer document in the space that corresponds to the question number. Completely fill in the space that has the same letter as the answer you have chosen. *Use only a No. 2 lead pencil.*

Sample Question:

1.   Which of these cities is farthest north?

    A.   Buffalo

    B.   New York City

    C.   Rochester

    D.   Albany

The correct answer to this question is C. You would indicate that on the answer document as follows:

1.   Ⓐ Ⓑ ● Ⓓ

You should answer all questions. Even if you are unsure of an answer, it is better to guess than not to answer a question at all.

The directions for the written assignment appear later in this test.

Answer Sheet

1. Ⓐ Ⓑ Ⓒ Ⓓ
2. Ⓐ Ⓑ Ⓒ Ⓓ
3. Ⓐ Ⓑ Ⓒ Ⓓ
4. Ⓐ Ⓑ Ⓒ Ⓓ
5. Ⓐ Ⓑ Ⓒ Ⓓ
6. Ⓐ Ⓑ Ⓒ Ⓓ
7. Ⓐ Ⓑ Ⓒ Ⓓ
8. Ⓐ Ⓑ Ⓒ Ⓓ
9. Ⓐ Ⓑ Ⓒ Ⓓ
10. Ⓐ Ⓑ Ⓒ Ⓓ
11. Ⓐ Ⓑ Ⓒ Ⓓ
12. Ⓐ Ⓑ Ⓒ Ⓓ
13. Ⓐ Ⓑ Ⓒ Ⓓ
14. Ⓐ Ⓑ Ⓒ Ⓓ
15. Ⓐ Ⓑ Ⓒ Ⓓ
16. Ⓐ Ⓑ Ⓒ Ⓓ
17. Ⓐ Ⓑ Ⓒ Ⓓ
18. Ⓐ Ⓑ Ⓒ Ⓓ
19. Ⓐ Ⓑ Ⓒ Ⓓ
20. Ⓐ Ⓑ Ⓒ Ⓓ
21. Ⓐ Ⓑ Ⓒ Ⓓ
22. Ⓐ Ⓑ Ⓒ Ⓓ
23. Ⓐ Ⓑ Ⓒ Ⓓ
24. Ⓐ Ⓑ Ⓒ Ⓓ
25. Ⓐ Ⓑ Ⓒ Ⓓ

26. Ⓐ Ⓑ Ⓒ Ⓓ
27. Ⓐ Ⓑ Ⓒ Ⓓ
28. Ⓐ Ⓑ Ⓒ Ⓓ
29. Ⓐ Ⓑ Ⓒ Ⓓ
30. Ⓐ Ⓑ Ⓒ Ⓓ
31. Ⓐ Ⓑ Ⓒ Ⓓ
32. Ⓐ Ⓑ Ⓒ Ⓓ
33. Ⓐ Ⓑ Ⓒ Ⓓ
34. Ⓐ Ⓑ Ⓒ Ⓓ
35. Ⓐ Ⓑ Ⓒ Ⓓ
36. Ⓐ Ⓑ Ⓒ Ⓓ
37. Ⓐ Ⓑ Ⓒ Ⓓ
38. Ⓐ Ⓑ Ⓒ Ⓓ
39. Ⓐ Ⓑ Ⓒ Ⓓ
40. Ⓐ Ⓑ Ⓒ Ⓓ
41. Ⓐ Ⓑ Ⓒ Ⓓ
42. Ⓐ Ⓑ Ⓒ Ⓓ
43. Ⓐ Ⓑ Ⓒ Ⓓ
44. Ⓐ Ⓑ Ⓒ Ⓓ
45. Ⓐ Ⓑ Ⓒ Ⓓ
46. Ⓐ Ⓑ Ⓒ Ⓓ
47. Ⓐ Ⓑ Ⓒ Ⓓ
48. Ⓐ Ⓑ Ⓒ Ⓓ
49. Ⓐ Ⓑ Ⓒ Ⓓ
50. Ⓐ Ⓑ Ⓒ Ⓓ

51. Ⓐ Ⓑ Ⓒ Ⓓ
52. Ⓐ Ⓑ Ⓒ Ⓓ
53. Ⓐ Ⓑ Ⓒ Ⓓ
54. Ⓐ Ⓑ Ⓒ Ⓓ
55. Ⓐ Ⓑ Ⓒ Ⓓ
56. Ⓐ Ⓑ Ⓒ Ⓓ
57. Ⓐ Ⓑ Ⓒ Ⓓ
58. Ⓐ Ⓑ Ⓒ Ⓓ
59. Ⓐ Ⓑ Ⓒ Ⓓ
60. Ⓐ Ⓑ Ⓒ Ⓓ
61. Ⓐ Ⓑ Ⓒ Ⓓ
62. Ⓐ Ⓑ Ⓒ Ⓓ
63. Ⓐ Ⓑ Ⓒ Ⓓ
64. Ⓐ Ⓑ Ⓒ Ⓓ
65. Ⓐ Ⓑ Ⓒ Ⓓ
66. Ⓐ Ⓑ Ⓒ Ⓓ
67. Ⓐ Ⓑ Ⓒ Ⓓ
68. Ⓐ Ⓑ Ⓒ Ⓓ
69. Ⓐ Ⓑ Ⓒ Ⓓ
70. Ⓐ Ⓑ Ⓒ Ⓓ
71. Ⓐ Ⓑ Ⓒ Ⓓ
72. Ⓐ Ⓑ Ⓒ Ⓓ
73. Ⓐ Ⓑ Ⓒ Ⓓ
74. Ⓐ Ⓑ Ⓒ Ⓓ
75. Ⓐ Ⓑ Ⓒ Ⓓ

76. Ⓐ Ⓑ Ⓒ Ⓓ
77. Ⓐ Ⓑ Ⓒ Ⓓ
78. Ⓐ Ⓑ Ⓒ Ⓓ
79. Ⓐ Ⓑ Ⓒ Ⓓ
80. Ⓐ Ⓑ Ⓒ Ⓓ
81. Ⓐ Ⓑ Ⓒ Ⓓ
82. Ⓐ Ⓑ Ⓒ Ⓓ
83. Ⓐ Ⓑ Ⓒ Ⓓ
84. Ⓐ Ⓑ Ⓒ Ⓓ
85. Ⓐ Ⓑ Ⓒ Ⓓ
86. Ⓐ Ⓑ Ⓒ Ⓓ
87. Ⓐ Ⓑ Ⓒ Ⓓ
88. Ⓐ Ⓑ Ⓒ Ⓓ
89. Ⓐ Ⓑ Ⓒ Ⓓ
90. Ⓐ Ⓑ Ⓒ Ⓓ

Practice Test 2

1. The following data represent the ages of seventeen people enrolled in an adult education class:

$$32, 33, 34, 35, 36, 42, 43, 50, 51, 61, 61, 62, 63, 68, 79$$

Adina organized the data as follows:

3	2, 3, 4, 5, 6
4	2, 2, 2, 3
5	0, 1
6	1, 1, 2, 3, 8
7	9

The display Adina used is called which one of the following?

A. box-and-whisker plot

B. stem-and-leaf plot

C. cumulative histogram

D. pictograph

2. When infants and their mothers have strong attachments,

   A. the parents are of higher economic status.

   B. the parents are usually strict disciplinarians.

   C. the children generally become socially competent.

   D. there is no correlation with social skills.

3. The Ungerville cafeteria offers a choice for lunch on its Mexican Day special. You can choose either a taco or burrito. You can choose a filling of chicken, beef, or beans, and you have a choice of six different beverages. To determine the total number of possible different lunches consisting of a taco or burrito, one filling, and one beverage, which mathematical process would be most useful?

   A. factor tree

   B. conditional probability

   C. factorials

   D. counting principle

4. Research on the effectiveness of day care shows that

   A. IQ scores will always go up for children in day care.

   B. the children will have better social skills than those not in day care.

   C. intellectual performance of underprivileged children will increase.

   D. negative effects in forming relationships with others may occur.

5. A family consists of two parents, three sons, and two daughters. The mother clearly favors her eldest son, the "momma's boy." This son does very well in school and in his career. This exemplifies the concept of

   A. ego involvement.

   B. meritocracy.

   C. experimental effect.

   D. self-fulfilling prophecy.

6. A topographical map is one that shows the

   A. population distribution of a region.

   B. climate of a region.

   C. landscape and water of a region.

   D. political boundaries of a region.

7. The spinner shown below is divided into equal sections.

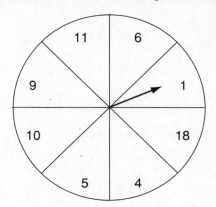

What is the probability of landing in a section with a number that is a multiple of 3?

A. ⅝

B. ⅚

C. ⅜

D. ³⁄₁₀

8. The culture of a people consists of its

      I. religion.
     II. language.
   III. social organization.

A. I only

B. I & II

C. II & III

D. I, II & III

9. The monotheism of the ancient Hebrews spread throughout the ancient world and led to the formation of Christianity and Islam. This is an example of

A. cultural diffusion.

B. religious homogeneity.

C. global interdependence.

D. demographic data.

10. A nomadic lifestyle would most likely be found in the

    A. English countryside.

    B. Scandinavian fjords.

    C. Sahara desert.

    D. Canadian Rockies.

11. Andy Warhol's portrait of Marilyn Monroe was done in which genre?

    A. Impressionism.

    B. Cubism.

    C. Pop art.

    D. Dadaism.

12. Which of the following are research tools?

    I.   the library
    II. the Internet
    III. interviews

    A. I only

    B. I & II

    C. I & III

    D. I, II & III

13. This form of exercise emphasizes breathing techniques, stretching, and relaxation:

    A. yoga.

    B. pilates.

    C. aerobic conditioning.

    D. spinning.

14. BMI represents

    A. body movement index.

    B. body mass index.

    C. binary motion index.

    D. bilingual maturational index.

15. Physical education goals for children include all of the following EXCEPT

    A.   aerobic conditioning.

    B.   sportsmanship.

    C.   joining a sports team.

    D.   strength training.

16.

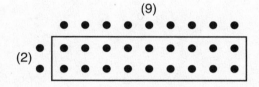

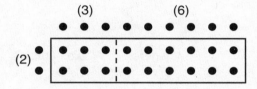

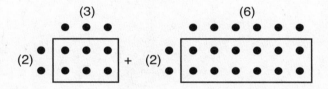

The diagram above could be used to model which one of the following?

    A.   distributive property

    B.   associative property of addition

    C.   commutative property of multiplication

    D.   associative property of multiplication

17. Ms. Rosenberg writes these words on the chalkboard:

        Igneous
        Sedimentary
        Metamorphic

She is going to teach a lesson on

    A.   geography.

    B.   biology.

    C.   chemistry.

    D.   geology.

18. Given the numbers –2, –1, -½, 0, 1, 3, which Venn diagram expresses the characteristics of the numbers correctly by type?

A.   Integers   Whole numbers

1, 3

0

–2, –1

$-\dfrac{1}{2}$ Nonpositive numbers

C.   Integers   Whole numbers

1, 3

0,
–1, –2

$-\dfrac{1}{2}$ Nonpositive numbers

B.   Integers   Whole numbers

0, 1, 3

–2, –1

$-\dfrac{1}{2}$ Nonpositive numbers

D.   Integers   Whole numbers

1, 3

0    $-\dfrac{1}{2}$

–2, –1

Nonpositive numbers

19. The diagram below displays a factor tree for the number *x*.

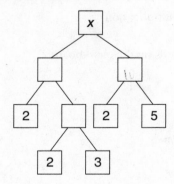

What is the value of *x*?

A. 14

B. 80

C. 100

D. 120

20. The average speed of a plane was 600 kilometers per hour. How long did it take the plane to travel 120 kilometers?

A. 0.2 hours

B. 0.5 hours

C. 0.7 hours

D. 5 hours

21. One type of allergic reaction results in constriction of the bronchial tubes, which interferes with the passage of air into and out of the lungs. This type of allergic reaction is most closely associated with

A. emphysema.

B. asthma.

C. bronchitis.

D. meningitis.

22. Given the point (1, 1), which one of the following points is the shortest distance from the point (1, 1)?

A. (5, 0)

B. (3, 4)

C. (−3, 2)

D. (0, −3)

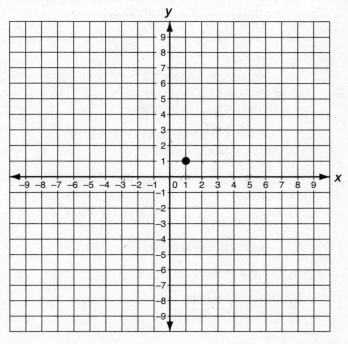

23. An example of a bone-strengthening exercise is

    A. weight lifting

    B. swimming

    C. bicycling

    D. meditation

24. Which of the following graphs best represents your height above the ground when riding a ferris wheel?

    A.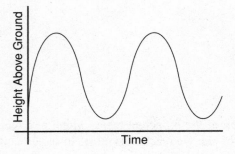

    C.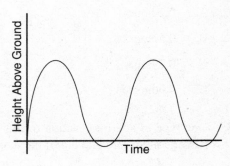

    B.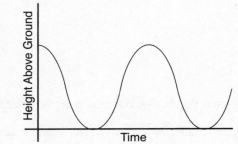

    D.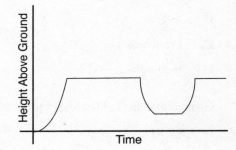

25. A teacher gave the following homework assignment to her class for the weekend: While riding in a car or walking on a street, bring paper and pencil. Look at car license plates and think of a phrase to go with the letters. For example:

    CST — Carrie Stood There
    NJL — Not Just Luck

    Write down three plate letters and the phrase that you made up. This teacher was trying to develop her students'

    A. auditory processing skills.

    B. kinesthetic awareness.

    C. language skills.

    D. visual tracking.

26. The price of a sweater was reduced by 50% during a clearance sale. In order to sell at the original price, by what percent must the new price be increased?

    A.   200%

    B.   50%

    C.   75%

    D.   100%

27. A teacher is doing a career awareness unit for his sixth-grade class. Which of the following would be appropriate?

       I.   Have each child take a personality inventory.
       II.   Use small groups to conduct class research projects on a particular field.
       III.   Bring in representatives of a number of careers to speak to the class.

    A.   I only

    B.   I & II

    C.   II & III

    D.   I, II, & III

28. The term *colonialism* would be used to describe

    A.   Spanish conquests in the sixteenth century.

    B.   the medieval system of guilds.

    C.   Haitian independence from France in 1804.

    D.   the Catholic Church's usage of indulgences.

29. A recipe for spinach pasta uses the following ingredients:

INGREDIENT	AMOUNT
Oranges	2
Scallions	¾ bunch
Cream	1 cup
Angel-hair pasta	12 oz.
Baby spinach	3 bags

This recipe serves 4 people and takes 17 minutes to prepare. To serve 10 people, how many ounces of angel-hair pasta are required?

A. 15

B. 20

C. 25

D. 30

30. Mr. DeVito's class is studying immigration to the United States. Which concept would be appropriate to introduce?

A. divestment

B. assimilation

C. feudalism

D. nationalism

31. Ms. Posner wants her students to have an idea about the subject they will be studying before they begin. Which strategy should she use?

A. outlining

B. previewing

C. rereading

D. note taking

32. A child in a second-grade class reads in a word-by-word manner and often stops between words. Which technique would NOT be useful to help the child?

   A.   using reading material at a lower level

   B.   giving experiences in choral reading

   C.   reading poetry

   D.   emphasizing left-right tracking

33. Given the following numerical computation,

$$\frac{5+3(4-2)^2}{4}$$

which operation should be performed first?

   A.   addition

   B.   subtraction

   C.   division

   D.   powering

34. A teacher takes a beaker of colored water and pours it from a long, slim vessel into a short, wide vessel. The teacher is illustrating the principle of

   A.   natural selection.

   B.   deduction.

   C.   conservation.

   D.   accommodation.

35 Which of the following were early influences on the Constitution of the United States?

   I.   The Magna Carta
   II.   The Declaration of Independence
   III.   The Articles of Confederation

   A.   I only

   B.   II only

   C.   I & II

   D.   I, II & III

36. Given the following balanced scales,

and

which one of the following is correct?

A.

B.

C.

D.

37. Which of the following would be considered proteins?

    I.   chicken
    II. shellfish
    III. cereal

A. I only

B. I & II

C. II & III

D. I, II & III

38. All of the following are aerobic exercises EXCEPT

A. jumping jacks.

B. walking.

C. squats.

D. swimming.

39. Which of these painters are considered Impressionists?

       I.   Monet
     II.   Rembrandt
   III.   da Vinci

A.   I only

B.   II only

C.   I & II

D.   I, II & III

40. The tango, samba, cha-cha, and bossa nova are all examples of

A.   African dance.

B.   Mid-eastern dance.

C.   Latin American dance.

D.   Indian dance.

41. Tchaikovsky, Rimsky-Korsakov, and Mussorgsky were

A.   Russian composers.

B.   Russian dancers.

C.   Polish musicians.

D.   American composers.

42. Ms. Rodriguez is teaching social studies and outlining skills. What would be the most appropriate heading for the following outline list?

       A. _____
       1.   More government regulation
       2.   Reform of corrupt political practices
       3.   Concern for the problems of workers

A.   Reconstruction

B.   The Progressive Era

C.   The Cold War Era

D.   The New Frontier

43. The widespread use of computers has led to a national concern over

    A. increased pollution of the environment.

    B. guarding the right to privacy.

    C. protection of the right to petition.

    D. a decrease in television viewing.

44. Jose conducted a survey of 20 classmates to determine their favorite breakfast drink. The results are shown in the following table:

BEVERAGE	NUMBER OF CLASSMATES
Orange juice	6
Milk	4
Tea	2
Soda	2
Other	6

To create a pie chart for this data, how many degrees should be used for the sector representing milk?

    A. 40°

    B. 72°

    C. 86°

    D. 90°

Questions 45 and 46 refer to the following paragraph:

1. One potential hideaway that until now has been completely ignored is De Witt Isle, off the coast of Australia. 2. Its assets are 4,000 acres of jagged rocks, tangled undergrowth and trees twisted and bent by battering winds. 3. Settlers will have avoided it like the plague, but bandicoots (rat-like marsupials native to Australia), wallabies, eagles, and penguins think De Witt is just fine. 4. Why De Witt? 5. So does Jane Cooper, 18, a pert Melbourne high school graduate, who emigrated there with three goats, several chickens, and a number of cats brought along to stand guard against the bandicoots. 6. "I was frightened at the way life is lived today in our cities," says Jane. 7. "I wanted to be alone, to have some time to think and find out about myself."

45. Which of these changes is grammatically correct?

    A. Sentence 1—Change *has been* to *have been*.

    B. Sentence 7—Delete *to have*.

    C. Sentence 3—Change *will have* to *have*.

    D. Sentence 5—Change *emigrated* to *immigrated*.

46. Which one of these changes would make the passage flow more logically?

    A.   Put Sentence 5 before Sentence 4.

    B.   Begin the passage with Sentence 4.

    C.   In Sentence 1, delete *off the coast of Australia*.

    D.   Begin the passage with Sentence 2.

47. In teaching higher-level reading skills, Mr. Chin wants his students to recognize editorializing. Which of these best illustrates editorializing?

    A.   Robert McGee was given a well-deserved round of applause.

    B.   Also discussed at the Board meeting was the condition of the South Street School.

    C.   The company received its charter in 1912.

    D.   Just before he sat down, Mr. McPherson asked, "Has the homework been completed?"

48. The creation of wildlife refuges and the enforcement of game hunting laws are measures of

    A.   conservation.

    B.   exploitation.

    C.   conservatism.

    D.   population control.

Questions 49 and 50 are based on the following excerpt:

" . . . But there are some occasions . . . when he considers certain laws to be so unjust as to render obedience to them a dishonor. He then openly and civilly breaks them and quietly suffers the penalty for their breach . . . "

49. This passage supports the use of

    A.   military force.

    B.   appeasement.

    C.   civil disobedience.

    D.   retaliation.

50. Which leader based his actions on the philosophy expressed in this passage?

    A.   Vladimir I. Lenin

    B.   Simón Bolívar

    C.   Yasir Arafat

    D.   Mohandas K. Gandhi

Questions 51 and 52 are based on the following poem.

In a unit on ecology for a fifth-grade class, the teacher presents the following poem:

> The days be hot, the nights be cold,
> But cross we must, we rush for gold.
> The plants be short, the roots spread wide,
> Me leg she hurts, thorn's in me side.
> I fall, I crawl, I scream, I rave,
> Tiz me life that I must save.
> How can it be, I've come undone,
> Here 'neath this blazin' eternal sun?
> The days be hot, the nights be cold,
> Me lonely bones alone grow old.

51. What physical setting is the poem describing?

    A. a forest

    B. a tundra

    C. a swamp

    D. a desert

52. The type of writing in the poem can best be described as

    A. colloquial.

    B. narrative.

    C. metaphoric.

    D. factual.

53. Use the diagram below to answer the question that follows.

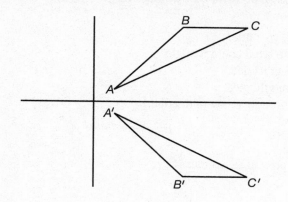

In the figure above, triangle *ABC* is transformed to triangle *A'B'C'*. This type of transformation is called which one of the following?

A. reflection

B. dilation

C. rotation

D. translation

54. Mrs. Nemetski is doing a unit on literary genres. She presents the class with the following story:

   A fisherman was trying to lure fish to rise so that he could hook them. He took his bagpipes to the banks of the river and played them. No fish rose out of the water. Next he cast his net into the river and when he brought it back, the net was filled with fish. Then he took his bagpipes again and as he played, the fish leaped up in the net.

   "Ah, now you dance when I play," he said to an old fish.

   "Yes," said the old one, "when you are in a person's power you must do as he commands."

To which genre does this story belong?

A. narrative

B. character analysis

C. editorial

D. fable

Questions 55–57 refer to the following:

A flea and a fly in a flue
Were caught, so what could they do?
Said the fly, "Let us flee."
"Let us fly," said the flea.
So they flew through a flaw in the flue.

—*Anonymous*

55. What form of poetry did the teacher present to her class?

    A. an elegy

    B. a ballad

    C. a limerick

    D. haiku

56. The repetition of the *fl* in *flea, fly,* and *flue* is called

    A. alliteration

    B. onomatopoeia

    C. imagery

    D. symbolism

57. A follow-up activity for this poem might include:

    I.   having students illustrate the poem.
    II. asking students to write their own poem in this form.
    III. having students clap their hands to practice the rhythm of the poem.

    A. I only

    B. I and II

    C. I and III

    D. I, II, and III

58. Given that the following sentence is true,

    "If turnips are not blue, then the sky is falling"

    which one of the following sentences MUST also be true?

    A. If turnips are blue, then the sky is not falling.

    B. If the sky is falling, then turnips are not blue.

    C. If the sky is not falling, then turnips are blue.

    D. If the sky is not falling, then turnips are not blue.

59. A cycling of materials is represented in the diagram below.

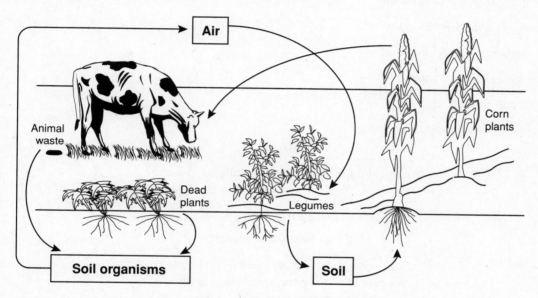

    Which statement is supported by events shown in the diagram?

    A. Materials are cycled between living organisms, only.

    B. Materials are cycled between heterotrophic organisms, only.

    C. Materials are cycled between the living and nonliving components of the environment.

    D. Materials are cycled between the physical factors of the environment by the processes of condensation and evaporation.

60. The proverb "Death is a black camel, which kneels at the gates of all" is an example of

    A. alliteration.

    B. simile.

    C. metaphor.

    D. hyperbole.

61. Mr. Chan is teaching his class how to recognize propaganda. He presents his class with the slogan "Buy a brand-new Whizzer bike like the ones all your friends have." Which propaganda device is he illustrating?

    A. bandwagon

    B. testimonial

    C. card-stacking

    D. glittering generality

62. Laura *tried* to do her best.

    The judge *tried* the case harshly.

    These two sentences illustrate

    A. grammatical errors.

    B. synonyms and antonyms.

    C. rules of spelling.

    D. words with multiple meanings.

Question 63 is based on the following poem:

Richard Cory

By Edwin Arlington Robinson

Whenever Richard Cory went down town,
We people on the pavement looked at him:
He was a gentleman from sole to crown,
Clean favored, and imperially slim.

And he was always quietly arrayed,
And he was always human when he talked;
But still he fluttered pulses when he said,
"Good-morning," and he glittered when he walked.

And he was rich—yes, richer than a king—
And admirably schooled in every grace;
In fine we thought that he was everything
To make us wish that we were in his place.

So on we worked, and waited for the light,
And went without the meat, and cursed the bread;
And Richard Cory, one calm summer night,
Went home and put a bullet through his head.

63. Richard Cory represents the

    A. wisdom of age.

    B. happiness of love.

    C. deception of appearance.

    D. contentment of youth.

64. A teacher presents the following sentences to her class. Which one is correct?

    A. I don't like hiking as much as I like cross-country skiing.

    B. I don't like to hike as much as I like cross-country skiing.

    C. I don't like hiking as much as I like to ski cross-country.

    D. I don't like to hike as much as I like going cross-country skiing.

65. The flowchart below shows part of the water's cycle. The question marks indicate the part of the flow-chart that has been deliberately left blank.

    Which process should be shown in place of the question marks to best complete the flowchart?

    A. condensation

    B. deposition

    C. evaporation

    D. infiltration

66. Joshua's tie has three colors. One-half of the tie is blue, one-fifth is brown, and the rest is burgundy. What fraction of the tie is burgundy?

    A. $^5/_7$

    B. $^2/_{10}$

    C. $^3/_{10}$

    D. $^7/_{10}$

67. Economic resources include all of the following EXCEPT

    A. land

    B. labor.

    C. capital.

    D. values.

68. Consider the following:

    I.   Education
    II. Age
    III. Sex
    IV. Health

    Of the factors above, which affect income in one's career choice?

    A. I and II.

    B. I, II, and III.

    C. I, II, and IV.

    D. All of the above.

69. Mr. Weintraub wants to introduce a unit on consumer awareness. Which one of the following would NOT be a useful introduction?

    A. taking a class trip to a supermarket

    B. discussing the work of Ralph Nader

    C. reading a biography of Donald Trump

    D. doing a price comparison of items in different supermarkets

70. Dawn draws a picture of a parallelogram on the board. All of the following are properties of a parallelogram EXCEPT

    A. opposite sides are equal.

    B. opposite angles are equal.

    C. diagonals are equal.

    D. diagonals bisect each other.

71.

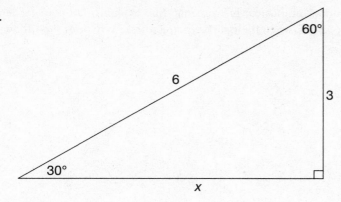

Given the figure above, which one of the following equations could NOT be used to calculate the value of x?

A. $\sin 60° = \dfrac{x}{6}$

B. $x^2 + 3^2 = 6^2$

C. $\tan 30° = \dfrac{3}{x}$

D. $3^2 + 6^2 = x^2$

72. In studying American history, a class is shown the film Modern Times starring Charlie Chaplin. The film illustrates the

A. class struggle.

B. evils of slavery.

C. negatives of industrialization.

D. horrors of war.

73. A microprocessor is used in which of these items?

A. calculators

B. incandescent lamps

C. jet engines

D. telegraphs

74. Ms. Yashamura is teaching her class a unit on musical instruments. She explains that percussion instruments are instruments that produce sound when their surfaces are struck. Which of the following are percussion instruments?

> I. drums
> II. bassoon
> III. cymbals

   A.   I only

   B.   I & II

   C.   II & III

   D.   I & III

75. Which composer is most associated with marching music?

   A.   John Philip Sousa

   B.   Johann Sebastian Bach

   C.   Cab Calloway

   D.   Stephen Sondheim

76. After a class has studied ancient Egyptian history, the teacher wants to show students some ancient Egyptian art and artifacts. Which would be the most appropriate place to take the students?

   A.   The Museum of the Moving Image

   B.   The Whitney Museum

   C.   The Metropolitan Museum of Art

   D.   The Guggenheim Museum

77.

A number diminished by 5 is 3 more than 7 times the number.

If we let *n* represent the number referred to above, which one of the following best represents the statement shown above?

   A. $n + 5 > 7n + 3$

   B. $n - 5 > 7n + 3$

   C. $n - 5 > 7(n + 3)$

   D. $n - 5 = 7n + 3$

78. According to research, what is true about suicide?

    A.   It occurs more often in males than in females.

    B.   It occurs more often during the day.

    C.   It is successful every time it is attempted.

    D.   It occurs more often after widowhood.

79. Mr. Jones, an art teacher, wants to teach the concept of perspective. In order to show distance, how should he have the students draw something in a work to show that it is in the background?

    A.   Draw the object where two lines meet.

    B.   Draw the object behind another object.

    C.   Draw the object darker than surrounding objects.

    D.   Draw the object lower in the picture.

80. In teaching social studies, a teacher puts these two quotations on the board:

    "By uniting we stand, by dividing we fall."
    John Dickinson, 1768

    "Yes, we must all hang together or most assuredly we shall hang separately."
    Benjamin Franklin, 1776

    These quotations illustrate the concept of

    A.   nationalism.

    B.   confederacy.

    C.   equality.

    D.   totalitarianism.

81. Diagrams, tables, and graphs are used by scientists mainly to

    A.   design a research plan for an experiment.

    B.   test a hypothesis.

    C.   organize data.

    D.   predict an independent variable.

82. Mrs. Korenge is teaching a unit on ecology. She tells her class,

> "A new type of fuel gives off excessive amounts of smoke. Before this type of fuel is used, an ecologist would most likely want to know . . .

    A.   what effect the smoke will have on the environment."

    B.   how much it will cost to produce the fuel."

    C.   how long it will take to produce the fuel."

    D.   if the fuel will be widely accepted by the consumer."

83. Mr. Galili is teaching the Civil War and its aftermath in social studies. He explains that the Jim Crow laws were attempts by

    A.   the federal government to improve the status of African Americans and Native Americans.

    B.   the state and local governments to restrict the freedom of African Americans.

    C.   the states to ban such organizations as the Ku Klux Klan.

    D.   the Radical Republicans in Congress to carry out reconstruction plans.

84. Pregnant women who drink alcohol are associated with

    A.   lower weight in the fetus.

    B.   higher heart rate in the fetus.

    C.   more premature births and stillbirths.

    D.   no differences from those women who do not drink.

85. The diagram below represents the percentage of total incoming solar radiation that is affected by clouds.

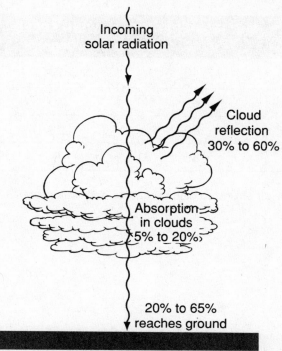

What percentage of incoming solar radiation is reflected or absorbed on cloudy days?

A.   100%

B.   35% to 80%

C.   5% to 30%

D.   0%

86. The data table below shows average daily air temperature, wind speed, and relative humidity for four days at a single location.

DAY	AIR TEMPERATURE °C	WIND SPEED (mph)	HUMIDITY (%)
Monday	40	15	60
Tuesday	65	10	75
Wednesday	80	20	30
Thursday	85	0	95

On which day was the air closest to being saturated with water vapor?

A. Monday

B. Tuesday

C. Wednesday

D. Thursday

87. Ms. Posner is doing a unit on plants with her class. She took three seeds and put them in three different locations. Each seedling was grown in the same soil and each received the same amount of water. At the end of six days, the results were put on this table:

DATA TABLE		
LOCATION	HEIGHT (cm)	LEAF COLOR
Sunny windowsill	7	Green
Indirect sunlight	9	Green
Closed closet	11	Whitish yellow

What hypothesis was most likely being tested here?

A. A plant grown in the dark will not be green.

B. The type of soil a plant is grown in influences how tall it will be.

C. Plants need water to grow.

D. Plants grown in red light are taller than plants grown in green light.

88. Mrs. Blanchard uses a strategy in which she has her students copy key words from the board and listen to cue words that reinforce these key words. Next, the students write down information about the key words using lines as bullets. Then the students write down the questions that are presented and the answers to these questions. Next, the students read the textbook at home and try to find the key concepts discussed in class. Finally, these concepts are written in the students' own words in their notebooks.

    Which skill is Mrs. Blanchard trying to reinforce by using this method?

    A. creative writing

    B. organizational strategies

    C. note taking

    D. comprehension of textbook chapter

89. Joel's reading teacher gives his parents some activities to do at home to develop his phonological awareness. The parents are to say a word. Joel must then repeat the word, leaving out the first sound. For example, the child would say *an* after the parent says *fan*. Which phonological skill is this activity developing in the child?

    A. reverse manipulation

    B. deletion manipulation

    C. segmentation naming

    D. substitution manipulation

90. The following symbols represent

    A. bass clef.

    B. musical scales.

    C. chords to be played.

    D. time signature.

Directions for the Written Assignment

This section of the test consists of a written assignment. You are to prepare a written response of about 150–300 words on the assigned topic. You should use your time to plan, write, review, and edit your response to the assignment.

Read the assignment carefully before you begin to write. Think about how you will organize your response. You may use any blank space provided on the following pages to make notes, write an outline, or otherwise prepare your response. However, your score will be based solely on the response you write on the lined pages of your answer document.

Your response will be evaluated on the basis of the following criteria:

- **PURPOSE**: Fulfill the charge of the assignment
- **APPLICATION OF CONTENT**: Accurately and effectively apply the relevant knowledge and skills.
- **SUPPORT**: Support the response with appropriate examples and/or sound reasoning reflecting an understanding of the relevant knowledge and skills.

Your response will be evaluated on the criteria above, not on writing ability. However, your response must be communicated clearly enough to permit valid judgment of your knowledge and skills. The final version of your response should conform to the conventions of edited American English. This should be your original work, written in your own words, and not copied or paraphrased from some other work.

Be sure to write about the assigned topics. Please write legibly. You may not use any reference materials during the test. Remember to review what you have written and make any changes you think will improve your response.

Written Assignment

Use the information below to complete the exercise that follows.

In a class of 20 fourth grade students, five are reading two grade levels above, ten are reading at grade level, and five are reading 1-2 grade levels below. How would you create a meaningful comprehension lesson that reaches all students? The lesson must illustrate the principles of a balanced reading program. Explain how you will ensure that reading comprehension is addressed. Specifically, describe a pre-reading activity you would use with a text, two instructional techniques that you would use to bolster comprehension of a story, and a post-reading activity that would help assess comprehension.

Practice Test Answer Sheets

Begin your essay on this page. If necessary, continue on the next page.

_____

_____

_____

_____

_____

_____

_____

_____

_____

_____

_____

_____

_____

_____

Continue on the next page if necessary.

Continuation of your essay from previous page, if necessary.

Continuation of your essay from previous page, if necessary.

Continuation of your essay from previous page, if necessary.

NYSTCE

Multi-Subject Content Specialty Test

Answers:
Practice Test 2

Answer Key

1. (B)	26. (D)	51. (D)	76. (C)
2. (C)	27. (C)	52. (A)	77. (D)
3. (D)	28. (A)	53. (A)	78. (A)
4. (C)	29. (D)	54. (D)	79. (C)
5. (D)	30. (B)	55. (C)	80. (A)
6. (C)	31. (B)	56. (A)	81. (C)
7. (C)	32. (D)	57. (D)	82. (A)
8. (D)	33. (B)	58. (C)	83. (B)
9. (A)	34. (C)	59. (C)	84. (C)
10. (C)	35. (D)	60. (C)	85. (B)
11. (C)	36. (C)	61. (A)	86. (D)
12. (D)	37. (B)	62. (D)	87. (A)
13. (A)	38. (C)	63. (C)	88. (C)
14. (B)	39. (A)	64. (A)	89. (B)
15. (C)	40. (C)	65. (C)	90. (D)
16. (A)	41. (A)	66. (C)	
17. (D)	42. (B)	67. (D)	
18. (A)	43. (B)	68. (D)	
19. (D)	44. (B)	69. (C)	
20. (A)	45. (C)	70. (C)	
21. (B)	46. (A)	71. (D)	
22. (B)	47. (A)	72. (C)	
23. (A)	48. (A)	73. (A)	
24. (A)	49. (C)	74. (D)	
25. (C)	50. (D)	75. (A)	

Diagnostic Grid: Questions Sorted by Subarea

SUBAREA I. LANGUAGE ARTS	QUESTION NO.
1. Understand the foundations of reading development.	32
2. Understand skills and strategies involved in reading comprehension.	31, 88
3. Understand and apply reading skills and strategies for various purposes (including information and understanding, critical analysis and evaluation, literary response, and social interaction).	12, 89
4. Understand processes for generating, developing, revising, editing, and presenting/publishing written texts.	45, 46, 47, 64
5. Understand and apply writing skills and strategies for various purposes (including information and understanding, critical analysis and evaluation, literary response and personal expression, and social interaction).	25, 61, 62
6. Understand skills and strategies involved in listening and speaking for various purposes (including information and understanding, critical analysis and evaluation, literary response and expression, and social interaction).	51, 57
7. Understand and apply techniques of literary analysis to works of fiction, drama, poetry, and nonfiction.	52, 56, 60, 63
8. Demonstrate knowledge of literature, including literature from diverse cultures and literature for children/adolescents.	54, 55
SUBAREA II. MATHEMATICS	
9. Understand formal and informal reasoning processes, including logic and simple proofs, and apply problem-solving techniques and strategies in a variety of contexts.	20, 58
10. Use mathematical terminology and symbols to interpret, represent, and communicate mathematical ideas and information.	1, 16, 18, 19, 22, 44
11. Understand skills and concepts related to number and numeration, and apply these concepts to real-world situations.	26, 66
12. Understand patterns and apply the principles and properties of linear algebraic relations and functions.	33, 36, 77
13. Understand the principles and properties of geometry and trigonometry, and apply them to model and solve problems.	53, 70, 71
14. Understand concepts, principles, skills, and procedures related to the customary and metric systems of measurement.	29
15. Understand concepts and skills related to data analysis, probability, and statistics, and apply this understanding to evaluate and interpret data and to solve problems.	7, 24
SUBAREA III. SCIENCE AND TECHNOLOGY	
16. Understand and apply the principles and processes of scientific inquiry and investigation.	65, 81, 87
17. Understand and apply concepts, principles, and theories pertaining to the physical setting (including earth science, chemistry, and physics).	17, 85
18. Understand and apply concepts, principles, and theories pertaining to the living environment.	48, 59
19. Apply knowledge of technology and the principles of engineering design.	82
20. Understand the relationships among and common themes that connect mathematics, science, and technology and the application of knowledge and skills in these disciplines to other areas of learning.	73, 86

(continued)

227

IV. SOCIAL STUDIES	QUESTION NO.
21. Understand major ideas, eras, themes, developments, and turning points in the history of New York State, the United States, and the world.	9, 28, 35
22. Understand geographic concepts and phenomena and analyze the interrelationships of geography, society, and culture in the development of New York State, the United States, and the world.	6, 8
23. Understand concepts and phenomena related to human development and interactions (including anthropological, psychological, and sociological concepts).	10, 34
24. Understand economic and political principles, concepts, and systems, and relate this knowledge to historical and contemporary developments in New York State, the United States, and the world.	42, 50, 67
25. Understand the roles, rights, and the responsibilities of citizenship in the United States and the skills, knowledge, and attitudes necessary for successful participation in civic life.	30, 49
26. Understand and apply skills related to social studies, including gathering, organizing, mapping, evaluating, interpreting, and displaying information.	80, 83
SUBAREA V. FINE ARTS	
27. Understand the concepts, techniques, and materials of the visual arts; analyze works of visual arts; and understand the cultural dimensions and contributions of the visual arts.	11, 39, 76, 79
28. Understand concepts, techniques, and materials for producing, listening to, and responding to music; analyze works of music; and understand the cultural dimensions and contributions of music.	41, 74, 75, 90
29. Understand concepts, techniques, and materials related to theater and dance; analyze works of drama and dance; and understand the cultural dimensions and contributions of drama and dance.	40, 72
SUBAREA VI. HEALTH AND FITNESS	
30. Understand basic principles and practices of personal, interpersonal, and community health and safety; and apply related knowledge and skills (e.g., decision making, problem solving) to promote personal well-being.	3, 21, 37
31. Understand physical education concepts and practices related to the development of personal living skills.	14, 15
32. Understand health-related physical fitness concepts and practices.	13, 23, 38, 78
SUBAREA VII. FAMILY AND CONSUMER SCIENCE AND CAREER DEVELOPMENT	
33. Understand concepts and practices related to child development and care and apply knowledge of family and interpersonal relationships.	2, 4, 5, 21, 84
34. Understand skills and procedures related to consumer economics and personal resource management.	43, 69
35. Understand basic principles of career development; apply processes and skills for seeking and maintaining employment; and demonstrate knowledge of workplace skills, behaviors, and responsibilities.	27

Detailed Explanations of Answers

1. **B**

   A stem-and-leaf plot shows the data in numerically increasing order. The leaf is the last digit to the right and the stem is the remaining digit or digits disregarding the leaf. For example, given the number 27, 7 is the leaf, 2 is the stem

stem	leaf
2	7

2. **C**

   Studies have shown the importance of the infant–mother bond. It is the first socialization for the newborn and leads to social competence. It has no correlation, however, with a mother's economic situation, nor does it relate to discipline.

3. **D**

   The counting principle states the following:

   > *If there are m different ways to choose a first event and n different ways to choose a second event, then there are m × n different ways of choosing the first event followed by the second event.*

There are three stages in this example:

Stage 1	*taco or burrito*	*2 choices*
Stage 2	*filling*	*3 choices*
Stage 3	*beverage*	*6 choices*

Total possible different outcomes: $2 \times 3 \times 6 = 36$

4. C _____

The only correlation between day care and other factors that was borne out by testing was the increase in intellectual and academic performance in underprivileged children who attended day care as compared with those who did not attend day care. No correlation was found in the social skills of the children. We cannot say that IQ scores will always go up for those in day care.

5. D _____

The concept of self-fulfilling prophecy is also called the Pygmalion Effect (named after George Bernard Shaw's play Pygmalion, *in which a poor cockney girl is transformed into seeming as if she were a lady of breeding). It says that if we believe someone has a particular quality or qualities, whether positive or negative, we generally communicate these beliefs and the person will try to match our expectations. Thus very often, the expectations come true. Ego involvement means that one is overly concerned with himself or herself and his or her needs. Meritocracy is a type of government ruled by those who deserve to rule. The experimental effect is the results that an experiment itself will give, regardless of what is being tested.*

6. C _____

The topography of a region is specifically the nature of its landscape—mountains, deserts, plateaus, oceans, and lakes. Population distribution would be shown on a demographic map. Climate and political boundaries are separate entities.

7. C _____

The probability of an event $= \dfrac{\text{total successful outcomes}}{\text{total possible outcomes}}$

Successful events are multiples of 3. This includes 6, 9, and 18. There are three successful events. The total number of possible outcomes is 8. Probability of landing on a multiple of 3 = ³⁄₈.

8. **D**

The culture of a people is the way in which the people live. It encompasses their religion, language, social organization, customs, traditions, and economic organization.

9. **A**

Cultural diffusion refers to the extending of an aspect of culture from one area to another and its inclusion in the culture(s) of other people. Religious homogeneity is the similitude of religion, not its spread. Global interdependence refers to the importance of one country to another, usually in terms of economics. Demographics is the study of population trends.

10. **C**

A nomadic lifestyle is one in which people do not settle in one area; instead, they roam from place to place and set up temporary living arrangements in each place. The desert is an area of nomadic lifestyle because it generally does not support agriculture and does not have sufficient water for people to settle there permanently.

11. **C**

Andy Warhol made the genre of Pop Art famous. Pop Art uses typical cultural icons, such as Warhol's Campbell Soup cans or Marilyn Monroe, to make a statement about popular culture. Impressionism was a nineteenth-century art form used by such artists as Monet to create a dreamy, "impressionistic" view of reality. Cubism, which Picasso made famous, separated reality into geometric figures. Dadaism, an early twentieth-century movement, is exemplified by Max Ernst and Marcel Duchamp. It was a rebellion against the times and preached that everyone had a right to his/her own interpretation of reality.

12. **D**

The library offers the student books, articles, journals, and so on with which to do research. The Internet is a very useful tool because of its convenience and its access to hundreds of sites. Interviews with relevant people can offer an important glimpse into the "personal" stories or issues of a topic.

13. **A**

Yoga, a form of exercise brought from the Far East, emphasizes correct breathing, stretching exercises, and relaxation techniques. Pilates is a method of strengthening one's "core" or abdominal area and back.

14. **B**

BMI, or body mass index, is a tool for indicating weight status. It is a measure of weight for height and helps determine whether an individual is overweight, underweight, or at a normal weight.

15. **C**

The physical education curriculum is designed to promote healthful living in students and to introduce them to a variety of physical activities. Thus aerobic conditioning helps train their hearts, strength training works on muscle groups, and sportsmanship teaches children how to behave with one another. Joining a team is an optional activity for children, not a goal of physical education.

16. **A**

The distributive property (of multiplication over addition) can be demonstrated algebraically as

$$a (b + c) = ab + bc$$

The diagrams in the example display as follows:

$$2(9) \quad = \ 18$$
$$2(3 + 6) \quad = \ 18$$
$$2(3) + 2(6) \ = \ 18$$

17. **D**

Igneous, sedimentary, *and* metamorphic *are terms that describe varieties of rocks; therefore, they would be taught in a lesson on geology, which is the study of the earth's history.*

18. **A**

Venn diagrams are overlapping circles that display elements of different sets. They show elements common to more than one set as well as elements unique to only one set.

–2, –1, 0, 1, 3	*are integers*
–2, –1, –1/2, 0	*are nonpositive (Note: Zero is neither positive nor negative.)*
0, 1, 3	*are whole numbers*

19. **D**

A factor tree decomposes an integer into its prime factors by continuously factoring a given number into two factors until there are no further factors other than one and the number. For example, the factor tree for 12 appears as follows:

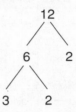

To work a factor tree backward (from the bottom up), multiply the factors to obtain the composite number they come from.

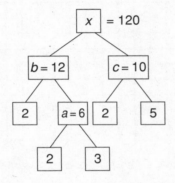

$$a = 2 \times 3 = 6$$
$$b = 6 \times 2 = 12$$
$$c = 2 \times 5 = 10$$
$$x = 12 \times 10 = 120$$

20. **A**

The plane travels 600 kilometers in 1 hour.

$$\frac{120}{600} = \frac{1}{5}$$

To travel 120 kilometers, you need ⅕ of an hour or 0.2 hours.

21. **B**

Asthma occurs when the bronchial tubes do not allow sufficient air to pass through to the lungs. Emphysema is a lung disease that is generally caused by smoking or air pollution. Bronchitis is an inflammation of the bronchial tubes, usually as part of a cold. Meningitis is an inflammation of the brain that affects the spinal cord.

22. **B** ───────────────────────────────

Plot the answer choices on the x-y coordinate plane.

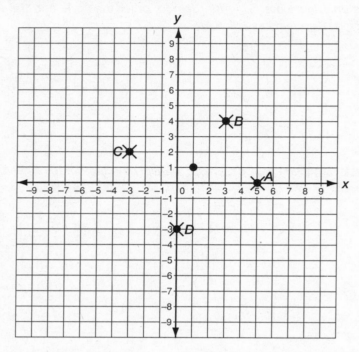

By careful examination, points A, C, and D are equidistant from the given point (1, 1). Point B is closest.

23. **A** ───────────────────────────────

Weight lifting is exercise specifically targeted to increase bone mass. Swimming and bicycling are aerobic exercises designed to increase the heart rate. Meditation is meant to calm and soothe; its focus is breathing.

24. **A** ───────────────────────────────

A person enters a ferris wheel at a height a little above ground level. He/she achieves a maximum height a while later and, after an equal amount of time, is back at the lower position. This cycle then repeats until the ride is over.

25. **C** ───────────────────────────────

Making up words using given letters is a language skills and requires that students think of words and phrases. Kinesthetic awareness deals with the sense touch, while auditory processing skills relate to the sense of hearing. Visual tracking is left-right tracking and is an important pre-reading skill.

26. D

The sweater's price was cut by half. Therefore, it needs to be doubled to sell at the original price. For example,

Original price: $20.00

50% sale: $10.00

To go back to the original price, you must double the sale price, which is the same as increasing it by 100%.

27. C

Taking a personality inventory is not necessary at the sixth-grade level. Researching different careers and listening to practitioners of the field are very useful for career awareness.

28. A

Colonialism is the extension of a nation's rule of beyond its borders by the establishment of settlements in which indigenous populations are directly ruled or displaced. Colonizers generally dominate the resources, labor, and markets of the colonial territory. In the sixteenth century, Spain extended its rule to parts of North America, South America, and the Caribbean. Guilds were the forerunners of modern trade unions, a system in which people who practiced similar crafts joined together. Haiti's independence from France removed the colonialism that France had imposed upon this island. Indulgences were practices of the Catholic Church in medieval times in which Catholics "bought" pardons from the church.

29. D

We establish a proportion relating the number of people to the ounces of angel-hair pasta.

$$\frac{4}{12} = \frac{10}{x} \quad \text{Then cross multiply.}$$

$$4x = 120 \quad \text{Divide by 4.}$$
$$x = 30$$

30. B

Assimilation is the process in which a minority racial, cultural, religious, or national group becomes part of the dominant cultural group. Divestment occurs when a country removes itself, whether it is economically, militarily, or socially, from something in which it had previously invested. Feudalism was a system in which people were protected by lords in exchange for their labor. Nationalism, or patriotism, is the feeling of pride and belonging that a people has for its country.

31. **B**

Previewing is a technique that, as its name implies, allows a student to get a foretaste of what is to come. Outlining is a method of organizing material. Rereading is used to find answers to specific questions, and note taking is a method of writing down important facts.

32. **D**

Reading in a word-by-word manner shows that a student is having trouble with the level of reading, so lower-level materials would be useful. Both choral reading and poetry reading give students an opportunity to practice rate of reading. Left-right tracking is a visual exercise for beginning readers; this would not be appropriate for the student.

33. **B**

*The order of operations requires us to do all operations **within** grouping symbols first. A parenthesis is a grouping symbol. The first operation to be performed is 4 – 2.*

34. **C**

The law of conservation states that a material will have the same volume regardless of the shape of the container in which it is placed. Accommodation and its sister concept, assimilation, is the way in which one incorporates new information in one's way of thinking. Piaget is the Swiss psychologist who did experimental work on these concepts. Natural selection is a Darwinian concept that states that a species will naturally evolve to retain useful adaptive characteristics. Deduction is a method of reasoning.

35. **D**

The Magna Carta is an English document signed by King John in 1215 that promised fair laws, equal access to courts, and a trial before imprisonment. It is the basis of our Constitution. The Declaration of Independence was the first step of our country's announcing its intention to break free of English rule. The Articles of Confederation, drafted in 1777, were in effect the first constitution of the United States and led to the present constitution. Therefore, all three influenced our Constitution.

36. **C**

We can analyze the four answer choices by converting each △ or □ to its ● equivalent.

A.

B.

C.

D.

37. **B**

Poultry and fish are considered proteins and provide energy over a period. Cereal is in the carbohydrate family.

38. **C**

An aerobic exercise is one in which large muscle groups are used, an exercise that can be maintained continuously, and an exercise that is rhythmic in nature. It is meant to challenge the heart and lungs and make them work harder. Jumping jacks, walking, and swimming all do that. Squats are an anaerobic exercise meant to tone and firm the hips and thighs.

39. **A**

The Impressionists were a group of painters who wanted to show their view of reality, not necessarily a photographic image of what appeared. They often used a pointillist style of painting, in which the painting consisted of dots of colors. Claude Monet is an acclaimed painter of this style. Rembrandt, a sixteenth-century Dutch artist, is famous for his use of chiaroscuro, or light and dark, to evoke emotions and senses. Leonardo da Vinci is the artist famous for, among his many other talents, his painting of the Sistine Chapel in the Vatican.

40. **C**

These dances all originated in South America, although they spread in popularity all over the world.

41. **A**

Tchaikovsky is a nineteenth-century Russian Romantic composer who created some of the world's greatest ballet music in addition to his symphonies. Mussorgsky is also a nineteenth-century Russian composer famous for the opera Boris Godunov. Rimsky-Korsakov is another nineteenth-century Russian composer who is famous for his operas. He also completed some of Mussorgsky's works.

42. **B**

The Progressive Era in the early twentieth century can be described as one in which government concerned itself with reform. The progressives, as they called themselves, worked to make American society a better and safer place in which to live. They tried to make big business more responsible through regulations of various kinds. They worked to clean up corrupt city governments, to improve working conditions in factories, and to better living conditions for those who lived in slum areas, a large number of whom were recent immigrants. Reconstruction took place in the years immediately following the Civil War, which ended in 1865 and concerned itself with putting the United States back together again after the war. The Cold War Era occurred in the aftermath of World War II. It involved great competition between the former Soviet Union and the United States. During the 1960 election campaign, the Democratic candidate, John F. Kennedy, had stated that America was "on the edge of a New Frontier"; in his inaugural speech he spoke of "a new generation of Americans"; and during his presidency he seemed to be taking government in a new direction, away from the easy-going Eisenhower style. His administration was headed by strong, dedicated personalities. The Kennedy staff was also predominantly young. Its energy and commitment revitalized the nation.

43. **B**

A great concern of educators, parents, and the general public is privacy in using computers. The Internet is a vast worldwide network, and users worry that what is sent over the Internet may not be secure.

44. **B**

Four of the twenty people chose milk. That is, ⁴/₂₀ or ¹/₅ of the people chose milk. Consequently, ¹/₅ of the 360° pie chart should be associated with milk.

$$\frac{1}{5}(360°) = 72°$$

45. **C**

The verb phrase will have avoided *implies that an action will occur in the future. However, it is clear that the author is describing what has already happened; therefore,* have avoided *is the correct verb usage.*

46. **A**

Sentence 1 ends by describing all of the animals who have made De Witt Island their home. The best transition to sentence 2 introduces Jane Cooper and then explains why she chose this particular place.

47. **A**

Editorializing is giving an opinion about an occurrence or an issue. Choices B and C are factual statements. Choice D is a straightforward question. Choice A's use of the words well-deserved illustrates editorializing because it gives the writer's opinion about the applause.

48. **A**

Wildlife refuges are places specifically created so that animals can have a safe haven. Similarly, game hunting laws prevent hunters from killing animals indiscriminately. Exploitation is the opposite: It means using a resource for our own ends regardless of the effects on the resource. Conservatism is a political point of view that espouses keeping status quo in society.

49. **C**

The passage discusses a person's willful breaking of a law, even though he knows that what he is doing is illegal. This is called civil disobedience. Military force is the act of using a country's military might to achieve objectives. Appeasement is a policy of giving in rather than going to war. Retaliation is revenge for a specific occurrence.

50. **D**

Gandhi is the famous leader of India who used civil disobedience to gain his country's freedom from Great Britain. Lenin was a major leader of the Soviet Union under Communist rule. Simón Bolívar, also known as the "George Washington of South America," was a general who helped many countries win their independence from Spain. Yasir Arafat was the leader of the Palestine Liberation Organization.

51. **D**

The poem describes a blazing hot environment with cold nights. Plants are small with wide roots, and no mention is made of rain; therefore, it would be a desert. The plants are not the type to be found in a forest, where there would be natural covering from the sun. A swamp would be rainy, and a tundra is a cold, icy environment.

52. **A**

Colloquial language is informal or conversational. The author's use of The days be hot, the nights be cold *and* Tiz me life that I must save *is nonstandard English; thus it is considered colloquial. A narrative is a long story, while factual writing, as the name implies, gives readers facts. Metaphors are comparisons without the use of the words* like *or* as.

53. **A**

A reflection is a transformation that "flips" the figure across a line to create a mirror image on the other side of the line. In our example, the triangle is "flipped" over the x-axis, creating its mirror image.

54. **D**

A fable is a story that teaches a lesson; therefore, the passage can be classified as a fable. A narrative is generally a long, fictional piece. A character analysis scrutinizes one or more characters that are presented. An editorial gives an opinion on a specific subject.

55. **C**

A limerick is a humorous poem in the rhythm a-a-b-b-a. The first two lines rhyme; the second two lines rhyme; and the last line rhymes with the first two lines. An elegy is a mournful poem. A ballad is a long poem that tells a story. Haiku is a form of poetry with a 17-syllable verse, divided into three units of 5, 7, and 5 syllables.

56. **A**

Alliteration is the repetition of consonant sounds. Onomatopoeia occurs when a word actually sounds like the sound it makes. Imagery is a way to portray something by comparison. Symbolism occurs when a word or phrase represents something else.

57. **D**

Illustrating the poem would allow younger children to visualize its humor, while clapping their hands as the poem is read reinforces its rhythm. Older children could write their own poems in this style.

58. **C**

In an if–then *statement, the phrase following the* if *is called the hypothesis and phrase following the* then *is called the conclusion. Given an original statement, only the contrapositive is guaranteed to have the same truth value. The contrapositive is obtained by swapping the hypothesis and conclusion phrases and also negating them.*

<u>*Note:*</u> *The negative of "turnips are not blue" is "turnips are blue."*

59. **C**

The diagram shows cycling among air, legumes, soil organisms, dead plants, live plants, and animals. This means that the cycling occurs between the living and nonliving parts of the environment.

60. **C**

A metaphor is a comparison between two items without the use of like *or as. In the proverb, death is called a* black camel. *A simile is a comparison that uses* like *or* as. *Alliteration is the repetition of a consonant sound, and hyperbole is an exaggeration.*

61. **A**

The statement tries to influence readers by telling them that all of their friends own this particular item. This device is known as bandwagon. A testimonial is a quote by someone, whether by name or anonymous, that vouches for the product. Card-stacking is the intentional organization and arrangement of material to make one position look good and another position look bad. A glittering generality is use of an emotionally appealing word or concept to gain approval without thinking.

62. **D**

The two sentences show two meanings for the verb try. *In the first sentence, the word means* attempted, *while the second very means* judged.

63. **C**

Robinson shows the reader that although Richard Cory seems to have everything—riches, grace, and respect of others—he was inwardly very unhappy and committed suicide.

64. **A**

These sentences illustrate the grammatical rule of parallelism. The phrase before the like, as, or than *have to match, or be parallel to the phrase after the like, as, or than. Choice B states: "to hike" and "skiing." Choice C states: "hiking" and "to ski." Choice D gives us "to hike" and "going cross-country skiing." Only Choice A shows parallelism in its use of "hiking" and "skiing." Therefore, A is correct.*

65. **C**

In order to turn water, a liquid, into water vapor, a gas, the process of evaporation must occur. Condensation is the reverse—turning a gas into a liquid. Deposition occurs when something is deposited in an area, and infiltration is the process by which one item permeates another item.

66. **C**

The blue and the brown comprise ½ + ⅕ of the tie. Use 10 as the lowest common denominator:

$$\frac{1}{2} = \frac{5}{10} \text{ and } \frac{1}{5} = \frac{2}{10}$$

Thus the blue and brown make up ⁷/₁₀ of the tie. The balance (1 − ⁷/₁₀) or ³/₁₀ belongs to the burgundy.

67. **D**

Economic resources are those that provide goods and services to people. Economic resources are considered to be scarce, while wants are unlimited. Therefore, land, labor, and capital are considered resources, while values are not goods or services that are limited.

68. **D**

(D) is the best answer. Education affects one's career choice and can affect income. One's age affects income also; young people just entering a career do not usually have an income as high as those who have been there for a few years. Unfortunately, women still do not have a salary as high as men. One's health affects one's ability to get an education, one's ability to secure employment, and one's salary. Because all the items do affect income, answer (D) is the best choice.

69. **C**

Taking a class trip to the supermarket would introduce students to comparative pricing of the same item in different brands, while comparing different supermarkets would show the students possible differences in pricing in the same brand. Ralph Nader is a very vocal activist in consumer affairs. Donald Trump, however, is a real estate developer.

70.

Properties of a parallelogram include

- *The sum of its angles is 360°.*
- *Opposite sides are equal.*
- *Opposite sides are parallel.*
- *Opposite angles are equal.*
- *Adjacent angles are supplementary (add to 180°).*
- *Diagonals bisect each other.*

Diagonals are only equal if the parallelogram is a rectangle.

71. **D**

The following math facts are used in this example:

$$\sin x = \frac{\text{side opposite angle } x}{\text{hypotenuse}}, \quad \tan x = \frac{\text{side opposite angle } x}{\text{side adjacent to angle } x}$$

$$(\text{leg})^2 + (\text{leg})^2 = (\text{hypotenuse})^2$$

Choice D: $3^2 + 6^2 = x^2$ *says* $(\text{leg})^2 + (\text{hypotenuse})^2 = (\text{leg})^2$.

72. **C**

Modern Times is a classic film that shows the dehumanization of industrialization. Its classic scene depicts Charlie Chaplin as a cog in an ever-turning machine.

73. **A**

A microprocessor is a circuit that directs the other units in the computer. It is used in a micro-computer. A microprocessor contains one silicon chip, so it is small enough to be used in small pieces.

74. **D**

Percussion instruments need to be struck in order to produce sound. Therefore, the drum and cymbals belong to this class of instruments. The bassoon, however, is a wind instrument since it produces sound when a musician blows into it.

75. A

John Philip Sousa was known as the "King of March." One of his most famous marches was "Stars and Stripes Forever." Johann Sebastian Bach was a classical composer, while Cab Calloway is best known as a jazz musician who led one of the greatest bands in the Swing Era. Stephen Sondheim is a contemporary composer who has written lyrics for many Broadway shows.

76. C

The Metropolitan Museum of Art has a famous permanent exhibition of Egyptian art and artifacts, including mummies and mummy cases. The Museum of the Moving Image, as its name implies, deals with films. The Whitney Museum deals with American art, while the Guggenheim Museum exhibits contemporary works of art.

77. D

Diminished *means* "made smaller." This implies subtraction; therefore, a number n diminished by 5 means n – 5. Three more than 7 times the number n is 7n + 3, and finally, is means "equals." Putting is all together, n – 5 = 7n + 3.

78. A

Research shows that suicide is attempted about three times more often in males than in females. None of the other statements has been shown to be true.

79. C

To show atmospheric perspective, one can draw something darker than its surroundings. This will make it seem farther away, because light colors "jump out" while darker colors seem to fade away, as if they were farther back in the atmosphere.

80. A

Both speakers are referring to the colonies that were later to become the United States of America. This feeling of togetherness and pride for one's country is called nationalism. Confederacy occurs when one group joins in opposition to another. Totalitarianism is the rule by a dictator—the antithesis of these quotes—while equality denotes equal rights.

81. C

Diagrams, tables, and graphs are different ways to display information. These would be most useful in organizing that information. They would not assist in predictions, test a hypothesis, or design a research plan but could be helpful in any of these endeavors.

82. **A**

An ecologist is concerned about environmental issues; therefore, he or she would be most interested in the effect of the fuel's smoke emissions. Cost and time factors do not concern the environmentalist, so Choices B and C are irrelevant. Similarly, consumer acceptance is not the domain of the environmentalist, so Choice D is not correct.

83. **B**

The Jim Crow laws were in existence from the 1880s (post–Civil War) to the 1960s. A majority of American states enforced segregation using these laws. States and cities could impose legal punishment on people for a variety of "infractions" dealing with African Americans. Intermarriage between the races was forbidden, and in both the public and private sectors, blacks and whites were separated.

84. **C**

Studies have shown that drinking alcohol while pregnant is associated with more premature births and stillbirths among the fetuses of these women. Drinking is not associated with weight or heart rate of the fetus.

85. **B**

The diagram shows cloud reflection to be 30% to 60% and absorption to be 5% to 20%. The question asks us what percentage is reflected or absorbed, so we must add the two percentages. This gives us 35% (30% + 5%) to 80% (60% + 20%).

86. **D**

Relative humidity measures the percentage of water vapor in the air. The higher the humidity, the more water vapor exists in the air. Thursday had the highest relative humidity (95%), so D is the correct answer.

87. **A**

The variable in this experiment is light. The plants were grown in the same soil and given the same amount of water, so Choices B and C are wrong. The experiment does not deal with red light, so Choice D is incorrect. The three plants were given different amounts of light, so Choice A is the correct answer.

88. **C**

This method is entitled "Call Up" and is a note-taking strategy. Choices B and D are incidental skills that are being taught by this strategy in which the focus is taking organized notes. However, organizational skills are the primary strategy that is being taught by this approach. Choice A is incorrect because this is not creative writing. It is writing to learn and interpret information.

89. **B**

This is an example of deletion manipulation. Choice A refers to reversing the sounds in CVC (consonant–vowel–consonant) words, as in top/pot. Choice C refers to naming different sounds in CVC words. Choice D involves changing one sound in a word, as in sell/bell.

90. **D**

Time signature shows the musician how many beats there are in each bar and which note is to be used as a beat. These musical notations are all written as one beat measure—therefore, all times will be _____:4 time. Certain time signatures lend themselves to certain styles of songs (e.g., most waltzes are written in 3:4 time, and the majority of rock songs would be based around 4:4 time).

Written Assignment Answer Earning 4 Points

Generally speaking, I would devise a balanced approach to teaching reading. Specifically, I would frequently assess my students as to their level so they could be placed into appropriate reading groups and they could move into and out of groups as needed. In this approach I would combine my use of whole-class guided texts with having students put into guided reading groups where the texts are on different levels according to ability. Ideally, the guided reading group texts would be united according to theme but differentiated according to the pre-assessed levels of students. For targeted strategies in comprehension, there are times when the teacher might use homogeneous grouping. In my classroom, there will be many times when I will use heterogeneous grouping, but given this particular situation, I would utilize homogeneous grouping in an effort to let students work on similar goals and to share strengths.

In terms of pre-reading, I would establish a purpose for reading through KWL, vocabulary introduction, and/or discussion of ideas that will acquaint readers with the background knowledge required for their text. I would conduct these pre-reading activities with the entire class. Then, I would homogeneously divide this group of 20 into smaller groups (five each) based on reading ability. I would initiate a guided reading program by using appropriately leveled reading materials for each of the groups. Likewise, I would set individualized goals for each of the groups.

When it comes to the lower-level reading group, I would focus their efforts on working on decoding and predicting strategies. I would take advantage of the opportunities for reciprocal reading among these learners in an effort to get them questioning, summarizing, clarifying, and predicting. I would have these students do some extensive vocabulary preparation activities so they are ready before they read. They would also have the text read aloud to them before they read it silently. I would outline some of the big ideas, supporting details, and content for them in a graphic organizer, parts of which would be left blank for the students to complete. I would also work on some decoding practice for the tougher words in the text. I would provide consistent and frequent assessment by observing them as they read the text softly or silently to themselves and as they read the text orally. Finally, I would check in with them for understanding and comprehension.

For the middle groups (in this scenario, there are two groups with five students in each group), I would focus on the goal of their making connections between their texts and other texts we've read. While I would use many of the aforementioned strategies, I would encourage partner reading activities as well as more independent reading. I would create graphic organizers for them, which would allow them to make those intertextual connections.

I would encourage the group of five who are reading two grade levels above to work on higher-level skills along Bloom's Taxonomy such as making inferences and evaluations about their assigned text. These students would be encouraged to do more pair-share reading and more independent work. I would devise a graphic organizer with higher-level questions asking them to synthesize what they have read. Perhaps I would engage them by asking them to illustrate the theme of the book in a different form. For instance, perhaps they would compose a short story or a poem that allows them to articulate their understanding of the theme.

While providing this kind of guidance to a specific group, I would ensure that students in the other groups are engaged in active learning of their specific literacy activity. In terms of post-reading activities, I would observe and provide guidance to individual students and differentiate my instruction by asking different kinds of questions of each student based on individual need. I would also ask specific questions to ensure that each text has been comprehended by the students. Given this homogeneous grouping, the assessment would take place through my observation of group work and through quizzes, tests, and student projects. Of course, these assessments would be individualized to the learning goals of the specific groups.

Features of the Written Assignment Scoring 4

Purpose. The purpose of the assignment has been achieved. All three questions have been addressed. The essay describes a meaningful comprehension lesson while illustrating the principles of a balanced reading program. The writer ensures that reading comprehension is addressed as well as provides viable post-reading activities that would help to assess comprehension.

Application of Content. By giving clear and specific use of a variety of reading instruction methods, activities, the writer accomplished the requirement to describe the lessons and activities that would be necessary to accomplish the stated goals of the lesson.

Support. References to specific tasks to support the reading needs of each group of 5 round out a well developed answer.

Index

Installing REA's TestWare®

SYSTEM REQUIREMENTS

Pentium 75 MHz (300 MHz recommended) or a higher or compatible processor; Microsoft Windows XP or later; 64 MB available RAM; Internet Explorer 5.5 or higher.

INSTALLATION

1. Insert the NYSTCE Multi-Subject CD-ROM into the CD-ROM drive.

2. If the installation doesn't begin automatically, from the Start Menu choose the RUN command. When the RUN dialog box appears, type d:\setup (where d is the letter of your CD-ROM drive) at the prompt and click OK.

3. The installation process will begin. A dialog box proposing the directory "C:\Program Files\ REA\NYSTCE_CST\" will appear. If the name and location are suitable, click ok. If you wish to specify a different name or location, type it in and click ok.

4. Start the NYSTCE Multi-Subject TestWare® application by double-clicking on the icon.

NYSTCE Multi-Subject CST TestWare® is **EASY** to **LEARN AND USE**. To achieve maximum benefits, we recommend that you take a few minutes to go through the on-screen tutorial on your computer. The "screen buttons" are also explained here to familiarize you with the program.

SSD ACCOMMODATIONS FOR STUDENTS WITH DISABILITIES

Many students qualify for extra time to take the NYSTCE Multi-Subject CST exam, and our TestWare® can be adapted to accommodate your time extension. This allows you to practice under the same extended-time accommodations that you will receive on the actual test day. To customize your TestWare® to suit the most common extensions, visit our website at www.rea.com/ssd.

TECHNICAL SUPPORT

REA's TestWare® is backed by customer and technical support. For questions about **installation or operation of your software**, contact us at:

> **Research & Education Association**
> **Phone: (732) 819-8880 (9 a.m. to 5 p.m. ET, Monday–Friday)**
> **Fax: (732) 819-8808**
> **Website: www.rea.com**
> **E-mail: info@rea.com**

Note to Windows Users: In order for the TestWare® to function properly, please install and run the application under the same computer administrator-level user account. Installing the TestWare® as one user and running it as another could cause file-access path conflicts.

REA's Test Prep Books Are The Best!
(a sample of the <u>hundreds of letters</u> REA receives each year)

" The gem of the book is the tests. They were indicative of the actual exam. The explanations of the answers are practically another review session. "
Student, Fresno, CA

" I just wanted to thank you for helping me get a great score on the AP U.S. History... Thank you for making great test preps! "
Student, Los Angeles, CA

" Your Fundamentals of Engineering Exam book was the absolute best preparation I could have had for the exam, and it is one of the major reasons I did so well and passed the FE on my first try. "
Student, Sweetwater, TN

" I used your book to prepare for the test and found that the advice and the sample tests were highly relevant... Without using any other material, I earned very high scores and will be going to the graduate school of my choice. "
Student, New Orleans, LA

" What I found in your book was a wealth of information sufficient to shore up my basic skills in math and verbal.... The practice tests were challenging and the answer explanations most helpful. It certainly is the Best Test Prep for the GRE! "
Student, Pullman, WA

" I really appreciate the help from your excellent book. Please keep up with your great work. "
Student, Albuquerque, NM

" I used your *CLEP Introductory Sociology* book and rank it 99%– thank you! "
Student, Jerusalem, Israel

(more on next page)

REA's Test Prep Books Are The Best!
(a sample of the <u>hundreds of letters</u> REA receives each year)

" I used [*the REA study guide*] to study for the LAST and ATS-W tests—and passed them both with *perfect scores*. This book provided excellent preparation ... "
Student, New York, NY

" The reviews in [the REA book] were outstanding ... If it wasn't for your excellent prep, I would not have stood a chance [of passing the NYSTCE]. "
Student, Elmira, New York

" I did well because of your wonderful prep books... I just wanted to thank you for helping me prepare for these tests. "
Student, San Diego, CA

" My students report your chapters of review as the most valuable single resource they used for review and preparation. "
Teacher, American Fork, UT

" Your book was such a better value and was so much more complete than anything your competition has produced—and I have them all! "
Teacher, Virginia Beach, VA

" Compared to the other books that my fellow students had, your book was the most helpful in helping me get a great score. "
Student, North Hollywood, CA

" Your book was responsible for my success on the exam, which helped me get into the college of my choice... I will look for REA the next time I need help. "
Student, Chesterfield, MO

" Just a short note to say thanks for the great support your book gave me in helping me pass the test... I'm on my way to a B.S. degree because of you! "
Student, Orlando, FL

(more on previous page)